Joseph Pennell, Hugh Thomson, Arthur Hamilton Norway

Highways and byways in Yorkshire

With illustrations by Joseph Pennell and Hugh Thomson

Joseph Pennell, Hugh Thomson, Arthur Hamilton Norway

Highways and byways in Yorkshire
With illustrations by Joseph Pennell and Hugh Thomson

ISBN/EAN: 9783337156640

Printed in Europe, USA, Canada, Australia, Japan

Cover: Foto ©Andreas Hilbeck / pixelio.de

More available books at **www.hansebooks.com**

Highways and Byways
in Yorkshire

BY ARTHUR H. NORWAY
WITH · ILLUSTRATIONS · BY
JOSEPH PENNELL AND
HUGH THOMSON

London
MACMILLAN AND CO., Limited
NEW YORK : THE MACMILLAN COMPANY
1899

RICHARD CLAY AND SONS, LIMITED,
LONDON AND BUNGAY.

CONTENTS

CHAPTER XV

CHAPTER XVI

CHAPTER XVII

CHAPTER XVIII

LIST OF ILLUSTRATIONS

HIGHWAYS AND BYWAYS

IN

YORKSHIRE

Whitby Harbour.

LIST OF PLATES

HIGHWAYS AND BYWAYS

IN

YORKSHIRE

HIGHWAYS AND BYWAYS

IN

YORKSHIRE

CHAPTER I

THE GREAT NORTH ROAD, BAWTRY, TICKHILL, THRYBERGH

"ONE may call and justify this," says sententious Fuller,
" to be the best shire in England ; " and he adds, with a quaint
reference to Tully's orations, *optima quae longissima*—the best
which is the longest.   Now while professing every regard for
Fuller, whose little quirks are not to be handled by the world's
blunt thumb and finger, but should be accepted gratefully as
pretty coruscations in a biographical waste which he might
have left so arid,—with all gratitude and love, I say, for my old
friend and comrade, I protest strenuously against the gauge
which he adopts.   For does one measure Madonna with a foot
rule, or estimate a mighty warrior by inches ?   Here is a shire
which from the first twilight of our stormy history has caught
all men's imagination by the strength and vigour of its life, a
stage on which the grandest dramas have been played out with
pomp and tragedy, a soil which has been drenched through
and through by the very noblest blood in England, a sturdy

E   B

bulwark thrust well nigh across the whole width of the country
in the track of Scotch invasion, a land of tradition, of romance,
and one withal of beauty so great and varied, so rare a medley
of exquisite river valleys falling out of wild moorland hills, of
high grassy dales along the wind-swept mountains, and of stern
seacoast as can be matched only in one other shire.   If life in
Yorkshire had been tame throughout all history, if its dalesmen
had been peaceful shepherds and its barons ready to give un-
questioning loyalty to every king who sat at Westminster, if its
townsmen had been placid traders and its great forests had
never bred an outlaw,—yet men would have wandered over its
mountains and gazed down its valleys with delight for their very
beauty.   To look on Wharfe stealing beneath Barden Woods,
or to watch Swale rushing black and swollen out of the highlands, must have been a pleasure even if those rivers flowed
through wildernesses where man had never dwelt.   But as it
is, the natural charm is stung into enthusiasm by some poignancy
of human interest which clings to every mile of the vast area
of Yorkshire, making of that county not only an epitome of
English history, but more than that, a monument of fierce
passions and bloody tragedies, of cruel raids and gallant expeditions, which cries out loudly for our sympathy and interest
even in these days of peace.   For many a century Yorkshire
life was a splendid pageant ; and though the banners and the
pennants have long since swept away elsewhere, though the
dales are silent which used to echo with the clank of spears or
harness, and the daws nest freely in the roofless castles of
Scrope and Mowbray, or defile the sacred precincts of Fountains
and of Rievaulx,—still those who listen rightly may catch some
echo of the distant music, clear and ringing through all the
generations which have come and gone.   A very little fancy
will people those valleys once more with the musters of sturdy
yeomen who rode to Bannockburn or Flodden, will raise again
the banner of the Five Wounds of Christ, or call up the picture
of the first messengers spurring into York from the field of

"The Great North Road."

[To face page 1.

Marston Moor, where, through the long summer evening, the
citizens knelt praying in their churches that they might be
spared that terror which was surely falling on them.

Ah, great old days ! I shall lose myself in retrospect if I do
not check the rush of memories which assails me as I set foot
on Yorkshire soil.   It was Fuller who misled me ; and probably I have said enough to show what it was that distressed me
in his ranking this great county by its miles and acres.   There
was time to make the protest, for I am not in Yorkshire yet,
though running fast a-wheel along the last few miles of that
highway which goes northwards through Grantham, Stamford,
Newark and a dozen other famous towns, and is yet known
commonly as the Great North Road.   Whether it was great or
otherwise is of little moment now, except to cyclists and ragged
beggarmen ; for they alone out of the whole community travel
its deserted ways which were once so full of noisy life, and mark
how the ancient wayside inns have lost their occupation and
descended into farms or cottages ; while as each easy hill surmounted discloses new lengths of the broad old highway
running straight and smooth between wide grassy borders, the
very spaciousness and emptiness of the road possess a certain
dignity and grandeur which are suggestive of long vanished
pomps and noble spectacles such as we shall never see again.
It was not yonder sleepy farmer jogging home from Doncaster
in his gig, that the makers of this highway had in mind ; nor
was it the herdsman who walks cautiously before his sheep,
checking them with his staff in front while his dog brings up all
stragglers in the rear.   It was for quite other travellers that the
width and length of the Great North Road were designed,—for
Roman armies marching northwards where their greatest peril
always lay, for the progresses of kings bent on hunting in the
great forests north of Trent, or called hastily to arms by some
revolt of Barons whose power was regal and whose loyalty a
phrase, for bands of pilgrims journeying to the shrines of St.
John of Beverley or St. Wilfrid of Ripon or to the Roode of

Doncaster "at the brigge end," places so holy that in the old
days when faith was living they drew towards them vast numbers
of strong men and tender women submitting voluntarily to
dangers and privations such as even money would scarce tempt
us to undergo.   It was for packhorses with their high-piled
burdens, for stage wagons like that which Roderick Random
chased so many weary miles afoot, agreeing at last to pay the
wagon master ten shillings for his passage to London, on the
understanding that when he was disposed to walk, his friend
Strap should get in and ride in his place.   It was even more
particularly designed for post chaises, such as that in which Mrs.
Shandy, Tristram's excellent mother, used to drag her reluctant
husband up to London under that queer clause in her marriage
settlement ; but, most of all, the makers of the road as we now
see it had in mind stage coaches, like the " Regent," which
worthy old John Barker drove for many a year from the " George
and Blue Boar " in Holborn to Grantham within the day,
daunted by neither floods nor snow, so long as his team of
greys or chestnuts could plunge or stagger through.   And if it
was for coaches that this great roadway was designed, it was
surely in a sense designed for robbers too ; or at any rate it
served their purpose admirably.   In fact the whole North Road
had a somewhat unsavoury reputation, and those who travelled
by it went in constant peril.   " The York coach not forty yards
before me," wrote Lady Anne Irwin to her father, the Earl of
Carlisle, in April, 1776, " the York coach not forty yards before
me was stopped and robbed.   I saw the rogues do it, and could
expect nothing less myself, having no other guard than Tom
Bulfin ; but upon seeing him armed, they rid off with such
violence, either on purpose or design, they had near thrown
Tom from his horse.   Thus I fortunately escaped, but they
took in another stage coach about a hundred yards behind me
and got a good booty,—two watches and above twenty pounds.
People have seldom much money going from London, especially those that pay all their debts there "—surely the gentlemen

of the road need not have troubled their heads about this small
minority of the population,—"but I was charged with a com-
mission to your lordship . . . and have in bank-bills and
money near £160 to pay you." Happy Lady Anne to keep
this heavy purse, while lighter ones were being handed out in
her very sight ! Lucky Tom Bulfin to escape with a shaking !
Misfortunate robbers, who gained £20 and missed eight times
as much ! How our little chances in life go by without our
knowing it ! Well, let us be grateful that the roads are safe to-
day ; for even a cyclist, who, I take it, comes nearer to the
vacuus viator of an older age than anybody else among us, would
hardly like turning out his empty pockets at the bidding of a
dirty footpad.

Somewhere on the road, not very far from Bawtry, the Earl
of Dumfries was robbed in November 1649. At least he said
he was, for the two men whom he accused declared it was the
most innocent matter in the world ! His lordship with his
servant was riding over the corn. They asked him to desist :
whereupon the Earl got down and walked away without a word.
His servant did the same. The two horses were left straying in
the road : and they, good honest men, were taking them, for
greater safety, to the pound ! I blush for humanity when I add
that they were not believed.

But how the North Road is haunted by the phantoms of all
successive ages ! Deserted, lonely highway ! what tragedies has it
not witnessed ! Even in this blithe summer sunshine, when the
scent of the hawthorn is blown across my track from every
hedge, when the woodpigeons are calling in the cool woods, and
there is movement far and wide over all the face of the level
country, I cannot ride along without finding a hundred recollections chase each other through my memory. Was it not
upon this highway that the second Richard was hurried secretly
down from London after Bolingbroke had stripped him of
his crown,—poor, friendless monarch, travelling to an end so
doubtful that as he lay in state no more than his face could be

exposed ? How often this country must have been ravaged by
triumphant men at arms led by Warwick, the great Kingmaker,
marching north to Middleham or Raby ; or by the fierce
Edward, who won his throne at Towton Moor, not twenty miles
from here, where the cause of the Red Rose went down in seas of
blood and the little River Cock ran crimson underneath the
corpses heaped up in the snow ! How those who dwelt by the
wayside on this road must have known his features, and must
have known too his saintly rival, Henry, that gentle kingly man
who, as Hall tells us, deemed that by " his trouble and adversitie
his synnes were to him forgotten and forgeven," and whom the
men of the north country loved with such devotion that they
built shrines in his memory and prayed to him as to a saint, long
years after he came to his solitary and unhappy end ! Why,
there is scarce a king in all our history whom this road has not
seen riding by amid a gallant company, nor any tragedy which
has not sent its fugitives skulking at nightfall along the grass
borders in the shadow of the hedge.

But here is Bawtry breaking in upon my gloomy memories, a
red-tiled cheerful town, aligning itself along the North Road with
a frank admission that it owes not only its birth, but its continued
existence to that great highway. I am told that it was once a
seat of commerce, catching the stream which from very early
times has flowed out of the factory districts of the West
Riding towards the shipping ports upon the Humber. It may
be so ; but I look around at the long empty street, scarce more
than a double line of houses following the winding of the highway, and I doubt the magnitude of the commerce. At any
rate, Bawtry is nothing now but a resting place for travellers ;
and for those who come north with the intention of seeing
Yorkshire it is the most appropriate of all gateways to the
county. For here, in the ancient days of royal progresses, the
sheriff and gentlemen of the land of broad acres used to meet
their sovereign, greeting him with their loyal salutations on the
very border. Many a gallant troop of courtiers rode down this

street, not all of whom, as we may very well surmise, were
pleased to see their monarch coming. For strange things went
on among the baronage north of Trent. There were those
among them who cared little for the authority of any king, and
were for shaking off his yoke whenever he showed a tendency
to disagree with them, and there were others of less strength
whose loyalty was worth no more. So that when these happy
meetings occurred between the sovereign and his loving subjects,
the old street of Bawtry must have witnessed strange scenes of
dissimulation and veiled menace.

But I cannot stand here in the sun speculating upon the
precise worth of the loyal professions of men who have been
dust for three centuries and more. I have ridden far, and am
going into the " Crown," that picturesque old hostelry, for some
refreshment, over which the proverbial saying about the town
warns me not to hurry, lest I be overtaken by the fate of " the
saddler of Bawtry, who was hanged for leaving his liquor." I
vow he would have saved his life had he been a cyclist, and
ridden twenty miles along the Great North Road on a warm
morning. But who was he? I am sorry that I do not know ;
for even those local authorities who might be expected to have
certain information on a point so interesting disagree entirely
among themselves. What is certain, however, is that a traveller
who carried a good deal of money in his saddle-bags, and was
on his way to Doncaster, paused at Bawtry to refresh himself
and to have some alteration made in his saddle, which galled
his horse's back. He might have spared the saddler's fee, had
he known that as he rode out of Bawtry he would be robbed
near the King's Wood, which was a nice convenient shelter,
often used for cover by gentlemen waiting to accost travellers.
Now, instead of going on to Doncaster, when his saddle bags
had been lightened and his horse's burden eased, the traveller
returned to Bawtry in great indignation ; and making at once
for the dwelling of the saddler, he found a tankard of ale which
he had bestowed upon the fellow, to cement good feeling before

departure, standing still untouched, while the saddler was nowhere to be found. That a man in Bawtry should leave his
liquor to go flat was strange and suspicious. The country was
scoured, the saddler was caught, and very soon afterwards hung
at York. As I look through the glass at the bottom of my
tankard, tilted high above my chin, I declare he got no more
than his deserts.

This King's Wood at the end of Bawtry Lane, where our
traveller came to grief, was a place of evil reputation. I have
passed it at nightfall not without a qualm, half fancying that I
saw a horseman drawn up on the little piece of greensward in
the shadow of the hedge. It is not night yet, nor near it ; but
I will not go that way. I will make a circuit, and reach
Doncaster through some pretty places that I wot of which have
no evil memories ; and so I turn out of Bawtry half way up the
north side of its straggling street, calling to mind as I mount a
hill and see the old church below me, that other noted resident
who came to an end as sad and much more painful than the
saddler,—one Arthur Thistlewood, who laid a plot to kill a
whole British Cabinet at once, and was cut in pieces for his
pains,—you may see the axe at Newgate yet. I understand
that Bawtry people cherish his memory ; but for my part I am
glad to pass out of the town which reminds me of him. How
far away seem all conspiracies and treasons, as I ride once more
into the open country through the hush of the summer afternoon ! The high green grass is turning into bronze all over the
face of the undulating country. The shadow of cool woods lies
across the road. A little wind comes laden with sweet scents
of hawthorn, and under the bushes a weary woman sits and fans
herself, while her sodden husband lies back upon the bank
asleep. Other wayfarers there are none ; and so I ride on
silently until, topping the crest of a little hill, I see a wide plain
stretched out before me with the grand tower of Tickhill Church
standing up no more than a mile away. Behind the tower there
are the green ridges of swelling hills ; and towards the left, on

the summit of a tree-clad mound, a solitary flagstaff marks the
spot where from the earliest times there stood a noble castle,
centre of an inheritance so splendid as to be often chosen for a
queen's dowry, an "honour" which included portions of five
counties, and which when not held by royalty itself, was always
in the hands of great and noble barons.

In fact this quiet village, famed now chiefly for its walnuts,
was one of the principal resorts of chivalry in Britain, being in
the immediate neighbourhood of one of the only five places
licensed by King Richard I. for holding tourneys when after his
return from captivity he began to give encouragement to martial
exercises. Not even the ground on which these splendid jousts
were held can be identified to-day. The long and goodly village
streets, through which so often the pennants of half the nobility of
northern England must have fluttered, are occupied by flocks
of ducks waddling from the pond upon the common, where a
row of pollard willows bordering a sedgy stream invites the
grazing cattle to stand within cool shade, flicking their tails
drowsily. On the castle mound there are but few walls left;
only a handsome gateway reminds us of the warriors who rode
in and out beneath it. But for this gateway, it would be
difficult to see in Tickhill an ancient place of arms. Its moat
girdles the castle mound, still full of water as it used to be, a
wide brown waterway threading the woodland which has
invested the hillside. It lies there cool and beautiful in the
hot afternoon, shot over with gold flashes which penetrate the
overarching trees; but it has no terrors now, unless it be for
evil children, bird's-nesting unlawfully upon the slopes. Ah,
how far away seem those days, just after Marston Moor, when a
garrison of rake-helly cavaliers held the ancient fortress,
palisaded and defended by a strong moat and counterscarp, and
were "exceedingly oppressive" to the country round. But
Colónel Lilbourn came that way; and when he passed, the
last vestiges of feudal England at Tickhill had disappeared for

ever, and that deep peace had fallen on the country villages in which they are buried even yet.

Maybe it is just as well ; for in the old days I certainly should not have ridden where I will through the sunny country without inquiring carefully whether a party was out from Tickhill, and giving it a wide berth if it were. As it is, I pass on through the village without a care ; and when it lies behind me by a mile or so, I strike off to the right, where a rough lane passing through a farm brings me out on the main road from Rotherham to Worksop. It is a pleasant country, fertile and thickly wooded and by no means flat. For here one enters on the limestone ridges, and presently we shall climb up them and see their characteristic features. But now the road is running by tall woods which hide a spot of very curious interest ; and passing through a gate just where the open fields begin again, I follow a little winding path dropping down beneath limestone scars, up which shrubs and trailing ivy grow luxuriantly. This path descends into the valley of a little river by whose bank, half buried in the greenery, stands the stately gatehouse of Roche Abbey, set close beneath the precipice from which the monks, seizing the most striking feature of their valley with that quick sense of picturesqueness which distinguished the Cistercians, named themselves "monachi de rupe," Monks of the Rock. So the noblest of the homes of this order in the north was "de Fontibus," while their lordly colony in the far distant land of Norway was named "The vale of light." The warm glow of the afternoon falls into the valley in a flood. The little stream gleams with its reflexion as it steals along beneath the trees. In an open glade a trifle higher up a couple of red-roofed cottages stand shining in the sun, and the fowls go to and fro clucking in the short grass. In the abounding stillness one might fancy that all human life had ceased on the departure of those who planned and built the lovely walls which are now a shattered ruin, waiting in some enchanted slumber till their

master's hand shall set them up once more in their ancient glory,
and the sound of chanting roll again through the hollow and
over the short turf on the limestone crags above.   I sit down
in the shadow of the bank and rest awhile in this, the loveliest
spot that I shall see to-day.

Three hundred years and more have gone by since the monks
of the Rock were driven out of their little Eden, and still the river
runs down sparkling through the woods as if it were expecting
them to-morrow.   God knows with what extremity of pride or
greed this old house may have been filled when the great ruin
fell upon it.   Gross charges were laid against all monks for
many a generation before that evil day.

" You have three daughters at home," said a gentleman of
France to King Richard I., " whom you love more than the
grace of God ; they are Pride, Luxury, and Avarice."

" My friend," replied the King, " they are no longer at home.
I have married Pride to the Templars, Luxury to the Black
Canons, and Avarice to the Cistercians."

I note the taunt, and pass it by.   For in this life of human
men, where the loftiest ideals and the noblest hopes decay and
are corrupted so very fast, we may desire passionately to be
judged and measured by what was best and greatest in us, just
as a mountain is measured by its highest summit, rather than
by a balance struck between its heights and its abysses.   It is
mere justice so to judge ; and I will therefore think of the
Cistercians, not as they may have been on their dissolution, but
as they certainly were at the time of their foundation, full eight
centuries ago,—reformers, men revolting from the easy life and
lax practices which had crept into the monasteries of their day ;
men struck with fear for their salvation, fleeing into the wilderness, seeking places the wildest and most solitary they could
find, where toiling and fasting, in hunger and in peril of their
bodies, they might, according to their own hope, save their
souls alive.

Such a spot was this cleft among the limestone crags—no

pleasant hollow in a fertile country, as we see it now, but a
wild chasm in a land of dense forests and morasses, pierced
by no better roads than mule tracks, and by few of those;

Roche Abbey.

haunted by wild animals in great profusion, and by almost
equal numbers of desperate and outlawed men, from whose
necessities even monks could expect no more forbearing treat-

ment than full men have received from fasting ones in all ages
of the world. To this solitude, this valley filled with unknown
perils, came a little band of monks alone ; and here they
pitched their first rough dwellings, and endured the weather.
We do not know whence they came ; whether from Fountains, or
Rievaulx, or by direct secession from some older abbey ; but
amid the spiritual exaltation which occupied their loneliness
during the first years of their sojourn here, gazing long at the
irregularities of the rock face, they fancied that they saw on it
a semblance of Christ distended on a cross ; and that image
seeming to them a miracle, became very holy in their eyes, and
drew many pilgrims from all parts of England.

You will search vainly for the image now. Such as the scar
was in all ages, before the monks entered the narrow valley,
such it has become again, a rough sheer precipice, rising by
the north side of the abbey church so close that it must have
darkened all the space within. It is at this spot that one can
best appreciate the beauty of the great building which rose
slowly from the ground in what was then a wilderness ; and can
gain some comprehension of the vastness of the effort which
set itself unresting to the accomplishment of so great a task.
Let no one fancy that the fruits of this labour and struggle in the
desert have perished with the monks. In many another valley
of this broad land of Yorkshire, monks were toiling with as
much fortitude as here, following the light through cold and
hunger and every evil that can assail man's body, yet sur-
mounting every one, and leaving behind them triumphant
proofs of victory. Their hopes and aspirations may have been
right or wrong, their religion false or true ; I do not dogmatise
about it. But sure I am that while their actual achievements
are laid waste, even as I see them here before me, the life of
England was the richer and the stronger for their struggle ; and
as no group of men can follow out a great design laboriously
without bequeathing to their successors some depth of outlook,
some encouragement to strength of purpose, so there must be

among the twisted strands which form the life of England some
cord of power which would not have been there had not these
Englishmen sacrificed their ease eight centuries ago in accom-
plishing a high conception. Let us so think of the Cistercians
and of all other monks, as they meet us constantly in roving
round this land of Yorkshire; for we who deal with bygone
times, however lightly, are trustees of the reputation of the
dead.

It is time to move onwards. I climb slowly out of the solitary
valley, leaving it filled with the gold light of the waning afternoon, welling over with peace and silence ; and following my
road, I mount at last upon the limestone crags, where gray
peaks of splintered stone stand out among the short, sweet turf.
Deep below the road a valley runs, closed at length by the
shoulder of a hill, on which the red-roofed village of Maltby
stands shining pleasantly in the evening sun. It is a pretty
spot. The crags are fantastically piled ; a few sheep go
browsing in and out among them ; and from the depths of the
valley, coming out of I know not what cool region, there blows a
keen and stimulating air, growing sharper as the sun drops
lower in the sky. It is already late, and I have far to go. I
ride on quickly through the falling twilight, while the fresh
evening air brings out every scent of flowers in the hedgerows,
together with that odour of springing grass which blows across
the fields in no other season than the early summer. I have
turned off from the road which goes to Rotherham, a grimy
place visited by none except those whose interest in church
architecture is strong enough to brave the certainty of being
choked with smoke and blinded with coal dust. We will not
regret leaving Rotherham unseen ; but there is a little scrap of
ancient building lying no more than a few miles away upon my
left, which I should certainly have visited had I not lingered so
long in the pleasant valley of Roche Abbey. It is an ancient
cross at Thrybergh ; and since it is growing fast too dark to
see the outlines of the country, which besides is of no very

striking interest, I will tell the story of St. Leonard's Cross,
an ancient relic of the days of chivalry, when the district
of South Yorkshire was a pleasant land, unsoiled by the
smoke and smother which for its great good oppress it in our
day.

The cross is nothing but a weather-beaten fragment now ;
but in the days when knights and nobles from all Europe were
flocking to the Holy Land it was tall and stately, and stood con-
spicuously by the wayside calling travellers to prayer. If one
may trust the story told by Sir John Reresby, whose Memoirs are
excellent reading for those interested in the tale of Yorkshire
life in the Commonwealth and the time of Charles II., the saint
was of his own family, no less a person indeed than one Leonard
de Reresby, who, serving his prince in the Holy Land, was taken
prisoner by the Saracens, who held him captive near seven years.
Now it is a grievous thing for any spouse to lack her lord's
society for seven years. The law in its mercy admits as much :
and Dame Reresby knew it did. So when the seventh winter
had gone by, and there came to Thrybergh neither palmer nor
wandering minstrel charged with news of the absent lord, the
indignant lady resolved to set another in his place who might
appreciate her more.

But in his lonely cell in Palestine, her husband also had remembered how the law ran ; so that " being apprehensive of this
accident, by the power of prayer he was miraculously delivered
and insensibly conveyed with shackles and gyves upon his
limbs, and laid upon the East Hill in Thrybergh Field as the
bells tolled for his wife's second marriage." Indeed a very
striking miracle !—and I wish Sir John had gone on to describe
with what varying degrees of rapture the wedding party received
and greeted the poor, dirty, fettered prisoner whom they found
lying in the field on their way to church. What he said to
them might be amusing also ; but that is a story which everybody can tell himself.

It is no wonder that a knight who was served so freely by

the powers of Heaven should afterwards become a saint. The
very fetters which were taken off his legs hung at Thrybergh for
centuries, till a thrifty Dame Reresby, in the absence of her
lord, contemning their sanctity, beat them into ploughshares.
It was an impious act. I hope she won forgiveness. But I
am puzzled about the Crusading Reresby : for another story—
Sir John does not tell it, though it is the prettier of the two—
relates how he plighted his troth at this very cross, then old
and holy, and bade farewell to his promised bride, the
heiress of the Normanvilles. Years passed, and nothing
had been heard of Reresby. His betrothed did not falter in
her faith to him, but her friends were urgent, and she believed
him dead. By degrees she ceased to hope for his return ; and
at length she gave consent to another suitor. The bridal day
was at hand, when a secret message was brought to her,
bidding her go to St. Leonard's Cross by night. She went, and
in the gloom beside the ancient column found a palmer waiting.
Tremulously she went up to him, and began to question him
what he did there, and why he called her into the lonely road
by night, knowing full well that only one man would have named
that meeting-place ; and so the long troth was knitted up again
on the spot where it began, and the ancient cross gained a
warmth of human interest which it will not lose while any stone
of it remains.

It is dark enough now for many a lover to pledge his faith unseen in the warm, scented lanes. In the night time these old
stories seem real and very near us. For in the day, when every
modern alteration pins our thoughts down to the present time, it
is hard to project our fancies back into a world of which the outer
aspect was so different. But this curtain of the dark is the same
which every generation of mankind since the foundation of the
world has watched falling from the sky or stealing up amid the
fields ; so that when the colour goes out of the plains and hills,
and the outlines of the hedgerows grow indistinct and shadowy
in the coming gloom, I know that the face of the country is

taking on the aspect which was familiar to long-dead monks
and knights, and to others also who dwelt upon the earth long
centuries before they came.   The age of the Crusaders seems

Conisboro' Castle.

faint and distant in the sunlight.   But I am already in it when
night falls ; and the world grows young with each stride of the
coming darkness.

C

Those lighted windows which I pass are in the town of Conis-
burgh.   I can scarce see the keep of the old castle reared
against the gloom ; but it is as well.   Scott has told me all I
want to know of Conisborough ; and I will not strip the magic
from another story by visiting its scene in daylight.   Do wise
men search for the very rocks which Turner painted, or try to
see whence Richmond towered over Swale, as on his canvas ?
Plague on it ! we have not all the gift of eyes ; let us use his
thankfully who will lend them to us.   And as I run out into the
scented dark again, and all Conisborough spins away behind me
like a dream, let me say that as I go through Yorkshire I claim
full liberty to mention or to leave out what I choose.   I will
describe what pleases me ; I will write fully of the things which
catch my fancy ; and if questioned as to why I did this, or left that
undone, I will attempt no other answer than a child might make
who has gone through the hedgerows plucking this flower because
he liked its scent, and that because it had a glorious red colour,
and again another because it twined prettily among the rest, or
was pearled over with the dew, or for no reason at all, but mere
wilfulness.   I know well that I have left many a flower in the
hedges, and he who will may go and glean them after me.

CHAPTER II

I⟶ is a grey morning. Now and then a splash of rain whips across the window pane, or a sobbing wind slips in and stirs the curtains gently. The sky is dark with rough clouds, and there is every sign of breaking weather. I will not travel on the long road to York, stored as it is with very noble memories, until the sun shines and I can do them justice. In the meantime it is pleasant to linger in the comely streets of Doncaster, which is in a truer sense than Bawtry the gate of Yorkshire ; for in this town, built to command the passage of the Don, more than one north country storm cloud has broken and discharged itself in blood.

To me it seems that all the north country, properly so called, lies beyond the Don, if not indeed beyond the Humber. There is nothing in the aspect of Doncaster to-day which marks it as distinct from any other trim and prosperous town in the great midland shires, where burly, good-humoured farmers go about the streets, and life is slow and ruminating. From time to time the town wakes up to busy life and action ; but that is in the autumn, when the slim racehorses are brought out of the station with quivering nostrils and large, timid eyes, tossing their delicate heads and starting nervously at every sound. Then the crowds gather thickly under the tall trees that flank the avenues beside

C 2

the racecourse on the London road ; and the cool autumn sun
shines down on a scene of tense excitement which breaks into
roars like thunder when the horses get away from the starting-
post, and now one and now another draws before the rest.   But
in the months that lie between those tumultuous days of *fête*,
Doncaster slumbers as soundly almost as the Roman Emperor
who is fabled to lie buried at the corner of Hall Gate, forgotten
by the townsmen tramping to and fro above him.

Sleepy the town may be, but it is admirably comfortable ;
and thus we find that poets, who generally start upon their
loftiest flights from spots where their baser parts are best attended
to, have sung at some length the praises of its civic head :—

> " Sweet girls of Pindus, hither bring
>   Your drums and bagpipes hollow,
> The Mayor of Doncaster I sing,
>   Assist me, oh Apollo ! "

It was vastly well for the author of this tripping verse, aided by
the god whom he piously invoked, to celebrate the pomp of the
municipality.   But Apollo is not likely to help me with my
prose : and so I must choose humbler subjects.   I go wander
ing through the goodly, well-kept streets, till I reach the bank
of the deep and treacherous river, —

> " The shelving slimy river Don,
>   Each year a daughter or a son, "

as the half-forgotten rhyme puts it, with some trace of that old
pagan fancy which saw in a stream of flowing water a cruel,
sentient thing, drawing now one and now another to death
within its embraces.   On a little knoll stands the once ancient
parish church, an old building reconstructed, dominating the
town from this side with some grandeur : and before me lies the
town bridge, crossing the river in the very spot where all the
chivalry of Northern England on an October day in 1536 lay
beneath the banner of the Five Wounds of Christ, a gallant host
of thirty thousand men well armed and encamped on the

further bank of the river, in full face of the royal army which
King Henry VIII. had sent to check them, and against which
they were as four to one. Thus early in our wanderings in
Yorkshire have we encountered the most bitter of north country
tragedies,—one of which the scars and ruin will confront us again
and again in the records of ruined families and slaughtered
monks. Whatever may have been the truth of the charges
brought against the conduct of the monasteries, there was nothing
in this great armed protest against their suppression which was
not noble. Those who made it were the very pith and marrow
of the northern counties, men who all their lives had been
warders of England against the raiding Scots, veteran soldiers,
hoary statesmen, peaceful country gentlemen, hot-blooded lads,
all of whom had been taught to look with awe on the houses of
religion so richly endowed by the piety of their ancestors, so
exquisitely built when other dwellings had no beauty save that
of strength, hallowed by the most sacred associations of four
centuries, the burial-places of their fathers, the schools where
they themselves were taught. To the abbots and priors they
had resorted for advice in every difficulty ; from their number
they had chosen the executors of their wills and the trustees of
their estates—there was no intimate transaction of their lives in
which the monks were not concerned, and that not as intruders,
but as wise friends willingly consulted. These trusted counsellors
it was who were torn suddenly from the midst of the society which
relied on them, and which had no substitutes to take their place.
That society would have been base indeed if it had struck no
blow in their defence.

So there the host lay along the further bank of the river Don,
menacing and angry, a splendid and pathetic protest against
the progress of resistless forces which were even then moulding
the old feudal world into a modern shape ; and if it had attacked the King's small army, who can doubt that it might have
set back the hands of the clock for a few hours still ? But the
powers which rule events are not to be so flouted. Robert Aske,

that simple lawyer and country gentleman, who emerges from
obscurity as a leader of this great army, was filled with noble
scruples, and dispersed his troops on a pledge of redress of
grievances.   The action was as prudent as that of a swallow
which builds its nest in the crater of Vesuvius, trusting that
the fires will never break out again.   The King's wrath burst
forth ; the blood of noble gentlemen who trusted him was
poured out like water ; and the whole great tragedy swept
onwards to a close of which we can say nothing but " Alas,
alas ! "

It is long, very long ago since Robert Aske went bravely to
the scaffold, while the gibbets stood thickly by the wayside in
every part of Yorkshire.   But he and his comrades are not yet
forgotten, their sturdy manhood is a cherished memory in
Yorkshire, and it may be that he would not have deemed his
life a wasted one had he known how many of those who hear
his story told after three centuries can still say of him that he
did well.

It is time to leave Doncaster, yet before I go I have another
tale to tell, the story of one of those great feats of lusty daring
which have won their reputation for English fighting-men in
every age and country.   It happened in the great Civil War,
that sad conflict in which Yorkshire played a mighty part,
chiefly on the side of the Parliament ; and as the years drew on
towards the crowning tragedy of the King's death, his cause had
almost wholly perished in the north, save that it lived in the
hearts and secret counsels of a few brave and desperate men.
By what cunning stratagem a mere handful of these gentlemen
seized Pontefract Castle, that grim stronghold on the passes of
the Aire, I shall tell presently ; and there they lay in a fortress
reckoned to be impregnable, the last Royal garrison in the
north country, harrying the enemy as far as they could strike,
carrying off convoys, and flouting the military strength of the
Parliament with reckless dash and hardihood.   They were
joined by cavaliers from other parts of England ; and at last,

like a swarm of wasps settling on an orchard in September,
they stung so fiercely that the Parliament sent General Rainsborough with a substantial force to smoke them out. The
General invested the Castle with regular lines of attack ; and
while the siege progressed, he himself, for some reason of
strategy or comfort, lay in quarters at Doncaster.

  Now it seemed intolerable to this band of Rakehelly cavaliers
that a crop-eared General of the Parliament should presume to
interfere with their amusements, and they resolved to free themselves. Obviously the best way of doing this, since they had
not strength enough to drive off the besiegers by a sortie in
force, was to get possession of the General ; and they had a
double motive for attempting this, since the trusted leader of
the Royalists in the north, Sir Marmaduke Langdale, had been
taken, and was lying a prisoner at Nottingham, while an infamous
story ran from mouth to mouth to the effect that it was Rainsborough's intention to bring Langdale beneath the walls of
Pontefract, and give the garrison a choice between immediate
surrender and the execution of their general before their eyes.
" Upon this," says one who was himself among the garrison,
"Captain W. Paulden, who commanded all the few horse in
the Castle, laid a design to surprise Rainsborough in his
quarters in Doncaster ; not to kill him, but to take him prisoner,
and exchange him for our own general, and it was only his own
fault that he was killed, and not brought prisoner to the Castle.
This design seemed the more feasible, because the General and
his men were in no apprehension of any surprise ; the Castle
being twelve miles off, closely besieged, and the only garrison
for the King in England.

  " In order to execute this our purpose, Captain W. Paulden
made choice of twenty-two men, such as he most confided in.
At midnight, being well horsed, we marched through the gate
that was kept open, over the meadows, between two of the
enemy's horseguards, whom by the favour of the night we
passed undiscovered. Early next morning we came to Mex-

borough, a village four miles west above Doncaster, where there
was a ferry-boat.   There we rested to refresh ourselves and our
horses till about noon.

"In the meantime we sent a spy into Doncaster to know if
there was any discovery of a party being out, and to meet us as
soon as it was dark at Cunsborough, a mile from Doncaster,
which he did, and assured us there was no alarm taken by the
town and that a man would meet us at sunrise,—it being then
the beginning of March,—who would give us notice if all was
quiet.   Thither the man came accordingly ; the sign he was to
bring with him to be known by was a Bible in his hand."

Captain Paulden then divided his twenty-two men into four
parties ; six were to attack the main guard, six the guard on
the bridge, four were ordered to General Rainsborough's
quarters ; and the Captain with the remaining six, after he had
seen the four enter the General's lodging, was "to beat the
streets and keep the enemy from assembling."

It would be painting the lily to comment on the airy audacity
of this attempt by two-and-twenty men to kidnap the general of
a hostile army from out of his own quarters in broad daylight ;
and if anything could point the insolence of the design more
strongly than the bare recital of the facts, it is surely the
narrator's reproachful comment that it was only Rainsborough's
own fault that he was killed.   Now three of the parties into
which the little force was divided carried out their plans with
something like success.   "The four that went to General Rainsborough's lodgings pretended to bring letters to him from
Cromwell, who had then beaten the Scots.   They met at the
door the General's lieutenant, who conducted them to his
chamber, and told him, being in bed, that there were some
gentlemen had brought him letters from General Cromwell.
Upon which they delivered Rainsborough a packet wherein was
nothing but blank paper.   Whilst he was opening it, they told
him he was their prisoner, but that not a hair of his head should be
touched if he would go quietly with them.   Then they disarmed his

[To face page 25.

"*The Cavaliers cantered back across the bridge.*"

lieutenant who had innocently conducted them to his chamber, and brought them both downstairs. They had brought a horse ready for General Rainsborough upon which they bid him mount. He seemed at first willing to do it, and put his foot in the stirrup ; but looking about him and seeing none but four of his enemies and his lieutenant and his centinel, whom they had not disarmed stand by him, he pulled his foot out of the stirrup and cryed, 'Arms ! Arms !' Upon this one of our men, letting his sword and pistol fall, catch't hold of him and they, grappling together, both fell down in the street. Then General Rainsborough's lieutenant catching our man's pistol that was fallen, Captain Paulden's lieutenant who was on horseback dismounts and runs him through the body as he was cocking the pistol. Another of our men run General Rainsborough at the neck as he was struggling with him that had caught hold on him ; yet the General got upon his legs with our man's sword in his hand ; but Captain Paulden's lieutenant ran him through the body, upon which he fell down dead."

Thus this bold plot miscarried through the obstinacy of a hot-headed man who, having two supporters at his elbow and a thousand more within call, positively would not let himself be kidnapped by four troopers of the enemy, though they promised that they would not hurt him ! Unreasonable fellow, who could have foreseen his folly ? So the party from Pontefract chorused among themselves as they rode back sorrowfully without their man—for they all got clear away, having alarmed the Parliament men so much by their sudden onslaught that, if we may trust the account already quoted, the Roundheads were all running out into the fields in their nightgear when the cavaliers cantered back across the bridge.

See, the sky is breaking, and a gleam of sunshine falls over the old town as I ride out across the river, following the road to Pontefract. It is, at first, a very level country, the southern portion of that great plain which intersects Yorkshire through its whole extent from north to south. As we shall see later,

much of this plain is very beautiful, but here it lacks the
shadow of the hills which rise on either hand as one goes
north, and has thus no other charm than that which belongs
to every fresh, well-cultivated countryside. The land is richly
fertile ; for, is it not a portion of that paradise which Bishop
Tonstall praised so highly when he avouched, in riding to
York with King Henry VIII., that in all his travels through
Europe, east and west, he had not found its match, "there
being within ten miles of Haslewood"—of which old mansion
there will be more to say presently—"165 manor-houses of
lords, knights and gentlemen of the best quality, 275 several
woods, whereof some of them contain 500 acres, 32 parks and
2 chases of deer, 120 rivers and brooks, whereof 5 be navi-
gable, 76 water-mills for the grinding of corn . . . ." Indeed,
I have neither leisure nor patience to go on with the worthy
Bishop's statistics. I do not know what King Henry thought
of them. Perhaps he did not listen ; unless it be that his
very nimble mind followed the same course as mine, and
reflected what a land this must be to plunder. Do but think
of it ! "165 lords, knights or gentlemen of the best quality,"
not to mention their families and retainers, all going to and
fro by this road upon their lawful or unlawful occasions !
Consider the purses, the fat purses which must have gone
along this way in the pouches of poor, timid travellers, so
scared that a single whoop from an unseen farm-lad was
enough to send them scuffling to the nearest shelter—why
should a man not stretch his hand out when the plums hung
ripe and ready to drop into it ? So argued many a tall fellow
who knew well every turn and hedgerow of this road of evil
memories. Here is the spot named "Hanging Wood"—a
suggestive designation, which may have made more than one
bold lad shiver—a bit of copse hiding an ancient quarry, than
which no better cover could be wished. In fact it was a
favourite resort of that famous rascal Nevison, whose gallant
feats in lifting purses have snatched his name from dusty

oblivion, and shrined it high in the affections of northcountry-
men, who even claim for him the mythical glories of that ride
to York which has been ascribed without much reason to Dick
Turpin.   It was at this very spot—so the rustics will tell you
still with affectionate regret for the memory of one greater
than any of our own day—it was even here that Nevison
robbed the steward of Sir George Cooke of Wheatley of all
the money he had just collected from the tenants.   He had
ridden out from Doncaster with the steward, chatting very
affably, so that when he suddenly clapped a pistol to the poor
frightened servant's chest, told him who he was, and bade
him hand out the rhino, the wretched fellow had not a
moment to collect whatever courage he possessed, and so was
shorn as meekly as any lamb.

I fear there is something demoralising about this road
which may lead me down the primrose path as speedily as
it did poor Nevison and many another, if I do not contrive
to fix my attention soon on loftier associations ; and in the
very nick of time there is the old grey tower of the parish
church of Adwick Le Street standing up above the trees
upon my right.   That will do as well as any to restore the
tone of my morality.   For do not all good Americans, and
some others who pass this way, diverge to see the tombs of
the Washington family in the Thellusson Chapel of that ancient
House of God, and speculate upon the true solution of the
endless controversy whence, and from what branch of the
many-rooted family of Washington, came the immediate ancestors of that great man whom the world has united to
regard as one of the patriots least unstained by baser motives
whose actions history has recorded.   His fame has long since
passed into the rank of cherished memories for England,
whence he sprang, no less than for America for which he
fought ; and as the whole subject lies open to surmise, I
please my fancy with the speculation that it may, perhaps,
have been this quiet village, lost on the outskirts of the great

plain, to which George Washington's thoughts returned when
he remembered the Mother Country—this pretty cluster of
ancient cottages, up whose fronts the first roses are already
breaking into bloom, a peaceful, ruminating spot which has
lain silent through all the centuries, knowing neither noise nor
bustle since the old Roman highway which ran through it
dropped into disuse.

It is but a small détour which I have made, and I regain

Robin Hood's Well, near Doncaster.

the main road a mile or so beyond the point at which I left it,
undulating pleasantly for a little way, till at last I see by the
roadside a stone cupola supported on four columns, which is
really much too interesting to pass by without consideration.
For this, which is now dry and dusty, was the well of Robin
Hood, so called in every ancient record which we have, and
possibly not without some justification, though, indeed, most
wayside wells are so very old that one must seek for their first
origin in ages far beyond those to which the exploits of bold

Robin are accredited, and it may even be that this, as was suggested by Hunter, the historian of South Yorkshire, was in fact one of the springs made available for wayfarers by good King Aeduin full twelve hundred years ago. For that great ruler, says the venerable Bede, "took such care for the good of his nation that in several places where he had seen clear springs near the highways he caused stakes to be fixed, with brass dishes hanging at them for the refreshment of travellers ; nor durst any man touch them for any other purpose than that for which they were designed, either through the dread they had of the King, or for the affection which they bore him." At any rate, this well was a place of note sufficient to suggest that it had collected through long ages the repute of a spot meet for halting and refreshment ; and thus it was that when Henry VIII. rode this way upon his coronation he was met by the Earl of Northumberland and "a right great and noble company on Barnesdale, a little beyond Robbyn Haddez ston." That the well bears the name of Robin Hood may, of course, be nothing more than another instance of that curious tendency among the common people to give familiar names to those objects of which they do not know the origin — just as a group of ancient barrows on the East Coast bear the name of "Robin Hood's butts."

There, let us drop the antiquary, and be no wiser than a child again. For this is Barnsdale, and the wide country which we see to-day dotted with no more than fine clumps of trees, suggestive rather of pleasant parks than of virgin forest, was once the very heart of the greenwood, the chosen haunt of Robin Hood, and out of all the mighty Forest of Sherwood the most famous and most dreaded part.

> " The woodwele sang and would not cease,
>   Sitting upon the spray,
> Sae loud he wakened Robin Hood,
>   In the greenwood where he lay."

He may sing as he will now without wakening bold Robin ;
and, indeed, there are some too curious persons to be found
who deny that he ever could have done it : not meaning to
depreciate the woodwele's power of shrill piping, but being
minded to deny that there ever was a Robin Hood who slept
or wakened on this earth. The argument is, I understand,
that Robin was no more than "a faint western echo of the
heroes of solar mythology"; indeed, no better than poor
William of Cloudesley, "that good yeman," whom modern
wisdom has also relegated to the land of shadows, and who
has been identified, or very nearly, by some learned professor
with "the Nibelungs, the heroes of cloudland." It is not
now for the first time that I notice what a short and easy way
there seems to be from the studies of professors into cloudland.
But let the professors e'en go there if they will. Cloudland is
a long way off ; and it is moreover full of clever people, who
are always a nuisance to their neighbours. We will stay upon
the green earth, and watch the shadows sweeping by across the
trees, and smell the fresh scents of the springing grass, and
catch what we can of the lustiness of that strong, simple life
among the downs and woodlands of which the old ballad
writers sang in such incomparable language.

> " In somer when the shawes be sheyne,
> And leves be large and long,
> Hit is full mery in feyre Foreste
> To here the fowlys song.
> To se the dere draw to the dale
> And leve the hilles hee,
> And shadow hem in the leves grene
> Under the grenewode tree."

Is not the rush and trembling of those lines more excellent
than all the speculations of all the professors in Christendom ?
Ah, let us toss the books away, and come forth from the dusty
study into the green world and the bright sunshine and the

old plain faith in the stories which we loved when we were
young. Is it not enough to watch the dawn breaking over the
earth, or to see the green trees growing black as the twilight
steals out from the woods?

Since the days of those old ballad writers who knew so well
how to sing of the joy of earth, the whole face of this country
has been wondrously changed. Perhaps some effort of
imagination is needed when one tries to realise that this wide,
open meadow land was formerly a dark forest, and that the
sunny fields and copses by which the old road runs so pleasantly, were deep woodland glades where travellers went in fear
of violence, and desperate men herded together like the wolves.
I know not with any certainty what may have been the
boundaries of Sherwood Forest in ancient times, for that
excellent custom of the court of Regarders has gone out of use,
which was wont to impress the bounds so firmly on the
memories of those who dwelt in the locality. These Regarders
used to take a survey of the forest every third year, and in
their train went a number of boys collected willy-nilly from the
immediate vicinity. The boys were chosen because it was held
that the memories of the young are good; yet it was found
desirable to impress them firmly with the actual limits, lest any
wandering fancy should distract their attention at the important
moment, and so the boys were bumped heavily upon the
ground whenever the boundary was reached; or if the limit
were a stream, that was much better, for the urchins were
thrown in and "paddled about" until their attention was
awake. "Is that stream the boundary?" one of these
witnesses was asked in his riper age. "Ees," he answered
hastily, "Ees, that 'tis; I'm sure o't by the same token that I
were tossed into't, and paddled about there like a water rat till
I were haafe deead."

By such salutary measures the great area of the forest was
preserved intact for the king, who alone might hunt there law-
fully, since no subject could hold a forest; and all the beasts

that roamed the greenwood, whether "beasts of chase and
venery" or "rascals"—to adopt the division of good Dame
Juliana Berners—were the sole property of the king, guarded for
him by a great army of officials, Warders, Verderers, Foresters,
Agisters, Regarders, and I know not what besides, who con-
stituted the lawful population of the forest.   But besides these
officers who lived by administering the law, how vast must have
been the number of fugitives who lived by breaking it !   For
during the countless wars, invasions, and revolts which disturbed north country life generation after generation through
all our early history, each one followed by its chain of proscriptions and ruthless persecution of the losing side, there were few
hiding places so secure as these great forests, where a man
might lie hid for months and years in the deep secret glades,
having at least some shelter from the weather, and the best of
venison as oft as he chose to twang his bow.   And there was
merry company in the forests too, for in all the shires of
England vert and venison were protected by special courts and
judges, whose favourite punishment was outlawry ; and, human
nature in those days being much the same as it is now, those
courts were usually busy, turning out outlaws fast enough to
make the large forests populous.

      That this punishment of outlawry was so very frequent is no
mere guess.   The records of some at least among the courts
are available to this day, and the names of the culprits, with
their sentences and brief details of their offences, may there be
read and reckoned up.   Page after page of the coucher
book of Pickering is filled with records of such crimes ; and it
does not admit of doubt that if Robin Hood himself be
mythical, there were in Sherwood whole tribes of outlaws leading exactly such a life as is attributed to him.   Why, then,
should we doubt the tales which delighted us in our childhood,
located as they are in that very part of Sherwood which must
have been the most probable scene of such exploits ?   To what
part of the great forest could those who lived by plunder resort

with such certainty of a plenteous harvest as to this region of
Barnsdale, through which ran the great highway from north to
south, crowded in all ages by wealthy travellers, for the most
part very frightened, and ready to drop their purses and run off
at the first onslaught?

There, I have done with argument.

> " Then come with old Khayyam, and leave the wise
> To talk ; one thing is certain, that life flies."

It does, indeed, and I know not how we shall get round this
vast county of Yorkshire without a stricter attention to business
than we have shown up to this point. This is a country full of
occasions for digression ; let us gird ourselves up to resist
temptation. I turn away from the waterless well of Robin
Hood, and climb the hill with resolution to think no more of
him. When I reach the top I find an undulating road which
runs so pleasantly over the sunny country, that the mere joy of
motion is enough to give me satisfaction for the moment, and I
accordingly forget all else until I find myself mounting the
declivity of a long ridge under which the town of Pontefract
lies in a hollow, and stretches up the further slope towards the
ruins of the once noble castle. There is an old saw current in
some parts of Yorkshire, which says of anything very sure to
happen that it is "as sure as a louse at Pomfret." I did not
see a l . . . Cht ! What am I saying ? I mean only that the
town seemed to me a clean and comely one, though I did not
much regard it, being in truth over full of eagerness to see the
castle, which, after all, when found, is but a broken and a very
shattered castle. In old days I should have seen its heavy
battlements standing guard above the town as I top this road,
but the old walls have crumbled to a mere shadow of their
former grandeur, and the noble building which used to dominate
the prospect from every side is now difficult to see until one is
close upon it. Then one finds enclosed in a modern garden

D

a few broken towers and walls, roofless and blackened by the
weather, terrible to no one any longer, but speaking loudly to
all who care to listen of the vast changes which the last two
centuries have brought with them in the life of England, and in
the face and aspect of the country.   Yet broken and useless as
it stands to-day, Pontefract will not cease to be visited till one
thing has decayed and perished utterly which has more permanence than stone—that is the memory of man.

For this old fortress, standing on a site so important as to
draw on itself the chief attention of all those who fought in
northern England in every age of history, has gathered round

Pontefract.

itself so great a mass of tragedy and romance as is hardly to be
matched elsewhere.   "Ah, Pomfret, Pomfret, ah thou bloody
prison!"   Its Roman name, "Ad Pontem Fractam," at the
broken bridge, takes us back to that age of desolation which
followed the departure of the Romans, when their noble public
works fell into ruin, when those who had learnt the art of
engineering from them were hunted to the hills and slaughtered
by the inroads of Saxon pirates, and the broken bridge, pathetic
witness of the great tragedy of ruin and murder, must have
stood the most conspicuous object near the town.   Scarce any
echoes from those distant days of terror have reached our ears ;
but as we listen to the tale of history flowing down the

centuries towards our own the name of Pontefract arrests us again and again. I would that I had space to speak of half the memories of Pontefract, of the great Earl Thomas of Lancaster, who played the part of Simon de Montfort with less wit, and who was broken by the power of the King, and executed near this his own town of Pontefract, yet who leaves in history the memory of one who supported a true cause, and had the welfare of the country at his heart. It is a melancholy tale, but the pity of it pales before the tragedy of that poor, friendless king, Richard II., who fell so easily from his throne, and having seen his rival mount it, was hurried down to Yorkshire secretly, first to Pickering, and was at last brought hither, where without fear of question or chance of rescue the world believes that he was done to death. Yet there were those living at the time who did not believe that this foul deed was wrought at Pontefract ; and it is, perhaps, still a question that may, in some degree, be written down an unsolved mystery whether the king really perished in the year set down in history. For three years after his body, or that which passed as such, had been laid to rest in London, a wild story was whispered round the kingdom that Richard was living, and in Scotland. A lady of Irish extraction, born of the family of Bisset, met a poor vagrant in the Isle of Skye, and recognised him as the King, whom she had known upon his Irish expedition. Others caught up the belief. The outcast was sent over to the mainland, and the Duke of Albany took charge of him. The Friars minors fathered the report, and carried it with them to every part of the three kingdoms.

Was this fellow an impostor ? No other really than Thomas Warde, of Trumpington, a crazy varlet, who bore an accidental likeness to the poor dead King? He was, at any rate, able to keep up his imposture, if it were one, and eighteen years after Richard had been reported dead, his double was still in Scotland, attended by some followers who believed in

D 2

him.   It is a strange story, and we may, perhaps, leave it, as
did Wyntour in his chronicle :

> " Quethir he had bene king or nane,
> Ther wes bot few that wyst certaine.
> Of devotioune nane he wes,
> And seilden will had to here mes ;
> As he bare him, like wes he
> Oft half wod or wyld to be."

Poor hunted fugitive !   How his mind must have been
racked with nameless terrors during all these years of humiliating
pretension to a dignity which he never gained—terrors none the
less real "quethir he had bene king or nane"; for the arm
of the King of England was terribly long, and when one
remembers how many daggers he commanded, one marvels how
any fugitive who claimed his throne could have kept breath in
his body during twenty years.   Yorkshire is prodigal of tales of
hunted kings.

I know not how to tear myself away from Pontefract.   Yet
while I stand still upon the crumbling battlements, looking
down upon the tower of the fine old ruined church far below me
in the hollow, and catching now and then a glint of silver from
the windings of the Aire through the distant plain, I remember
one story, which I must tell for mere pleasure in its hardy
insolence.   It is the earlier part of that goodly narrative of
Captain Paulden from which I quoted the description of a merry
prank at Doncaster, and it tells the tale of the daring exploit by
which the handful of cavaliers, who made so much noise round
all the country, established themselves in the great old castle,
which was thought to be the strongest in all England.

The King's cause was at very low ebb in the year before his
execution, when half-a-dozen cavaliers began to look at Pontefract from afar off and sigh for it.   They had held it once and
had been smoked out of the eyrie.   By force they knew they
could not regain it ; but guile evens the weak with their

strongest foes, and thus these desperate men kept up their
hearts.   Colonel Cotterell was Governor of Pontefract for the
Parliament, and so little likely did it seem that any attack
would be made by the broken party of the King that the whole
force at his command consisted of no more than 100 men, of
whom the greater part were not even quartered in the
castle, but were billeted at their ease in the town.   Seeing their
enemies thus lulled in false security, the cavaliers entered into
secret correspondence with some members of the garrison, and
succeeded in seducing from his faith a corporal, who engaged
to be on duty on a certain night, and to offer no interruption
to any gentlemen whom he might see approaching the walls
with a ladder under cover of the darkness.   At the time arranged
certain plucky fellows did go to Pontefract with a ladder, but
the scheme had gone a-gley.   The friendly corporal was drunk.
Another sentinel stood in his place, a meddling fellow, who
fired on the gentlemen with the ladder and gave the alarm.
No very great harm was done by his officious conduct, for
none of the cavaliers was taken.   But Colonel Cotterell, re-
flecting on what might have happened, decided that it would
be better to have his whole force within the walls, and accordingly gave notice in the neighbourhood that he would
purchase at the castle on a given day as many beds as would
be required for the accommodation of his men.

Amongst others who heard that Colonel Cotterell wanted beds
were the guileful cavaliers, and they resolved to supply his
want themselves.   The necessary arrangements were soon
made, and a cartload of very nice beds was on its way to
Pontefract.   "With the beds," says Captain Paulden, " came
Colonel Morice and Captain W. Paulden, like country gentlemen with swords by their sides, and about nine persons more,
dressed like plain countrymen and constables to guard the
beds, but armed privately with pocket pistols and daggers.
Upon their approach the drawbridge was let down and the
gates opened by our confederates within.   Colonel Morice

and those who were with him entered the castle. The main-
guard was just within the gate, and there our company threw
down the beds, and gave a crown to some soldiers, bidding
them fetch ale to make the rest of the guard drink, and as
soon as they were gone out of the gate, they drew up the
drawbridge, and secured the rest of the guards, forcing them
into a dungeon hard by, to which they went down by about
thirty stairs, and it was a place that would hold 200 or 300
men.

"Then Captain W. Paulden made one of the prisoners show
him the way to the Governor's lodging, where he found him
newly laid down upon his bed with his cloaths on, and his
sword, being a long tuck, lying by him. The captain told him
the castle was the King's and he was his prisoner; but he without answering anything, started up and made a thrust at the
captain, and defended himself very bravely, till being sore
wounded, his head and arm cut in several places, he made
another full and desperate push at the captain and broke his
tuck against the bed-post, and then asked quarter, which my
brother granted, and he for the present was put down among
his own soldiers into the dungeon." Where I doubt not he
greeted them with winged words which would be worth the
hearing had any one recorded them.

Thus began the merry life of this garrison of brave cavaliers
at Pontefract. It ended in the only manner possible, when the
Parliament became triumphant everywhere; but what makes
the conclusion of the matter worth referring to is the fate of
Colonel Morice. In the final accommodation for the surrender
of the castle he and Lieutenant Blackburne with four others
were excepted, being regarded as rebels more pestilent and
dangerous than the rest. Yet General Lambert, admiring their
soldierly qualities, gave them a chance of dying nobly by
promising them their lives if they could cut their way out. The
whole number wished for nothing better, and sallied out with
desperate courage. Morice and Blackburne broke through their

enemies and gained the open country, but were taken a few days later near the coast of Lancashire, and brought to trial at York. In defiance of Lambert's promise, they were condemned to death, and lay in York Castle awaiting execution. On the last night of their lives they, by some friendly agency, got possession of a rope, with which they let themselves down the castle wall. Morice descended safely, and might have escaped with ease ; but Blackburne fell and broke his leg. Morice refused to leave him, and the guard found him standing by his helpless comrade, cheerful and undaunted, as he was still when a few hours later he mounted the scaffold side by side with his friend and went out of the world bravely in company with him. His portrait is at Sledmere. It shows a noble face.

Of the four who sallied out with him, one was slain and three were driven back within the castle. But the garrison did not desert them. They adopted a wonderful resource. In some disused portion of the castle they walled them up behind a screen of masonry, giving them provisions for a month, and there the three lay while the castle was surrendered and ransacked fruitlessly for them. When the pursuit was over, and the castle quiet, their friends succeeded in releasing them, and they all escaped.

Few have been the struggles in the stormy history of England in which Pontefract played no part ; and as I go down the steep hill past the ancient church, and over the level road towards Ferrybridge, I find myself plunging into a crowd of memories far more fierce and bloody than any I have named as yet, and entering a tract of country through which no one can pass even now without some throb of awe or pity for that infinite number of our forbears who fought and died among these sunny fields, casting off all ties of kindred, sons slaying fathers and fathers sons : a combat so terrible and unnatural that, used as men were to scenes of carnage in old times, no one among the ancient chroniclers can tell without some words of horror the story of a battle which was like no other battle

known to them, and of a slaughter so tremendous that for
forty-eight hours, it is said, the River Cock ran blood. It is
but a little way to Ferrybridge ; and here I will stand awhile
and begin my tale, while the River Aire, a wide and placid
stream, flows on beneath me through broad, level pastures
bronzed with buttercups and ruddy sorrel. A quarter of a
mile up stream is a little red-tiled village, having a square
church tower on slightly higher ground rising dark against
green woods. A keen wind blows the river into ruffles, and
the light changes quickly on the willow bushes by the bank.
To the eastward one can see nothing but bright gold and
green, and cattle grazing in the rich grass, with a dim line of
blue, hazy woods in the far distance—a silent, peaceful sight as
any one could find in England.

   This was the passage of the Aire which Pontefract Castle
was set to guard. He who held Pontefract, held this passage
also ; and he who held the passage had in his hands the key of
York, that great and noble city which was the military centre
of the north. Now in the crisis of the wars of York and
Lancaster, King Edward IV. lay at Pontefract, having with
him the Earl of Warwick, the great King-maker, and a vast
host, while at York were King Henry and Queen Margaret,
with Clifford, called "the Butcher," and an army which comprised nearly all the nobility of the North country ; for,
roughly speaking, the North was for Lancaster and the South
for York, and the hatred of the two was more deadly than has
since been known in England. Now, placed as these two
armies were, it was of consequence to both to hold the bridge
at this spot where I stand ; for so the Yorkists might keep
open a passage of retreat, while, on the other hand, King
Henry, if his troops could win the passage, might check
the enemy in crossing. So King Edward, knowing that the
Lancastrians had advanced as far as Towton, told off men-at-
arms to seize the bridge under Lord Fitzwalter and the Bastard
of Salisbury, brother to the King-maker ; but in the night of

March 27th the Butcher Clifford, at the head of a large force
of light cavalry, swooped down upon these meadows, surprised the Yorkists in their sleep, slew Fitzwalter and the
Bastard of Salisbury, and held the bridge himself. Now,
Hall, the chronicler, tells us that " when the Erle of Warwicke
was enformed of this feate, he, like a man desperate, mounted
on his hackney, and came blowyng to King Edward, saying :
' Syr, I pray God have mercy of their soules which in the
beginnynge of your enterprise have lost their lives ; and
because I se no succors of the world, I remit the vengeaunce
and punishment to God our Creator and Redeemer,' and with
that lighted down and slewe his horse with his sworde, saiyng :
' Let him flie that wil, for surely I wil tary with him that wil
tary with me,' and kissed the crosse of his swourde." Any one
may judge how this spectacle inflamed the passion which was
already raging under every banner in the army. It was pro-
claimed that in the coming battle no quarter should be given,
and further that any man who had no stomach for the fight
might then depart, but if he stayed, and wavered later, he
should instantly be slain. In this grim humour Edward, who
had the instinct of a born general, turned aside from the passage
where Clifford lay expecting him, and led his army across the
river at Castleford, three miles higher up, thus threatening to
cut off Clifford from his friends and block the road by which
he had advanced. Clifford saw his danger, and knew that
he had lost the stake for which he played. He retreated
instantly, and all along the undulating road through Sherburn
he skirmished with the advance guard of the Yorkist army,
hoping doubtless that as his own friends heard the din of
fighting they would throw out succours and beat back the
enemy who harassed him. Mile by mile he fought his way to
Dintingdale, where a lane, which may have been the old highway, strikes off upon the left to the village of Saxton lying in a
hollow. There the end came ; and the Butcher, who had
thrown off his helmet, perhaps for mere relief from weariness

and thirst, was transfixed with an arrow and slain. He was a bold and valiant soldier, and " Butcher " as he was, I know not if he was more bloody than other men in those fierce days. How he gained his tragic nickname I shall tell hereafter in its proper place. It is one of the mysteries left unexplained by the chroniclers why he was not succoured.

Let us turn off at this lane and go down to Saxton, by the way which the Yorkists' army must have followed as they came pressing on in this direction, over ground more open than it is to-day, till as they saw the church tower lying down below, they came in sight also of the host of Lancaster drawn up on the hill, which they had to cross ere reaching Tadcaster. It was late in the afternoon, and as the cold March twilight darkened down, Edward planted his standard bearing a sable bull on the height facing the Lancastrians, and drew his army up there through the night. When the dawn broke the two great armies looked in each other's face over a little hollow that divided them. It was Palm Sunday. I do not how far in the scattered farms and villages round about, men held their breath, or suspended the offices of life or of religion on that fatal morning. It may have been that even from Saxton Church, so close to the contending hosts, the sound of some chiming bell rose up on that last stillness of the dawn, bringing to all minds which were not wholly choked with hatred some memory of Him who died for all impartially ; and it can hardly be that fear had seized so utterly upon that country-side that from some House of God in the locality, prayer did not go up all through the day for those who needed it as sorely as any who have ever lived.

Early in the morning, some say at five, others several hours later, both armies gave a great shout, "and the same instante time," says Hall, " there fell a small snyt or snow, which by violence of the wyn was driven into the faces of them which were of King Henries parte, so that their sight was somewhat blemished and minished. The Lord Fauconbridge, who led the forward of King Edwardes battaile, being a man of great policie and of much experience in marciall feates, caused every archer under his standard to shot one flyght and then made them to stand still. The northern men feling the shoot, but by reson of the snow not wel vewing the distance between them and their enemies, like hardy men shot their schiefe arrowes as fast as they might, but al their shot was lost and their labour vayn, for they cam not nere the southern men by xl taylors yerdes." It is not easy to believe that the veteran generals of Lancaster were duped by so simple a device. But what is certain is that very early in the day the two armies were at close quarters, and that for many hours that great mass of men swayed backwards and forwards in the snow, hacking at each other with axes and with swords, amid a din of shrieks and battle cries such as no man's fancy can re-create, till at length when midday was far past, the throng of that bloodstained press began to move in one direction, and the Lancastrians were driven, fighting desperately, up that hill on which they had stood in pride a few hours earlier, past their stations, and down the old highway to Tadcaster, which drops by a steep descent to the River Cock. Up to this point they maintained some order ; but as the beaten soldiery crowded down the precipitous incline, and saw their triumphant enemy pressing over the hill-top, slaughtering without mercy all whom their swords could reach, the courage and discipline of the fugitives failed them, they lost all formation and became a mere rabble, trampling over one another in their hurry to escape. Then ensued a scene of carnage on which it is better not to dwell ; the bodies fell in the River Cock so thickly that they filled its channel up, and friend and foe alike swarmed over the little stream on a bridge of still living men. It is said that the river ran blood for eight-and-forty hours, while all over the hills blood was trampled into the snow in such quantities that when a thaw came all the furrows of the fields ran red.

Such was the fight on Towton Moor, the most terrible and

deadly which had been seen in England since Harold fell at
Senlac.   I stand on the hill above the village of Saxton,
looking down upon the slopes where the thickest of the fight
occurred.   All the fields are full of green, waving wheat, and a
plover rising from some sedgy hollow by the stream wheels round
in circles overhead shrieking plaintively.   The cottage gardens
in the village are full of budding roses ·   Scarce one of them is
old enough to have seen the battle, or to have harboured the
dying men who must have been helped down that slope in
crowds.   Far away to eastwards stretches the great plain,
roughened with green trees, softened by blue haze, stretching
infinitely distant from the roots of the ridges where I stand.
Summer has its hold upon the land, and here, where the
hacking of the swords was loudest, there is no sound breaking
the drowsy afternoon, save the calling of the plover overhead.
I go on past the Bloody Meadow, past Towton Dale Quarry,
and so up to the old steep road, down which the routed troops
crowded in confusion, and leave behind me the whole fatal
ground, over which to this day there grows in large, irregular
patches, a small dwarf, creeping rose, whose white petals are
slightly splashed with red, while its stems are of a dull, bloody
hue, which, even more than the flowers, recalls the day when
the noblest chivalry of England, Yorkists and Lancastrians,
White Rose and Red Rose lying piled together, fell in the snow
and perished upon Towton Moor.

The Palace, Bishop's Thorpe.

CHAPTER III

HASLEWOOD, TADCASTER, YORK, AND BEVERLEY

I DO not know that any topographer need desire a nobler subject than is thrust in the way of those who wander round the Ainstie of York. The Ainstie, a name of which I do not see that any one can give a wholly satisfactory explanation, is the district lying between three rivers, the Aire, the Ouse, and the Nidd, and extending westwards as far as Otley, a region both fertile and picturesque, and including the domains of as many families of note as would provide lively material for more than one stout volume were their deeds and the romance of their exploits but adequately told. And to me who love the great-ness of the past somewhat more than the achievements of our

own day, and dwell with higher pleasure on the story of a
Knight of Malta than on that of a successful mill proprietor, it is
a genuine embarrassment to find myself dragged by a sense of
duty at high speed through this treasure-chamber of romance,
where I would fain linger till I have despoiled it all. Would
that I might loiter slowly by the banks of Wharfe! But
how then should I see the coast and mountains of this vast
province? From Beverley, from Flamborough, from Richmond,
Barnard Castle, and the Dales, there come voices which call
me on ; but some leaves I will snatch from the laurels of this
great district as I go by, if only to show how rich a harvest of
stories, grave and gay, is to be reaped and garnered in the Ainstie.

When I stood upon the Field of Towton, I was no more than
a short three miles from Haslewood, an ancient house where
the great family of Vavasour have been settled since the
Conquest. For many centuries no name stood higher than that
of Vavasour in all the north country, and the little chapel which
stands beside the house is a perpetual monument of this esteem,
since it is said to have been the only one to which, in the days
when the worship of Roman Catholics was proscribed, the
privilege of celebrating mass was granted, and has been held
without any interruption to the present day. The house stands
nobly on a lofty ridge, a plain, squared building. having two
shallow wings ; and being left a little lonely and deserted, serves
the better as a stimulant to the imagination, recalling a dozen
stories of the noble family which owns it. But I will have
none but merry ones to-day, for, indeed, the tales of slaughter
which I have been telling, weigh a little heavily upon my mind,
and therefore I set aside the baronial grandeur of this family,
and take down from the shelves a certain cheerful publication
over which the readers of three centuries ago were wont to laugh
until they were both stiff and sore. Why should we not laugh
where they did, for all the extra wisdom we have gained? The
book is called "The Hundred Mery Talys," and among them
is one of Mr. Justice Vavasour.

"There was a Justice but late in the reame of England, callyd Master Vavasour, a very homely man and rude of condycions, and lovyd never to spend mych money. Thys Master Vavasour rode on a time in his circuite in the northe countreye, where he had agreede with the Sheriff for a certain some of money for hys charges thorowe the Shyre, so that at every inn and lodgynge this Master Vavasour payd for hys own costes. It fortuned so that when he came to a certayn lodgynge, he commanded one Turpyn, hys servant, to se that he used good hosbondry, and to save such things as were left and to cary it wyth hym to serve at the next baytynge. Thys Turpin doynge by his Maystre's commaundement, toke the broken bred, broken mete, and all such thing that was left, and put it in the clothe sake. The wyf of the house perceiving that he toke all such fragments and vytayle with him that was left and put it in the clothe sake, she broughte up the podage that was left in the pot, and when Turpyn had turned hys bake a lytyl asyde, she pouryd the podage in the clothe sake, whych ran upon his robe of skarlet and other of his garmentys, and rayed them very evyll, that they were much hurt therwith. Thys Turpin sodeynly turnyng hym and seeing it, revyled the wyfe therfore, and ran to hys mayster and told hym what she had done ; wherfore Mayster Vavasour incontinent callyd the wyf and seyd to her thus : 'Thou drab,' quod he, 'what hast thou don ? Why hast thou poured the podage into my clothe sake, and marred my raiment and gere ?' 'Oh, syr,' quod the wyfe, 'I know wel ye are a judge of the reame, and I perceive by yon your mind is to right and to have that is your owne ; and your mynd is to have all thing with you that ye have paid for, both broken mete and other thynges that is left, and so it is reson that ye have, and therfore because your servant hath taken the broken mete and put it in your clothe sake, I have therein put the podage that he left, because ye have wel and truely payd for them.'" To this elaborately "Mery Tale," the moral is— What ? One would never guess it, it is so recondite : " Here ye may se that he that playeth the niggarde over mych, som tyme it torneth hym to hys owne losse." With which smug piece of mediaeval wisdom stored up safely in our minds, we lay aside this mediaeval jest book, and stop laughing with our ancestors.

What am I to say of Tadcaster, that old dull town with its many breweries and its lack of modern interest? I know it was a Roman station; but I cannot stay here to talk of camps and legions where there is scarce one relic to be seen, while at York, no more than nine miles away, every detail of the life of those old days lies realised and palpable before our eyes. I care naught for Calcaria when Eboracum is so near, and prefer to hasten onwards with what speed I may. But as I run out upon the high road, once so smooth and good, but now neglected to a degree not creditable to the local rulers, a few miles of jolting surface bring me in sight of an old grey building standing back across two fields upon the right, by which I cannot go without remark, not upon the building, interesting though it be, but on the family which built it and dwelt there for many a generation. Indeed it is not possible to go through the Ainstie without thinking of the family of Fairfax, whose great capacity and restless energy twined themselves so tightly in the history not of England only, but of other and more distant lands.

Not many years after Towton Field the first stones of that old house were laid by Sir Guy Fairfax, who supported the White Rose strenuously, and profited by his valour, laying the foundations of this branch family of Steeton, to whose fame his brother Nicholas contributed even more than he. For in those days when the English nobles, worn out and spent with fighting and proscriptions, settled down to a peace of utter lassitude and exhaustion, Nicholas Fairfax cast his eyes about to see in what quarter of the world he might find adventure, and saw his opportunity in the ceaseless hostilities of the Knights of Rhodes with the Grand Turk, who, scarce a generation earlier, had established himself at Constantinople, where he lingers yet, to the eternal shame of Christendom. There is no more gallant story in all history than that of the great deeds of the Knights of Rhodes. While all Europe dallied and applauded idly a courage which they dared not imitate, this handful of brave men held the outpost of Christianity, and grew grey in fighting manfully against crushing odds, till at length the Sultan Solyman attacked the island with a resistless force. While his countrymen were preparing for the final assault, Fra Niccolo Fairfax was sent to cut his way through the Turkish fleet in a small galley and bring back succour from Candia. It was a daring feat, but Fra Niccolo accomplished it and brought back reliefs. His skill and bravery could not change the final issue, for the small band of knights was overwhelmed at last, and retired to Candia in two great ships, of which Fairfax commanded one. Ah, valiant Fra Niccolo ! had only ten thousand more been found in all Europe with thy spirit and thy passionate contempt for Moslems, how many penalties we should have been spared which we have now to pay for the cowardice of our ancestors and our own !

Well, Fra Niccolo's deeds must be read in Bosio ; I cannot transcribe them here. Another Fairfax of this great family was with the Constable Bourbon at the sack of Rome in 1527, and could have told us of George Frundsberg and the motley gang of Lanzknechts who followed him in that bold dash across the Alps, and whether it was indeed the fact that Bourbon was slain by Benvenuto Cellini, as the cunning goldsmith boasts in his incomparable memoirs, and how much more which comes rushing on the mind at the mere mention of that awful disaster to Rome and Christendom. Wherever hard fighting was going on in those ages you will find the traces of a Fairfax ; and if there be indeed records of all that members of that family wrought and saw, the world will some day receive a book such as it has rarely gloated over for its enjoyment.

I may very well talk about the Fairfaxes upon this road, which

E

truth to tell, owes any attraction it may possess to its associations, its surface being of the vilest possible, and, as every story, if it does not reach the end, should at least begin at the beginning, I will turn back to what was a very good beginning for Fairfax of Steeton, the day, that is to say, on which he carried off Isabel Thwaites from the clutches of the Abbess of Nun Appleton, which had closed on her with the peculiar grip which Mother Church reserved for heiresses. Had Isabel been no better than an heiress, Mother Church might possibly have maintained her hold. But she was beautiful to boot, and when one is seventeen, and beautiful, and it is spring time and the sap is rising, how can one not listen to the devil?

The devil was William Fairfax. He likewise was not old, and he had hot blood which called to Isabel and bade her heed him rather than the nuns. He came from Steeton, as I say, and Nun Appleton, where Lady Anne Langton, the Abbess, sat guard over Isabel the heiress, is scarce four miles away down over the hill near the banks of Wharfe. It is lamentably spoilt. One need not go to see it now. Four miles is not much; and moreover, Isabel was allowed to go out hunting. Fairfax hunted too, and was besides, a gentleman of birth and property. What more natural than that he should visit at the nunnery, where even the Cistercian rule permitted some intercourse with pupils who were rich? I daresay no harm was meant to Mother Church. Very likely half-a-dozen hot words spoken stealthily in the nuns' old garden did the mischief; the stubble was on fire in an instant; the Abbess raged, the maiden wept, and as for the hot-headed stripling who had caused the trouble, he tried fair words, but they failed; resorted to the law, but that failed, as it did very often when levelled at the Church; and then turned his hot head to what never fails, namely force, and came and carried off his bride. That must have been a pretty scene. Isabel was shut up in the church. I don't know how Fairfax got her out, but history tells us that no great while afterwards they were married at Bolton Percy, and there was scarce any

end to the riches which this stolen bride showered down upon
the happy thief.   No wonder that the lady Abbess fumed.   It
is long odds that she never had such a chance of wealth again.
But it would have come to just the same thing in the end, and
it is that which makes the story so instructive.   For this
Abbess lived to see the Dissolution, and to whom was the
nunnery granted ?   Why, to the Fairfaxes, and it was to the
son of William and Isabel that the old Abbess handed over
all her keys.   What a lesson on the folly of opposing fate !

It was from this marriage that those Fairfaxes sprang who
were so great and terrible in the civil wars.   I would there
were more like them in these days, for England has need of
servants 'who are not only faithful, but strong as well, and
few there are who can put both qualities to the work which she
has waiting for them.   I know another story about Nun
Appleton—the tale of one Sister Hilda, who was no better
than she should be, who accordingly became a spectre, incurred
the humiliation of being conjured by an archbishop, and
disappeared at last in a crash of thunder together with an
erring friar and a strong smell of sulphur, while the candles
went out on the altar, and everybody was alarmed.   But I
really cannot stay to rake up these old scandals ; for see, a
turn of the road has brought in sight two noble towers standing side by side some three miles away, while at their base
lies a crowd of buildings which can be no other than York.
The first sight of that noble city drives out of my mind both
erring nuns and their hot-headed lovers ; and I hurry on my
way scarce noting the pleasant houses of the suburb, or the
green turf of the race-course, till I enter York itself beneath
the massive arch of Micklegate, and stand in the narrow
streets which still retain the aspect borne by them when the
city was a fortress.

For York has never yet been modernised ; our dull life has
touched but not absorbed it.   There are still the winding
streets of ancient timbered houses nodding each towards the

other, the old crumbling churches thrust out into the roadway
and splitting it into two narrow lanes by which the traffic
must filter onwards as it may.   The small, quaint alleys
winding to the river have not been improved away; the

Micklegate Bar, York.

pleasant gardens here and there about the walls are as green
and fresh as when the Stuart Kings or their wild courtiers
jested there on summer evenings ; the ancient gates and bars
can still be closed when the rulers of the city will ; and best
of all, the traveller of to-day may walk round nearly the whole

circuit of the walls and gaze forth still from the embrasures
whence in old days the warders looked for the smoke of

York from the Wall.

beacons in the north, or watched some jaded rider spurring
towards the city from Berwick or Carlisle.

These walls, once so formidable, are very quiet now ; and
you may pace up and down in solitude nearly all day long,

while the sun flickers through the trees and gardens of the
Deanery, while the swallows wheel and skim around the
Minster towers, and the sound of chanting reaches you across
the sweet, keen, northern air. You will walk onwards and
note the great height which the walls have had. You will
mark the towers and bastions which strengthened them; and
going further you will see the blackened keep of the ancient
castle standing by the river's bank, grim and strong, a clear
witness even yet to the fact that those who fortified York
anticipated no child's play, but feared assaults against which
the best defences they could rear were not a whit too much.
So, gradually, the modern peaceful aspect of the city falls
away, and one sees York as it was, the ancient military centre
of all England, the bulwark of the realm against the constant
peril of the north.

How shall we, who look on Scots as our fellow countrymen,
understand what York and England thought of them? Here
is an old document which tells us clearly; and I make no
apology for quoting it, since no one can understand the part
which York and Yorkshiremen played on the great field into
which we are going without a knowledge of the mutual feeling
between Scot and Englishman. "To all trew Cristen people
this present wrytynge seyng, redyng or heryng, George th'
Abbott of the Monastery of Our Lady of Alnewick, Sir Rauf
Grey of Chelvingham in the Countie of Northumberland,
Knyght, Sir Richard Brown, Vicar of Heddon . . . . . .
grettynge in our Lord God Everlastyng. Unto whom it ap-
perteigneth due and humble recommendacioun. Be it known
to your universities that whereas we be enformed yt oon
Bartram Dawson of the Citie of York, drapour, is seynesterly
defamed that he shulde be a Scottyshman borne, whereby he
is grevously hurt in his name and goodes; and for so much as
meretory and medful it is to record and testyfie ye truth in
every matter duely required, that for the concelement thereof
prejudice be not engenered to the innocent; we, therefore,

testifie and recorde yt the same Bartram Dawson was gotten and borne in the towne of Wardene in the Parishe of Bamburgh. . . . Wherfore we besech and desyre youe and yche oon of youe to admyt repute and take the said Bartram as an Yngles-man, not yeving credence to such defame and detraction. . . ."

Consider this document. It must have cost money. Knights and Abbots did not testify for the advantage of a draper out of sheer love of justice. Bartram must have paid heavily, and it is clear, therefore, that he wanted the document badly. Thus the suspicion of being a Scot had involved him in some serious trouble at the hands of his fellow townsmen, from which he could escape only by proving the suspicion ground-less. In plain words, what this document shows us is the fierce and unquenchable hatred which burnt between Scotland and England in all the middle ages, and which in this proud old city, head and centre of the greatest of the six northern counties, never waned till the union of the two countries into one government took their occupation from the border raiders, and let the old feuds die away into oblivion. What it was that Bartram Dawson feared, or what had actually been done to him, I know not; but if he were thought by the townsmen to be a Scot, it is odds if he carried off his life in safety out of the ruin of his smoking shop. It would have been easy on any night in York to make up a mob of men who had seen the cruellest deeds wrought by the Black Moss-troopers, and who would have been glad enough to pay them out on the goods and body of a fat draper in the Skellgate. There will be more to say of the border warfare as we go through Yorkshire; for the waves of that great sea of troubles surged over the actual marches and broke again and again among the Yorkshire dales. For the time it is enough that we note the bitter hatred that existed; and remember the fact that the great mission of York from the first day when its low walls rose at the inter-section of two streams was to keep a set watch northwards and to face the peril from the Scots.

Let us go on following the lanes that skirt the river's bank till we emerge at the garden of the Yorkshire Philosophical Society, a pleasant stretch of shady turf and winding gravel walks enclosing a group of ruins and remains which takes high rank even in Yorkshire for its beauty, and for wealth of human interest is unsurpassed. For here, cropping out upon a little knoll whence one looks forth upon the river and the swans which float down slowly on its silver stream, there is still a many-angled tower which formed one corner of the Roman walls. Now, to many of us in these days—I speak as one who is himself an ignoramus—the Roman occupation of these islands is a sort of fairy tale, the story of some temporary raid, some huge adventurous army which came and went, leaving about as much memory of its presence as the shadow of a summer cloud upon the earth. It is strange that we English, of all people, should think lightly of an occupation which was so like our own great task in India. Who has not heard from Anglo-Indians of the bitterness of the long separations which their life involves, of the continued craving for the sights and speech of home which assails a man whose days are passed in some lonely station on the plains, or how willingly even the highest rank and the greatest honour in that far, strange country are exchanged for the modest life of a private citizen at home? But these were the thoughts, these were the sorrows and pre-occupations of the Roman garrison at York. The sentinel who kept watch upon that old red tower, looking across the river and up the slope beyond, crowned with the baths and villas of his chiefs, while from the guard-room down below the songs and laughter of his comrades rang out clearly through the falling night, was thinking all the time of some vineyard on the Sabine Hills, or of some white walled town on the sunny coast of low Apulia, where the night fell how differently from the misty darkness of this cold northern land, and the stars came out warm and large and golden in the sky.

Do we ever think that this strange Roman occupation of our

land lasted longer than our own stay in India has been as yet? The sixth Roman legion, that one which, with a regimental pride worthy of our sympathy, wrote itself on every one of its inscriptions—"Leg. vi. Victrix"—was in garrison at York for full three hundred years. Think of it, as long a period as from the days of Queen Elizabeth unto our own! Is it not possible even now to catch the human interest of that long period of exile, to think of the men who ruled here in York neither as shadows nor abstractions, but as having like passions with ourselves, subject to the same griefs, and dominated by the self-same pride of race? It can be done by any one who will walk across the well-kept turf from the old, many-angled tower, till he reaches an ancient grey building near the water's edge, in which he will find stored as many relics of the Romans as will set his fancy working for many a day to come.

For there, in the silent rooms of this old building, lie not only the outward signs of the presence of the Romans on this ground, where they have been so long but half remembered, not only their statues and their mile-stones, their altars and the vessels of glass or pottery which served them for their daily use, but also their more intimate possessions, their ornaments and jewels, their rings, their bracelets and the armlets which their children wore. There are the trinkets of a Roman lady put together by the hands of those who loved her and laid beside her in her coffin, and there, too, are the childrens' toys, their whistles, their little messes of red paint, the scraps of glass and earthenware, with which they played hop-scotch, the shells they gathered at the seaside, and brought home to York as treasures. Do we not know how children love these trifles? All these, and many more, which childish fingers played with so many centuries ago as long as they had strength to hold them, and which, when the little lives which drooped and pined in the cold winters of this wild north land went out at last, were gathered all together at the end, and slipped in beside the child so that it might still hold the things it cherished in its nightly sleep. Ah, how human it all is! Does this old world ever change at all in any of its realities? You go downstairs into the lower room and find the inscriptions which the officers and soldiers of the legion carved on the graves of their wives and children: "To the Gods, the Manes, to Simplicia Florentina, a most innocent child, who lived ten months; Felicius Simplex, her father, of the Sixth Legion Victorious, dedicated this." How suddenly the barrier of ages is swept away as one reads these old inscriptions! Eighteen centuries count as nothing, and out of the long darkness of the past Felicius, the soldier, stretches out towards us a hand which trembles with emotion.

"Altera Roma," our second Rome, was the name which these proud conquerors bestowed on the noble city they had built as a military base and centre of the province of Britain, and stretching northwards from it they held a long chain of forts and stations set at easy intervals of marching up to the great wall which spanned the neck of the kingdom from Carlisle to Newcastle. Further off, again, there was a second wall; and within this double line the province slept securely, while the forces of the wild Picts spent themselves vainly outside the barrier. So here at York there grew up a rich and cultured life. The great plain which occupies all the level valley, cleaving Yorkshire like a gash from north to south, was dotted over with sumptuous houses and with pleasure gardens, while at Aldborough, some fifteen miles away, lay the summer villas of the officers, how stately, one may still see from the fragments lying in the cottage gardens. It was a luxurious and splendid life; and by rights there should have come down to our day a group of buildings which would have shown us Roman life upon its grandest side. But the dykes which fenced the Roman empire were growing leaky, the courage and resource of the great nation were sapped by luxury, the barbarians were stealing through the ill-kept watches on every side of the vast domain.

Rome had no longer strength for guarding Britain. She withdrew her soldiers, and what then remained in Britain? Why,
the cultured life, the luxurious buildings, the outer shell of
military organisation, without the sturdy courage and the
manly qualities which had kept the wolves at bay so many
generations. I may not stay to trace the progress of the
tragedy. For a while the mere terror of the Roman name
kept off the pirates from attacking the rich spoil for which
they lusted. The fabric stood as yet, but it tottered, and
men held their breath waiting for the crash of that mighty
ruin. It came at last. The fierce northern pirates swarmed
in on the second Rome; their axes went on hacking all
through the streets of the noble city; the sky was blackened
by the smoke of burning temples; and all through the plain
the work of slaughter and of desolation was continued till
the whole of that splendid civilisation lay buried underneath
a pile of blood-stained ashes. Of the actual details of the
slaughter we know next to nothing; but in a cave in the wild
moorland, near the town of Settle, where dripping water falls
continually from the roof in the semi-darkness, there have been
found the bones of some of the poor fugitives, with the trifling
articles which they could carry with them in their hurried
flight. So there it ended, this great and costly Roman
domination, which taught the people how to live in peace and
cultivate the soil, which gave them plenty and prosperity and
comfort in their daily life, and warded off from them the barbarians whom they feared. It ended in a race of terrified
men, women, and children away from their crops and orchards
in the fertile valley lands into a wet cranny of the rocks,
where in cold and darkness, crouching in daily terror of discovery and murder, they dragged out the scenes of a tragedy as
bitter as any that has happened in the whole history of the
world. Meanwhile the pirates wasted all the country, and this
is why we have so few evidences of what the Romans wrought
in the fair land of York.

Come, we have said enough about the Romans, and have left ourselves no space to talk of all the stories usually told in the handbooks, of how the Emperor Severus died at York, and the greater Constantine was born there, and of St. Helen, the mother of that great ruler who, on very doubtful evidence, is set down as a Yorkshire woman, and has countless wells dedicated to her on that presumption. There is, too, that odd tale of how somebody groping under the church of St. Helen on the walls found, during the middle ages, a vault in which a lamp continually burnt, and recognised it as the tomb of the Emperor Constantius, to illustrate which pretty tale, Camden quotes the opinion of one Lazius, who held that the ancients had the art of reducing gold to "a consistent fluid "—whatever that may mean—by which they kept fire burning in vaults for a long time. They did, indeed, if this story may be relied on, for when the vault was opened the Emperor had been dead full twelve hundred years, and the lamp was still alight! I suppose the foolish fellow who found it put it out to demonstrate that he could do as much ; otherwise we might ourselves have seen the wonder, and perhaps have even learnt this very useful art.

I cannot go away from this pretty garden without saying something of the ruined abbey of St. Mary, which stands on the highest part of the slope. "There are some," said Camden, manfully, "who take it ill that I have mentioned monasteries. I am sorry to hear it ; but—not to give them any just offence— let 'em be angry if they will." If he can snap his fingers at his readers and write of monasteries as he will, I suppose that I may do so, too, and, therefore, I will walk across the grass and see the shattered ruins. Time would scarce have hurt the massive columns of this exquisite old abbey ; storm and weather would but have touched the mouldings with an added grace, or lent a greater softness to the tendrils of the vine shoots that trail in the hollow at the head of every pillar, had not man, stupidest of all the animals, torn down wilfully the beauty which he was too blind to care for. One may still see the wall and the splendid windows of the north aisle of the nave, and the huge group of clustered columns which supported the tower arch upon that

St. Mary's Abbey, York.

side—enough, perhaps, to enable any one who will sit down by the broken arch of the old west door, while the shadows steal across the sunny grass, and the birds hop confidently round the broken walls, to see again in fancy the grand church as it was, a

glorious witness to the strength of purpose with which men of
old days followed their ideals.

There had been older monasteries in the north than this one
dedicated to St. Mary, but the Danes, who wasted Yorkshire
with fire and sword two hundred years before the Norman
conquest destroyed all these, and left the country such a savage
wilderness that, as the old chronicle tells us, "The country
people never heard the name of a monk, and were frightened
at the very habit." Into this pagan desert—for heathen creeds
can be traced there even now, and the dead leaves of to-day
must have been a mighty forest then—into this rank field of
superstition and mistrust came a handful of Benedictine monks
from Winchcombe, and its neighbour house of Evesham, eager
to restore those ancient dwellings of their Order which had
once fed the poor, and taught the children, and housed the
traveller who came down at nightfall from the lonely moor.
Some they restored, and this one they founded on a new site ;
and there they followed the mild rule of St. Benedict, losing,
doubtless, something of its old simplicity as their wealth
increased, made, perhaps, a little worldly by the doings of so
great a city just outside their close, till at last their easy life was
ruffled by the news that certain strangers from another land
had found a rougher road to heaven, and straightway the hearts
of a few brethren of St. Mary's leapt towards the new rule and
they yearned to follow it.

It was not a wholly alien rule which was practised by the
new comers, the Cistercian monks of Rievaulx, but one which
professed, like the brethren of St. Mary's, to draw its inspiration
from St. Benedict. Yet for that reason its stricter precepts
were the more detested by the Benedictines, to whom they
seemed, not only a personal reproach, but even an act of
internal treachery, dividing their ancient household against
itself. And so all Benedictines had been bitterly hostile to
the disciples of St. Bernard for a full generation when the
first of them came into Yorkshire, and the whispered rumours

of a life far holier than their own stole into the abbey of
St. Mary.

And there those whispers stirred the hearts of two or three
made of stronger fibre than their brethren, men who it may be
had long wearied of their easy life and the light burden of
their vows, and who now at last saw, as by a quick illumination,
that for them the road to heaven did not lie along the level flat
where they had been sauntering, but must be sought for in the
wilderness, with suffering and labour, must be followed over
rocks and stony ground, cold and fasting, taming the body with
shrewd pangs so that the spirit might burn the brighter.

In those days such ideas once conceived did not perish, but
rather spread from heart to heart as fire runs along the stubble.
Ere long there were thirteen of the monks of St. Mary who
could no longer rest in ease, and the Prior was among them.
At length they told their story to the Abbot, an old man worn
with years, who saw no way of rooting out the heresy save by
sternness and by discipline.

Poor, perturbed, old Abbot! He had, perhaps, never seen
souls in anguish for their salvation, and knew not how to deal
with them. He threw the weight of his authority against
them, and it did not count. He threatened them, and found
they did not fear him. There was a great ferment in the
Abbey.

One Churchman in great place in York was wiser than the
Abbot—Turstan, the Archbishop, "one who loved all religion," says the Chronicler; and to him as to a man who
cared for essentials more than forms, the prior told his story.
It may be that Turstan recognised in the eager words something which human opposition could not quench; or, it may
be that he caught at an opportunity of playing for his own
hand in the constant strife between the Bishops and the
Monasteries. At any rate, he promised his protection, and
declared that he would visit the Abbey on an early day.

The day arrived—it was October 6th, 1132, an epoch in

the history of St. Mary's Abbey, and an epoch too in that of
Yorkshire. Early in the morning Turstan came riding to the
Abbey, and he, with his attendants, having left their horses at
the gate-way, advanced towards the Chapter-house. On the
very threshold their entrance was barred by the Lord Abbot,
backed by a great crowd of angry monks, not only of St.
Mary's, but from other monasteries also; and so supported,
the Abbot demanded that Turstan should dismiss all his
attendants and enter alone into that hostile gathering.

Now, if Turstan had come that day, as he declared, in a
spirit of lenity and peace, he may very well have been pained
by this exhibition of mistrust; and indeed, the passions which
glared at him through the open door of the Chapter-house were
hot enough to give pause to any prudent man. He pointed
out that it was scarce reasonable to expect him to discuss
affairs of consequence without the counsel of his friends; but
he had hardly spoken when his words were drowned by a
storm of shouts and hooting such as seemed—so Turstan said
himself—to come rather of the riotousness of brawling
drunkards than of the humility of holy men. The Chapter-
house seethed with angry men; and those who were inside
pressed out shaking their fists and vowing that they would go
at once if the Archbishop's friends came in.

Turstan stood facing them in sheer amazement. At last
the clamour dropped and the Archbishop spoke: " I take
God to witness," he said, " that I came hither as a father,
having no evil toward you in my heart, wishing nothing but
peace and Christly brotherhood. But since ye try to strip my
office of its authority, now I strip you for the time being of
your functions. Your church is closed." In answer there
came a defiant shout, " We care not if it be closed a hundred
years," and the words were greeted with a roar of acquiescence
from the maddened monks, while some cried, " Seize them!
Seize them! " And others, laying hands on the Prior and his
comrades, strove to drag them away to the prison cells. They

clung to the Archbishop, imploring aid from him and from
St. Peter ; and, at length, Turstan and his friends tore away
the rebels by main force, and carried them into the church,
pursued up to the very door by a raging mob.   There they
sat, protector and protected, not without fear of violence even
in the sacred building, till at last the storm died down and
Turstan was able to carry off his friends in peace.

Such is the tale as it was told a whole life-time afterwards
by a very aged monk of Kirkstall who, verging as he was upon
his hundredth year, had seen the whole, and whose memory
was still untouched by time.   It was not solely for its interest,
nor for the light it throws on monastery life, that I told this
striking story.   It is, indeed, no more than the first chapter
of a story, for, from this great upstirring at St. Mary's, came
the glorious Abbey of Fountains, through what toil and suffering I shall tell hereafter when I reach the lovely country in
which that most noble ruin stands.

As I turn to leave this garden, which is to me one of the
most interesting places in all England, the shadows are lying
heavy on the grass, and the streets are hot and shadeless.   It
is long past noon, and with relief I seek the shadow and the
cool aisles of the Cathedral, concerning whose great beauty I
can never speak without a throbbing of the heart.   For, indeed, York Minster is to me a place of dreams too exquisite
and too impalpable to be set down in words.   Let other and
more phlegmatic men attempt in cold blood to analyse a
building which is beautiful enough to be the gate of Heaven.
I turn my memory back on all the hours I spent there, and
can recall nothing but the flushes on the stone-work as the
warm sun streamed red and golden through the ancient glass,
or, falling down in one long, lofty beam from the topmost
region of the clerestory, cast green flickering reflections on the
worn stone pavement.   It is to me a place of ancient pomps
and ceremonies, of long streams of blue-gowned pilgrims kneel-

F

ing at the shrine of St. William, or venerating the relics of the
murdered Archbishop Scrope, who wrought so many miracles
after he passed out of this mortal world. Ah ! how the ancient
arches are steeped in memories of Kings and Cardinals, of the
gorgeous processions of the Corpus Christi, or the quainter
mummeries of the Boy Bishop, whom the choir boys chose
each year from out of their own number to attend a great State
service on the day of Holy Innocents. They are gone ; all
these splendid pageants have passed out of English life, and the
echoes that ring through the lofty arches are those of a simpler
and (if you will) a purer worship. But what remains to Yorkshiremen of the tradition of their Minster is the better part of
all its magnificence,—the consciousness, I mean, that in every
generation it has been the very heart of Yorkshire life, the
full epitome of the best and worst which has befallen that
great shire.

The air is cooler as I emerge from the great Cathedral into
the picturesque old winding streets, and ride slowly and regret-
fully towards the bar that spans the road to Beverley, where I
must be ere night falls. It is a dull road at first, and I am loth
to turn my back on York. It were surely pleasanter to watch
the twilight dropping down upon the clustered beauty of the
great west front than it is to plough through the dust of this
much travelled road, over which the last heat of a fierce June
sun seems to scorch with twice the violence it had in York,
and where scarce any shade of trees abates it. The undulating
country has but little character ; and I resign myself with some
ill-temper to a ride which scarcely promises to be interesting.

Suddenly I am refreshed by a whiff of cooler air ; and giving
my attention once again to the scene around me, I perceive
that on the east and south the land is sinking to a level plain
which lies far in front of me without a hill, while, on the other
hand, the higher ground has gathered itself into ridges on my
left, where a line of low rounded summits falls by steep in-

clinations to the level pastures through which my road is
winding. The sun is dropping low, and over all the fertile
country there is shed a gold light which is infinitely soft and
lovely. Sweet and steady, this rich glow lights up the bronze
pastures and the cool woods which separate them, while from
the red-roofed farm on the first rising of the hills it glows like a
signal fire. Is this the country which I was told is dull and
ugly?

The road runs on as if it were on velvet, bordered with fine
oaks, from which the piping of the blackbirds grows louder
and more continuous as the sultry afternoon gives way to cooler
breezes. For over the face of the whole heat-stricken country
a keen air is blowing softly from the sea, and every creature
which has slumbered through the drowsy day wakes and turns
its face to meet it. Here at Kexby is an ideal scene of peace.
A little bridge carries the road over a sedgy stream, bordered
with elder and hawthorn bushes in full bloom, and beyond
them pollard willows, with here and there a patch of sprouting
bulrushes. The stream coils away and is lost to sight among
the level meadows, which stretch green and golden as far as a
dim line of woods three miles off across the plain. Half a
dozen red cattle are munching knee-deep in the buttercups,
but there is no other sign of motion on the surface of the
lonely country.

Such are the scenes which are presented at every turn of the
long road to Market Weighton, a road which has no feature of
strong interest, but which, on such a summer evening as this,
is as pleasant as the most jaded traveller could wish. At the
old town, which has such interest for archæologists, and so
little for the ignorant, the road turns up over a spur of the
chalk hills, from the first summit of which one sees the level
plain lying stretched out far and wide, with scarce one undula-
tion up to where its misty surface grows dim and indistinct in
the soft distance. The setting sun throws silvery mists over the

wide flats, and far away upon the left, at some unseen change
of light, there starts into sight a gleaming line of water, where
the Humber, like a gash given by some enemy, cuts up into the
heart of the country.

I might pause here and say much of the pirate boats which
found so easy an entrance through that gash ; for, indeed, the
muddy inlet of the Humber, too wide to blockade or protect in
any manner known in ancient days, was a fatal weakness to the
country, and many were the sorrows which entered by that
gate.   But it is growing dusk already, and I ride on, therefore,
lurching now and then into one of the deep hollows which are
characteristic of the roads across the wolds, till at length the
highway drops down by a pretty red-built hall, through deep
wooded banks, into the charming village of Bishop Burton,
where a large pond lies on the green, and over it a fine church
rises from the trees.   There is but one more hill to climb, one
more pleasant run along the ridge, and then a gate swung
across the roadway is opened with alacrity by the keeper, and
there is suddenly disclosed a view of charm so utter and
bewildering, that as I looked on it for the first time in the soft
twilight of that night in early summer, I wondered if sometimes
the pilgrims who came chanting over the wolds in old days,
footsore and weary, did not drop upon their knees as they
topped this hill and came out upon the Westwood, and saw
far down below the slender Minster towers, the goal of all
their hopes and prayers, the full satisfaction of their toil and
weariness.

Indeed, one needs not the simple faith of a mediæval
pilgrim to be deeply stirred by the beauty of the scene.   Far
down below, at the foot of a green hill, the slender Minster
towers stand up clear and sharp out of a mass of verdure and
of silver blossom.   For the wide fresh pastures on which the
roadway has emerged, and which lie undulating like a sea into
ridge and hollow as far as the eye can follow them on either

hand, are broken here and there by patches of very ancient
hawthorn trees in blossom, whose gnarled and twisted trunks
are old enough to have seen the pilgrims coming over this
sweet down, or to have given a first shelter to the fugitives who
were fleeing from justice to the sanctuary of St. John.   Beyond
the hawthorn trees an old red-roofed town lies along the foot of
the incline, and just where the houses cease upon the left, the
noble tower and octagonal turrets of St. Mary's Church complete the view.   As I linger on the top of the hill the last glow
of sunset fades, the feathery moon grows warm and luminous,
and a single star hangs close above the trees, gaining brightness
every instant.   I go down over the short elastic turf, and at the
foot of the hill pass into the town beneath an old red gateway,
which admits me to a wide street and market place, full of
silvery lights and shadows, while the bewildering richness of St.
Mary's Church glows down upon me one moment as if it lived
and moved, and the next is hidden as a sudden cloud sweeps
across the moon.   The streets are almost empty ; only now and
then a figure flits across the large moonlit spaces.   The night
is pervaded by a little wandering wind, which carries on its
wings the sweetness of lilacs and of may from some old town
garden, and stirs the blood with suggestions of warm summer.
On such a night Beverley is of no age, or rather of all ages ; and
I look round among the heavy shadows of the houses half expecting to see a band of those north country minstrels who
used to meet at Beverley out of all the country between Trent
and Tweed on the Rogation days, making night melodious
with their rebecks.   But they are gone long since from Beverley,
gone even from the memories of most who dwell there ; and
out of all the many-coloured pageants of the past,---knights,
chanting pilgrims, or minstrels with their sweet-tuned instruments,
no one has left more traces of itself than remains on the smooth
surface of a pond, when the rings have died away which a fish
made in leaping, save only the belief that every night Sir Jocelyn
Percy drives a team of headless horses through the ancient

town, stopping always at a certain house where he wrought some foul and shameful deed.   Is it not by this way that he comes?   I would not meet him.   And so I gain my inn, looking on St. Mary's Church, from out whose frosted richness the softest chimes steal all night long through my open window.

Beverley Gate.

CHAPTER IV

"Shake a bridle over the grave of a Yorkshireman," so says the ancient proverb, "and he will arise and steal a horse." I know not to whose wisdom we owe this curious reflection, nor whether it is indeed the case that the last sleep of a native of the county of broad acres may be so lightly broken. Certain it is, however, that horses, whether stolen or honestly acquired, are very much in evidence at Beverley, and as I stroll across the Westwood in the early morning, gaining an appetite from the keen breezes which blow up that way from the sea, I find a sufficient number of noble beasts cantering across the turf to set me wondering how far a man might be to blame if he did snatch up an unappropriated bridle, and slip it over the delicate head of any one of them which caught his fancy. "'Pon my life," sighed Major Monsoon, "I could never tell why temptations are put in our way unless it is for the pleasure of yielding to them." It is a simple creed. I fear that in old Yorkshire life there may have been some who held it. Long ago, in an old hotel in a midland county, where the landlord gratified a sporting taste by collecting any work of art which dealt with horses, or with pigs, for he combined both tastes, I saw a curious wooden panel, which the proud owner described to me as "The Yorkshire Coat of Arms." It was such a shocking slander that I hesitate to speak of it. Yet if people who are traduced do not hear what is said of them, how can they rebut the scandal? Shall I not therefore act the part of friendship, and repeat it?

This scurrilous old panel was shaped in the form of a shield, and as crest it bore a horse proper, the signification of which was that Yorkshire is the best county in which any man can buy a horse—which I make no doubt is perfectly true. But mark what followed—Ah! had the artist but only ended there. The shield was in four quarters, adorned respectively with a fly, a flea, a limpet and a piece of beef, and these enigmatical devices mine host explained gleefully as follows. " A Yorkshire· man," quoth he, " can drink like a fly, he can bite like a flea, he can stick fast like a limpet, and lastly, he is no good at all until he is hung." There,—it was not I who said it!—is it not shameful and atrocious? Will not every Yorkshireman desire to find and burn this panel? It was in Warwickshire that I saw it. Let those who list take that cue, and search diligently till they find it.

It is a cool morning, and the streets of Beverley are full of soft, sweet sunshine. I have come up to the top of the hill again to find the ancient cross that marked the outer limits of the sanctuary. For the kindness of St. John towards all criminals was not exercised only in his church, but extended for a full mile into the open country on every side ; and evil men, however stained with blood, even if it were the blood of priests, could not be seized by their pursuers save under heavy penalties, if they once gained the shelter of the holy bounds. All criminals loved St. John of Beverley ; debtors, murderers and thieves knew well the road across the wolds, and if in some parts of Yorkshire transgressors liked better to flee to the peace of St. Cuthbert of Durham, who was astonishingly potent in saving the lives of men who deserved to lose them, and who accommodated murderers at the rate of about four a year, yet over the Westwood men came constantly slinking through the dusk, or, speeding breathless from their pursuers, clung panting to the threshold of the sanctuary. How, one wonders, did the

monks receive these blood-stained fugitives who came knocking
at their gate in the dead of night? Was there no repulsion
from admitting to sit with them in the refectory some wretch
who had but that day slain a fellow creature out of lust or
passion? "William Hall, late of York, Tailour, on the feast of
St. Andrew the Apostle, in the nineteenth year of the reign of
King Henry the Seventh came and sought the peace of St.
John of Beverley, for that he had slain his wife, Margaret Hall,
and that peace was granted him." Did this scoundrel show

Beverley.

any grace or penitence when he presented himself before the
holy brethren of St. John? Penitent or not, it was their duty
to protect him, to feed and entertain him well, for thirty days.
But then came the penalty, for the fugitives in sanctuary,
though they escaped the ordinary law, were not relieved from
punishment. Within forty days they were brought before the
Coroner, and to him they confessed their crimes and abjured
the realm. His officer thereon branded them on the brawny
part of the thumb with the letter A, standing for the word

"Abjure," so that all men might know in what relation they stood henceforth to society. When that was done, the Coroner named a port to which the outcast should journey forthwith, and taking passage with what speed he might, should leave the country. If he found no passage over sea, he was bound each day to walk out knee-deep in the water, in proof of his goodwill to make the passage. All these were irksome penalties, but it was probably much more painful to be hanged, and so business was always brisk not only at Beverley, but at all other places where the privilege of sanctuary was maintained.

I fear I may be doing some injustice to St. John, and giving no true impression of his character, by speaking of his considerate treatment of the vicious before bringing him in person on the scene. The company of saints is apt to be esteemed a trifle tedious in these days,—a prejudice at which we cannot wholly wonder when we turn over the monkish chronicles and see how pointless and insipid their conversation reads. But let us in justice recollect that the charm of conversation is as evanescent as the colours on a bubble, and that few who snatch at the iridescent thing, succeed in carrying off more than the little smudge of soap from which it sprang. Perhaps even St. Cuthbert himself . . . but how I wander when I begin to talk of saints. Let me sit down here on the turf beneath the hawthorn blossoms, where I can look full upon the slender Minster towers which are sacred to St. John, and so will surely keep me to my text. Sitting here in the cool morning shade I could tell many stories about his holiness, but I will content myself with one which has the additional advantage of being about racing too.

Does any one know how old the sport of racing is in Yorkshire? I see that many of those who have writ thereon trifle with a matter of three or four centuries, fearing to plunge into the blackness of the past. But I, who do not pretend to have exhausted the antiquity of sport, leap back at one bound full twelve hundred years, and base myself on the high authority

of the Venerable Bede. For in the year of grace 685 — so that
renowned old author tells us—one Herebald, an excellent
though light-minded man, who, sobering a little as his years
advanced, presided creditably in the end over a monastery " at
the mouth of the river Tyne," was living among the clergy of
St. John of Beverley, not having, as he frankly owned, cured
himself of a love for youthful pleasures. This levity of
character had not escaped the keen vision of St. John, and so
it happened that on a certain day, as the Saint and all his
followers were riding together, they came to a plain and open
road well suited for racing their horses. Now the vain young
men who accompanied the Saint implored his leave to institute
a race ; but he refused, saying, truly enough, it was an idle
request. I daresay he said it with a smile and with a yielding
heart, for he too was a Yorkshireman, born at Harpham in the
East Riding, and doubtless knew as much of horseflesh as any
man among them. At any rate he did give way, but very
properly excepted Herebald from the freak, and kept him by
his side, perhaps to act as starter.

Now this was not to Herebald's mind, for he bestrode a nag
as good as any one he saw about him ; and having sat unwillingly beside St. John while his friends, with shouts and
laughter, contested several heats, he could bear it no more,
but gave his beast the spur and started off in chase, leaving
the Saint alone. " Alas, how much you grieve me ! " said the
Saint, as he shot off, but not for such reproof did the reckless
youth rein in. It was compulsion and not duty which brought
him to a stand ; for his horse, treading on a slimy stone, pitched
him off, so that his thumb was broken and the suture of his
skull was loosened, and he lay like one dead. He was carried
home and lay speechless all that night, while his friends looked
on him as but a lost sportsman, for they thought he could not
live. Indeed, the Saint, who probably knew more upon this
subject than any of the others, was so uncertain about it that,
after having spent the night in prayer, he came up early in the

morning to ask what Herebald thought of it. "Can you
live?" asked the Saint, doubtfully. "I may, through your
prayers," suggested Herebald, and the answer seemed to please
the Saint, for he at once asked several questions about the
patient's baptism, and, finding that the manner thereof had
been defective, he redressed the mischief, catechised the
penitent, and then blew upon his face, on which Herebald
found himself much better; and St. John, calling the surgeon,
ordered him to close and bind the skull where it had been
loosened. Then Herebald got up, and the next day was well
enough to resume his travels with the Saint, cured, for the time
at any rate, of his passion for the vain sport of racing. Ah!
what subjects for his treatment the Saint might find over there
behind me on the Westwood every year in the early days of
June, would he but come to life again and walk up to the race-
course.

Well, there is now in Beverley neither saint nor sanctuary;
and never a pilgrim comes across the Westwood chanting in
our day. Yet pilgrims come, though unmelodiously, and will
always do so while they can see the lovely casket in which the
men of old enshrined their faiths, and the red town lying at
the foot of the breezy pastures, just as men saw it lie four
hundred years ago and more. I come down slowly over the
short turf, and enter the cheerful street under its old, red gateway, and go by the pillared Market Cross until I come to the
Minster, and pass in by the north-west door. I do not
think that many men can have stood by the western door of
Beverley and looked along the delicate vault of that most
noble Church without drawing one deep breath of wonder and
delight.

From Beverley it is but a little way to Hull, and I know
of nothing that calls for mention by the road. Of Hull, what
shall I say? What can any one say but the thieves' litany,
well worn though it be—"From Hull, Hell, and Halifax, good
Lord deliver us!" I do not wish to be profane, or even un-

Hull.

mindful of the great benefit which Yorkshire has derived from
the trade of this black and ugly seaport, which turns to gold the
sludge which was once churned up by the Danish pirate ships ;
and, indeed, it is but in the justice of things that this inlet of
the Humber, through which came so many sorrows for those
who dwelt in Yorkshire in old days, should make wealth and
comfort for their modern representatives. Of all this, and
much more of the same cast of wisdom, I remind myself as
vigorously as I can in going round the mean and dirty streets ;
and yet it is of no use—I do not like Hull, and I wish that
the trade were still at pretty Beverley, or even at Ravenspur,
which is sunk beneath the sea. There was a time when Hull
was jealous of the trade of Ravenspur, and feared the merchants
who did business where the waves break white upon the shingle
now—so curious have been the turns of fortune on this un-
stable coast. For the scour of the currents running south along
the whole low coast from Flamborough to the mudbanks of the
Humber is for ever washing stealthily away now one and now
another bank ; and were it not that on Spurn Head itself—
which has no rock or even chalk wherewith to fend itself
against the tide—the action of these currents is counteracted
by other forces from within the estuary, the headland would
long since have vanished, and Hull itself might have been a
mere lost memory like Ravenspur, or Auburn further north, or
many another town or village where the children's playgrounds
are now open to the gambolling of crabs and starfish.

Now the land of Holderness—of which Beverley is the glory
and Hull, I had almost said, the blot ! but let me say rather the
greatest proof of modern energy—is a pleasant one to travel
through in early summer, when the woods are in fresh leaf, and
the corn is springing, and the wind blows softly from the sea
across the level flats. I turn my memory back on it and find
it stored with pictures of rich fertile fields where the lush grass
grew knee-deep beside some slowly flowing stream, where
pollard willows made a little shelter from the sun, and the

golden growth of buttercups shot through all the field. Far
away this wealth of gold and green lies stretching to the limits
of the sight, while here and there the red roofs of some goodly
farm gleam warm and homely in the sun, and a comely range
of well-kept buildings by its side speaks of comfort and
prosperity. All day I ride on through such sights. Sometimes I come out on the low seacoast, where a little range
of bluffs, scarcely to be spoken of as cliffs, mark the windings of the shore—a lonely, solitary beach, given over largely
to the gulls, who sit all day upon the shining sand in the
first wash of the waves. Far away to northwards I see
Flamborough lying like a cloud, and Hornsea, a little place
growing out of all knowledge now, but which for many a
century, until Hull people took the fancy of seeking sea-breezes
there, was as lonely a little town as any one might desire to
dwell in. In old days men did not unfrequently desire to dwell
in lonely towns upon the shore, where they might practise in
seclusion those ways of growing rich which the sea, great
demoraliser of the human race, as it has been in all ages, cast
freely in their way. Now I gather that the men of Holderness,
who are nothing if not discreet and reticent, do not deny that
there was a time in the long distant past when things were done
at Hornsea which were not consonant to any but an easy view
either of law or of morality. There were bad men in Hornsea
once, but the whole of them turned right round and led con-
verted lives in the year 1732, since which time not even a
breath of slander has been heard against the town. It was a
thunderstorm which wrought this marvel, and if the tales are
true of the damage which it wrought, it must have been a portent as startling as that sent to terrify the reprobate who was sitting
down in Lent to an *omelette au rhum*. "*Mon Dieu*," shrieked
the poor sinner, pushing back his chair from the table on
which the smoking dainty had just been uncovered, "*tout ce
bruit pour une omelette au rhum!*" and he hurled the omelette
out of window. Had the parish clerk of Hornsea known the

story of this judgment, it may be that he would not have used
the crypt of the church to which he was unworthily attached as
a receptacle for smuggled goods. But so he did, and on the
night of the 23rd December, 1732—since it is a moral epoch,
we may as well be particular about the date—on this night, I
say, of the cheerful Christmas season, the vault of Hornsea
Church was full of things which ought not to have been there.
And there, too, was the parish clerk, gloating over the lace and
hollands, and paying no heed whatever to the rising of a storm
without, till the din of the wind and the crash of falling trees
called his attention away from dreams of wealth, and bade him
fix it on the preservation of his life, for the church was in the
grip of the fiercest hurricane ever known along that coast. It
rose from Hornsea Mere—as is said by men who tell the story
still—and travelled seawards, stripping off the roofs of the
vicarage and over twenty other houses. It threw down a wind-
mill and carried the millstones across the fields full a hundred
and fifty yards. The poor clerk, crouching in the church,
heard the crashes which accompanied this ravage, and as the
whole building shook and quivered under the furious buffets of
the wind, he feared each moment that tower and arches must
come crashing down upon him, since no work of human hands
could endure beneath such violence. The great east window of
the church came flying into the choir in fragments ; and as
the wind tore howling through the arches the wretched clerk
fell back in a fit. When found next morning he was paralysed,
and the neighbours, good sympathetic people, said it was a
judgment, and added that there would have been no storm
at all if the clerk had been more circumspect in his behaviour.
This may or may not be a true view of the case, but at
any rate it is claimed that the lesson was not thrown away,
but was laid to heart by all those who dwelt in Hornsea ; and
that may be why I, who spent some time and labour in searching
for indications of what had been going on in past years on this
lonely coast, found so very little to reward me for my trouble.

For a long while ere reaching Hornsea I have lost the rounded chalk hills on my left, and have seen nothing but the wide green plain, as level as the sea itself. But I have not travelled far from the ancient town, with its large freshwater mere lying somewhat picturesquely near the very margin of the sea, when the hills begin to steal up again towards me, the plain shrinks to a narrow tongue of land, and once more I see nestling on the roots of the ridges the pretty church towers, and the clustering red roofs of the villages upon the wolds—for I have almost done with Holderness—that large strange expanse of fertile land which, in some far-distant days, the sea laid at the feet of the chalk hills, and withdrew and left it dry and fit for the habitations of mankind. The strangest impression of instability is left on the mind of one who rides quickly through this lush, flat country, catching sight from time to time of the line of hills inland. There, one thinks, is the true coast of the East Riding, and there it may be once again in the long future, when the sea has torn away the gift it gave—how many centuries ago !

As I draw near Bridlington I have little else to think of than the aspect of this hill country which juts out so boldly into the sea at the great headland of Flamborough. It was, and indeed is still, a strange, lonely district, abounding in traces of some long-vanished people who, in days before the dawn of history, scattered their camps and funeral mounds over every slope and valley of the hills. But not to stray into days so ancient, it is worth noting that this large district of the wolds was not enclosed until some sixty years ago. It formed till then no more than one large sheep-walk, and its scanty population were shepherds, formed into a society among themselves. Into this guild—if that term be really applicable—young men were not admitted till they could say by heart the Psalm in which the sweet singer of Israel sang that the Lord was his shepherd, Who made him walk beside still waters and through green pastures ; while on the second Sunday after Easter, when the Gospel con-

G

tains another declaration, "I am the good Shepherd," these
men, who found a simple pride in hearing their own occupation
consecrated by such associations, came to church in their full
numbers, so that the day was a kind of festival among them.
There are fewer shepherds now among the chalk hills ; there is
greater wealth there too, and the life has grown less simple.
Yet the district still retains many ancient customs and ways of
speech which are long forgotten in the more thickly-peopled
country.

These wolds are rather curiously subject to great cloud-
bursts, whence come floods that, sweeping down the deep
hollows of the hills, have from time to time done much damage.
Such a flood occurred at Langtoft, some seven or eight miles
inland, in 1892, and as an illustration of the perils which hover
at long intervals over these hill districts, the circumstances are
worth noting, especially since the catastrophe was by no means
unexampled.   It was a Sunday afternoon, the 3rd July, and the
morning had been hot and cloudless.   As the day passed the
sun went in, the breeze dropped, the air grew perfectly still and
oppressive, and a heavy copper-coloured sky brooded over the
surrounding country.   Gradually this blight upon the heavens
was seen to be gathering itself together into darker spots or
clouds of very striking weight and blackness, and about the
time of evening church these clouds began to travel rapidly
across the sky in the direction of Langtoft, drooping more and
more towards the earth, till, as they reached the hill above the
village, there was a terrible crashing of thunder, the sudden
lightning streamed over all the sky, the cloud tapered downwards in several twirling columns, the peaks broke, and the
whole volume of water descended with furious violence on the
hillside.

At the point where it struck the ground, a series of deep
rents were torn through grass and chalk which resemble nothing
so much as the devastation of an earthquake.   From top to
bottom of the hill, a full hundred yards, these great fissures lie,

attesting the mighty power of the water which went whirling down the valley six feet deep, sweeping away haystacks and cattle, sapping walls and houses, and putting the lives of many village people in the gravest peril. At the same moment there fell a shower of hail, and out of the black sky the thunder rolled continuously. It was an awful day, and none who passed through it can speak of their remembrances without some trace of terror, or recall the seething flood which rushed into their houses, without a shudder.

Bridlington Quay.

There is a noble church at Bridlington ; but the eager tourist will find little else to please him, save a seafront which many people love, and which therefore no one ought to condemn hastily, a wide blue bay, which one may easily learn to love, especially when all the lucent surface is broken into white by the light winds of early summer, and a distant range of cliffs which change in colour all day long, now pearl grey, now gleaming white, and again standing out sharp, black and riven against the oncoming night.

I think few sights in Yorkshire are more striking than the abrupt termination of the low coast of Holderness in the massive chalk cliffs of Flamborough. Here is no slow or gradual elevation of the coast-line. The chalk turns out across the sand, the line of hills inland sweeps onward to the coast and plunges out to sea, forming a promontory so striking that it can in no age have been other than notable and famous. Indeed, had there been on either side of this huge barrier any creek or inlet which could have been enlarged by art into a safe or defensible harbour, we might have looked for the story of a great sea life upon this coast. But Filey is an open bay, and Bridlington no better than a fairly sheltered an- chorage, on which, indeed, the energy of the sturdy Yorkshire- men constructed piers, doing their best, as their neighbours did at Scarborough, to make a harbour out of nothing. And doubtless they used their scanty chances well and boldly ; but the truth is, that from Hull to Whitby there is no natural harbour, nor was there at any time a fair chance of resisting those bold French and Flemish pirates who, in mediæval times, were constantly ravaging the narrow seas. "I have before sent a letter to the Privy Council," wrote Anthony Atkinson in 1599, " by the foot-post of Hull, concerning the Dunkirkers on this coast. Since then, four or five of our Hull ships have come home that have been ransacked of all they had . . . . They chase all the poor fishermen ashore, and those they take they strip naked. They put the whole country in fear about the Spurn Head and Flamborough."

The real grievance in this complaint was doubtless that, owing to their want of commodious ports, the men of Yorkshire could not make reprisals. They were but little subject to fear when they could strike in their defence ; but no man without a weapon in his hand cares to meet a well-armed enemy. Half a dozen fat Dunkirk merchantmen towed into Bridlington would have made a wondrous difference in the public feeling, and sent the youths of Holderness coursing the Channel as

boldly as any sea-wolves of Brittany or Cornwall. But, as it
was, those lusty energies found small outlet on the sea ; and
the coast remained a lonely one, frequented by smugglers,
and known as an apt spot for the landing of any persons who
had reasons for wishing to be unseen. Thus, in the latter
days of Queen Elizabeth, the Lord President of the Council of
the North, watching, as was his duty, all solitary lines of coast
on which Jesuits or other disturbers of the peace might land,
apprehended three persons who had just arrived at Flamborough,
namely, Father Walpole, the priest and Jesuit, his young
brother, and a noted conspirator named Lingen. Whereupon
one Richard Topcliffe, who seems to have been in attendance
on the President, wrote to the Lord Keeper Puckering, to
"signify how far they have digged into the hearts of these
unnatural traitors." In truth, the Lord President, though
labouring "with incredible toil, day and night, with assistance
of his chaplain, a very mild divine," had digged no way at all
into the hearts of the two men whose matured courage fitted
them to meet him on equal terms ; but with the undisciplined
terrors of the lad he had been more successful. Poor boy,
how could he withstand the fierce Lord President with the
penalties of high treason at his elbow ?   " An amiable youth,"
Topcliffe says he was, " and not so far gone as the others . . .
And all the truth, secret and matter, even against himself and
the others, flowed from him as fast as his Lordship could put
the questions . . . ." After the Lord President had examined
them all, he sent the Jesuit and Lingen to rest ; but to prove
young Walpole's honesty, he sent him well guarded to the
shore to see if he could find the place where he had buried
twelve compromising letters which he carried. The bundle
was found, though wet and soiled with rain, and brought to
his Lordship who leaped for joy. After tenderly handling
them before a fire, twenty-two were unfolded without blem-
ish. . . . God thus blesses Her Majesty by discovering
disloyal men and women about London and in sundry coun-

ties in England and Ireland ; she will see what a toiling Lord President can do."

So it was worth while for Lord Presidents to watch this coast, and they caught strange fish upon it when they kept their eyes wide open. As for the Revenue Officers, who were a kind of modern decadent symbol of the Lord President's power, I do not fancy that they caught much, for the things they looked for were all of a kind that might be hid in caves, and remain there for months, if not for years, without much damage, while the chances of finding them, I should imagine, were practically nothing. There may be headlands elsewhere so perforated and tunnelled with labyrinthine caves as Flamborough, but I myself have never seen one ; and if any one should say that there still lie kegs of hollands or good French brandy lost and forgotten in some hollow of the chalk, I should reply that I think it very probable.

It is on the northern face of Flamborough that the cliffs are loftiest, and as one trudges on from Bridlington, the rock faces, though high and sheer, have but little of the striking beauty of those which look to Scarborough and catch the full drift of the northern storms. But the air is golden as I walk over the short turf. It was hot upon the mainland, but here on this great bastion of chalk, over which the wind plays out of three of the four quarters, fresh and pungent from the North Sea, the heat is scattered and the sun does no more than flash gloriously on the undulating surges, catching now and then a quick gleam from the white breast of some sea bird that skims near the surface of the water. Far behind me, Bridlington begins to assume the aspect of an ocean city rising out of the sea, its towers and spires softened by a melting yellow haze, while the low coast of Holderness fades away dim and blue and distant, till I can no more distinguish it from the dull banks of cloud on the horizon. Here in the shelter of the headland, where half-a-dozen boats lie fishing on almost steady keels, the wind is no more than enough to blow the water into ruffles. But further out the setting of the tide has brought rougher water, and as I gaze at the horizon, distinguishing now one and now another vessel which the haze concealed from any but a steady look, I see that all are pitching as if they had encountered heavy weather. Such, surely, may have been the aspect of the ocean on that August day—how many years ago !—when one, sitting on this headland, saw the galleys heave in sight which were bearing Mary Stuart from the kingdom of her bridal to the kingdom of her birth. "One of the galleys, being the greater, was all white, the other, coloured red, was well trimmed and appointed. She wore a white flag with the arms of France, and in her stern another white flag, glistening like silver."

That is by no means the only memorable sight which has been witnessed by watchers on this headland.

> " You have heard of Paul Jones,
>   Have you not ? Have you not ?
> .   And you've heard of Paul Jones,
>   Have you not ?
> He was a rogue and a vagabond,
>   Was he not ? Was he not ? "

Vagabond he may have been, but I am not disposed to give him any harder name. At any rate, he fought what is probably the most desperate naval action upon record, within full view of these white cliffs. It was a September evening in 1779, when Jones, in command of an American squadron of three ships, encountered a convoy of merchant vessels escorted by the *Serapis*, Captain Pearson, and the *Countess of Scarborough*. The convoy slipped into port ; the *Countess of Scarborough* was taken after an hour's combat ; but between Jones' ship, the *Bonhomme Richard*, and the *Serapis*, the fighting was as fierce and deadly as was ever seen upon the sea. The armament of the *Serapis* was superior, and had she been well handled she must have won ; but by some blunder, Pearson allowed Jones to grapple him, and while the two ships lay locked together, a hand grenade thrown down the main hatch of the *Serapis* exploded a great pile of ammunition, disabled many guns, and caused appalling slaughter. Still, both ships were so shattered that it was an open question which would strike first ; and when Pearson hauled down his colours, the *Bonhomme Richard* was in a sinking state.

Here was a sight, indeed, for the fishermen of Flamborough ! The North Landing, that small cove, which is, with one exception, the only place upon the headland accessible to boats, must have been seething with excitement, such as not even a smart chase by the Revenue men could have occasioned, when some lugger, with a guilty knowledge of what lay hidden in the wet caverns of the chalk cliffs, went flying out to sea with the exciseman's cutter hanging on her wake. What noble hiding places there are in those white precipices ! What deep and intricate recesses, impossible of access save to those who know the exact locality of every sunken rock upon the coast !

As I go onward from the North Landing, following the rough, steep path which skirts the margin of the cliffs, I find myself climbing steadily though slowly, and indeed it is not until I reach the northern end of the Danes' Dyke that I have attained any great elevation above the sea. But from that point the chalk towers up into a majestic wall some three miles long, in which there is neither break nor inlet, nor any elevation falling much short of three hundred feet. The summit of the cliffs is an almost perfect solitude, their ledges are for the most part inaccessible except with ropes, and that is doubtless why they have been chosen by the sea birds as a breeding ground.

Here is a white cliff somewhat blackened by the weather, dropping sheer some hundred and fifty feet or more to where a grassy shoulder juts out for another fall. The precipice is roughened by myriads of little ledges, and at first one does not see what it is that stirs on the face of the inaccessible abyss, giving a perpetual appearance of slight motion to the solid rock. But presently some signal or alarm startles those who sit upon the ledges. There is a wild whirring caw, and instantly a

flight of thousands of birds wheels off the face of the cliff,
flashing gloriously black and white in the sunny air.   To and
fro they wheel in crowds, coming and going in countless multi-
tudes.   Out beyond the shadow of the rocks their white breasts
gleam like foam flakes on the water ; yet, infinite as must be
the number of those which sit there basking on the sea, you
can none the less see them crowded close together, dark hooded
and white breasted, on every ledge down all the vast height of
the precipice, while here and there, if you look closely, you may
distinguish a blue egg laid in some shady crevice of the cool
white rock.   There is a perpetual caw and chatter among the
inmates of this huge abyss.   Fighting and squabbling are in-
cessant for the best places on the ledges.   There comes a
jackdaw sailing on steady pinion past one ledge after another,
seeking vainly for a place where he may alight.   The gulls will
have none of him on their domain.   At last he settles on a
vacant space, but is pecked off with a wild, angry cawing, and
sails away round the shoulder of the cliff spluttering in wrath.

As I go on towards the mainland again, the path winding in
and out shows me every moment a new cliff face, roughened
all down its vast height by the presence of these birds.   If I
sit down on the cliff top, where the chalk rises from below in
high, tapering columns, I am not more than twenty yards from
the ledges where the gulls sit crowded side by side ; I can watch
them lighting and taking wing, or waddling to and fro and
stretching their long black necks towards each other.   A little
way beyond me a small wooden hut stands on the grass near
the edge of the cliff, and while I am wondering idly with what
object it was placed there, I see that four men have emerged
from it, and are sauntering along towards me.   One carries a
coil of rope which he pitches down upon the grass just above
the precipice which I have been watching ; while one of his
companions drives into the ground two pulley spikes, each
carrying a wheel over which the rope will run with no risk of

chafing, placing one spike dexterously at the extreme edge of
the cliff. Meantime another man has been slipping over his
legs and fastening tightly round his body a kind of sling
sufficient to support his weight with comfort, and when his
equipment is complete all the others sit down on the grass,
holding firmly to the rope, while the climber lets himself go
confidently over the cliff edge, and swings down easily among
the birds. Far down the cool shadow of the white rock he
drops towards the blue sea below, pausing every now and then
as his quick eye catches the blue gleaming of an egg, which he
transfers deftly to a canvas wallet by his side. And now he has
dropped as far as he desires, and the most difficult part of his
journey begins, for in going down he swung almost free of the
cliff face, descending easily as the men above paid out the rope.
But coming up strains every muscle in his agile, well-knit frame,
and as he strikes out with his legs, catching now one and now
another shelf of rock, on each of which his weight hangs for
the fraction of an instant, the tension of his muscles is evident
enough, and one realises in watching him how great must be
the strength and the agility needed to accomplish the ascent.
Seven eggs rewarded the bold climber, and as I moved away
another man was about to try his luck.

A mile or so beyond this point the chalk dips inland
suddenly, and the precipices end in low bluffs of red marl. I
stand on the sweet turf in sight of the last cliff and look out
across a lovely bay, towards which the sunny country falls gently
from the wolds far away upon the sky line. It is all soft and
beautiful in the warm summer glow. The blue sea washes in,
white and broken, on the chalky strand. The red bluffs gleam,
and down below an old wreck lies black and solitary amid the
breakers. Far away, the little town of Filey stands low upon
the curving strand ; and further off again, at the extremity of
the redder cliff which terminates the bay, the sea is foaming
white and mountainous over the deadly Brig. Far out under

the discoloured sea that perilous reef projects, stabbing like
a swordfish snout every solid thing that the waves wash up
within its reach.   From the buoy which lies tumbling just
where the sea grows blue again, the tolling of a heavy bell just
reaches my ear, a dull warning note carried over miles of water,
while the Castle Rock at Scarborough closes in a noble sea view,
standing up grim and solid above the pearly haze.

I conceive that few of those who visit Filey have any expectations of finding beauty on the land.   It is as well ; for,
indeed, there is but a bare landscape, look where one will
over the swelling country.   The last undulations of the wolds
are by no means picturesque, and it is the more fortunate,
therefore, that the sea views are of rather striking beauty.   I
will not plunge into that great quarrel which rages still upon
the question whether Filey was not the "well havened bay"
known to the old Greek geographer Ptolemy ; in fact, I should
like it neither more nor less were it proved that half the ancient
world—Greek, Persians, or they of Babylon itself—thought
well of it.   For me, it is enough that on this warm summer
afternoon the whole bay has the colour of one translucent
beryl.   The town lies in shadow.   The great precipices by
which I came this morning tower grey and black in the far
distance.   The wind blows freshly out of a sunny sky ; and
over the scattered boulders of the Brig, that singular reef where
the chafing waters never slumber, but are torn perpetually into
foam, the sea breaks green and white, flashing now and then
into a dazzling jet of spray, cool and translucent.   Further out
the colour changes every moment ; now it is a soft green, and
now a softer blue, and now a mere steely shimmer, as the sun
shines out more brightly, turning the brown seaweed into gold
by the brilliance of its wet reflection.   Far away upon the left
stretches a fine range of sheer dark headlands, and further off,
again, a craggy point rises over a mass of houses which can be
no other than the ancient town of Scarborough.

Come, let us go forward on our long road. For the charm
of Filey is not one admitting of exact description. It depends
upon no singularities of beauty or of interest ; but rather on
the memory of long, quiet days spent strolling on the breezy
cliffs, where the wind at evening comes in from the North Sea
with a freshness that whips the colour into one's face after the
hottest day. Simple pleasures, such as are the most fragrant
to remember, are still the hardest to describe ; and those alone
are found at Filey. I turn up through the wooded road known
as the Ravine. It is the first of many such which gash the
coast line throughout all its length as far as where the hill
country drops at last to insignificance again, and the Tees,
spent and wearied by its long course over moors and fells, creeps
out to sea between the flats of Middlesbrough.

We shall travel many a mile before finding level ground
again ; but, for my part, I do not complain of that, since in
toiling up the rough hills that lie between Filey and Scarborough, I am refreshed by the cool breeze that rises as the
sun falls lower, and enticed onwards by constant glimpses of
the Castle Rock, which comes and goes from sight again as the
level of the road changes. At last I gain the town, and turning
to the right I come out upon the South Cliff, and see the Castle
towering before me on its huge green crag, while the blue sea
washes round its base, and in a sheltered hollow at its foot
lies an ancient, red-roofed town, nestled into the warmest corner
of the hill. Two curving piers enclose a little harbour, and
towards its mouth half-a-dozen brown-sailed boats are slipping
through the oily sea, each one leaving a wide track that grows
grey in the fading light. The beach, which curves round
towards me from the town, is crowded still with people. Far
out the sea is stained red by the setting sun. At the bottom
of the cliff beneath my feet a lighted lamp gleams brightly out
across the water ; and the strains of some pretty waltz are
blown upwards by the gentle wind. It is a perfect summer

evening ; so still that the ripple of the waves is clearly audible,
and the shouts of children climbing on the Castle Hill ring
plainly through the clear air. But the night is falling fast. One
by one the visitors go home. The light below me is put out.
The band is silent. The lamps on the pier-head cast a red
reflection on the sea ; and overhead the stars shine out soft and
luminous in the warm sky.

CHAPTER V

WHEN a town has given itself to pleasure so utterly as Scarborough, how shall it find those who will listen with patience to its history? What care they who haunt the Spa and the Aquarium, or take pleasure in the gildings of the Grand Hotel,— what care have they, I ask, for the stories I could tell them of the lighted brands which the Danes hurled down from the captured castle on the doomed town below, or of the many sieges which the old fortress stood, and the tales of woe and daring which have gathered round it? "How came priests and bishops," demanded Corporal Trim, "to trouble their heads about gunpowder?" "God knows," said my Uncle Toby; "His providence brings good out of everything." In such words, with the same tolerant contempt, will the votary of Scarborough reply when asked questions concerning what went on there in past days.

"God knows." Even out of those dull old times His providence has produced these restaurants and bands! What matters it that from the Castle Crag a great voice calls for notice down all the empty centuries? Let it go on calling, while we eat our oysters and sip our lager beer.

Well, let it be so, then. All my ancient history shall be tossed into the dustbin. But one yarn among the number is very fit to be told in the pauses of the band; and surely the

Scarborough.

most gay-hearted tourist will be pleased to hear how the Mayor of Scarborough was tossed in a blanket.

It all happened so long ago that nobody need be concerned at the propagation of the scandal. King James II. was at the bottom of it all, as he was the author of most of the mischief done in his brief and miserable reign. It is well known how he spent his ingenuity in trying to favour the Roman Catholic religion, and how, when he could achieve that end in no other way, he tried to reach it by a decree of freedom for all religions, which decree he ordered to be read in every church throughout the realm. Now the Mayor of Scarborough received a copy of this precious document, and, as in duty bound, sent it to the rector of the parish, with a transcript of His Majesty's commands, making no doubt that he would loyally obey them. But the parson was a sturdy Protestant, and smelt a Popish rat even under the roses of universal tolerance. I know not in what terms he conveyed to Mr. Mayor that he would not read the decree, but whether sour or deferential, they annoyed the Mayor, who went to church next day vowing that if the orders of the King were not obeyed, he would do a deed that should be remembered in the town of Scarborough. So quickly does the civic spirit rise to the level of heroic actions ! And the Mayor's threatenings were by no means froth and vapour. They were the ordered warnings of a resolute temper, prompt to vindicate the slighted authority to him entrusted by the citizens ; and accordingly, when he heard the appointed portion of the service read without any mention of the decree, Mr. Mayor sallied forth from his pew, where he sat in state among the Aldermen, walked up the aisle with great dignity in the face of the astonished congregation, and then and there, in the most public way, caned the minister in his own pulpit.

Here, surely, is a man who ought not to be forgotten by posterity. Imagination reels in trying to depict the scene when Mr. Mayor, casting down the culprit on the ground, walked back, flushed and majestic, clothed in all the dignity of the law,

To face page 97.

"*On the Bowling Green.*"

and begged that the service might proceed. But not every one has the calmness of a Mayor, and I surmise that neither castigated minister nor startled congregation paid much more attention to their devotions. Next day Scarborough was still seething with excitement. On the old bowling green, where a gentleman, vaguely described as "a captain in the army," was trying to explain to a group of friends the precise meaning to be attached to the term "brawling in church," the feeling grew so warm that they decided to send for Mr. Mayor to explain it to them. That dignitary was unwise enough to disregard a courteous summons. So they repeated it by a file of musketeers, who brought back the Mayor, willy nilly. I know not in what terms he rebuked them for their presumption in handling the chief magistrate of Scarborough roughly; nor do I think the wags on the old bowling green gave him much time for spouting, for somebody had brought a blanket out, and some-body stood at each of the four corners, and somebody tripped up Mr. Mayor's heels and upset him with all his dignity into the bosom of the blanket, and somebody gave a hoist with lusty goodwill, and sent Mr. Mayor up to the stars and down again, and bumped him on the turf, and shot him up again to heaven, and rolled him over and spun him about, till he felt that all his inmost parts . . . . Ah! who does not yet recall the sensations he went through when six strong boys tossed him in the dormitory? Just so they treated Mr. Mayor, and if I know anything of mankind, I think when he came out of the blanket he must have been rather angry.

There was but one quarter in which the monstrous nature of this outrage could be represented properly, and accordingly the Mayor set out for London to complain to the King, not doubt-ing that his Majesty would be distressed out of measure on hearing what troubles had befallen a faithful servant who tried only to execute his will. But let men beware how they count on the support of kings. The Captain rode to London hard on his adversary's heels, and by dint of influence, or the power

H

of the purse, or the prevailing force of merriment, which set the
whole town laughing at the cost of the Mayor, got the matter
settled all his own way. So when at last the Mayor had a
chance of stating his sorrows before the Council, it was but to
hear the captain's pardon read, and to be dismissed to muse on
the uselessness of trying to do one's duty in a corrupt and
naughty world.

   There is a sharp whistle in the wind this morning, and the
sea is breaking heavily round the harbour walls. From time
to time a surge heavier than the rest sends a cloud of brown
spray flying over the wharves and quays where the fishing crates
are stored, and as I watch, a drift of flaky foam torn from the
crests of the grey breakers whips past the red roofs of the old
town and is driven slowly by the wind across the green slopes
of the Castle crag. As far as the dim skyline, where the stormy
clouds hang down and touch the tossing waters, there is nothing
but a wilderness of grey and angry sea ; but out of the torn
sky, coming I scarcely know from whence, a gleam of sunshine
falls upon the blackened Castle ruin, so that its shattered walls
begin to glow with a warm light which spreads and widens till
with a sudden burst of splendour the sun is shining over all
the hill, and the plumage of the seagulls wheeling up and down
the cliff flashes nobly under the dark sky. It is thus that I
love to think of Scarborough, that stern and blackened ruin
which has tasted of the worst that Time can do, and still faces the
storms of the North Sea as if it looked yet for the coming of
the Danish pirate boats. It is a typical north-country view,
a little grim, a trifle lacking in that colour which wins so many
hearts for the softer west, but an outlook full of grandeur and
of strong romance, one of those prospects whose very memory
sends a certain throbbing through the heart, like the first sight
of the Abbey on the cliff at Whitby, or the hoary battlements
of Bamborough darkened by the beating of a thousand winter
storms.

   Now I have said already that from Flamborough until one

comes in sight of Tees there lies a country of unbroken hill
and moor, intersected only by deep gorges or ravines, which
for the most part are exquisitely wooded, and occupied by
streams as beautiful as the heart of man could wish. For
when the rain clouds which drift above the moors have caught
and broken on the summits, and their stores of water come
rushing down the wooded clefts, each one of them has its
noisy waterfall and its brown foamy pools under the shade of
trees, so that the sound of water is never lost through all the
stillness of the dell till it is overpowered by the murmurs of
the sea chafing on the rough coast to which the stream is
hurrying down. All these narrow valleys are worth seeing,
and indeed a man might spend many days in loitering through
Hackness and Hayburn Wyke, or climbing the great peak of
Ravenscar till he sees the wide red curve of Robin Hood's
Bay lying far below him, and the small red town crushed all
together on the further cliff. There is always a choice of ways
in this noble county ; but I, who do not find the romance of
Yorkshire, nor even its most striking beauty, on the coast, will
turn westward through the wide arm of level ground which the
central vale of York projects to the sea at Scarborough.

It is a long road and a dull one ; for the great plain extends
so far that the barrier of the Cleveland hills in the distance on
my right seems scarcely loftier than the low ridges under which
I travel on the other hand. It is a scene which possesses a
certain wild freshness, but is lacking in dignity and interest.
I pass it by as quickly as I may, running on through Sherburn
and Rillington, and that somewhat dull old town of Malton on
the Derwent, where I might doubtless discover things of
interest had I time to stay and search for them. Does not
William of Newburgh in point of fact . . . but indeed the
worthy William himself, who loved this country well when he
walked about it in the flesh, would not have stayed me at this
moment to inflict his prolix stories on me. He would assuredly

H 2

have put aside his anecdotes with one wave of his canonical
hand, and bid me stretch my eyes across the wide level to the
distant blue line of the hills sweeping steadily towards me, or
watch the crimson poppies glancing by among the wheat fields,
or look out for the ivy-clad castle of Slingsby, less a fortress
than a Tudor dwelling house, which would have served the
worthy Canon as a text on which to preach to me of the
grandeur and vast strength of the barons who fixed their
dwellings in this fertile valley land, of the pomps and tragedies
which sprang out of their stormy lives. For my part I lend a
willing ear to the tale of all this long-past splendour, prolix
though it be ; yet I know there lies among the hills not so very
far before me a place of which I shall have to say so much, that I
am warned to save my breath until I come to it ; and therefore, as
I ride on through the pleasant country, I will mention only the
remarkable fact that on the road from Slingsby to Hovingham,
which pleasant byway I am now following, there dwelt long
ages since a monstrous snake, no less than a mile in length.
It occupied a cave by the wayside, and issuing therefrom at
such seasons as it pleased, occupied itself in devouring not
only the crops of the peasantry, but even their children and
themselves, so that in the end it became a quite intolerable
pest, and one Marmaduke Wyvill of Slingsby Hall vowed that
he would destroy it. I know not how he did the deed, and it
is as well, for the details were doubtless very gory. At any
rate he lies now all carved in stone in the church at Osgodby,
with his dog who helped him bravely ; and the whole story
serves to set on foot some speculation as to whether any spark
of truth may lie in the tales of dragons which occur at half-a-
dozen places in the northern counties ; whether any vestiges of
a race of Saurians such as roamed these islands in older geologic
ages did in fact remain here and there in the swamps and
caves of solitary districts, and linger on, strange and terrible
survivals of extinct worlds, until a period late enough to touch
the roots of traditions which are living yet.

It is a curious question, if an idle one, but while we have
been talking of it, all the face of the country through which
we are running has been changed. The plain has gone, and
the road is carrying us into the first valleys which pierce the
slopes of the Cleveland hills. Helmsley lies but a little way
before us, and the grey old stonework, glinting through the
trees upon the left, is the ancient castle which we must turn
aside to see, not only for the beauty of its site, but for the
grandeur of its associations. For hither George Villiers, duke of
Buckingham, "that life of pleasure and that soul of whim,"
brought down the dissolute Court life of the Restoration, and
through this gateway he rode out on the hunting expedition
which brought him to his end at Kirby Moorside. He it was
who repaired the walls left shattered by the cannon of Sir
Thomas Fairfax, who marched hither after Marston, and got a
bullet in his shoulder for his pains ; and, indeed, about these
mounds and ridges, where the trees are now the last invaders,
planting their green banners on the very walls, there has
been much fighting since the Norman barons of Espec and De
Ros built them as a stronghold, whence Scotch raiders might
be held in check ere they reached the fertile valley lands of
York and Mowbray.

De Ros is long forgotten in this district, but the name of
Espec is still on the mouth of every visitor, kept there by the
magic of a pitiful tale told of the loss of his only son, killed by
falling from his horse, and of a vow made by the heart-broken
father that, having no heirs, he would endow Christ with his
goods. Alas ! the pretty story is not true, for Espec had no
son, and though he founded Kirkham Priory and the great
abbey of Rievaulx here close at hand, he did it out of other
motives not a whit less noble than the desire to perpetuate the
memory of a broken heart. Come, let us go and see what it
was that this great baron did ; and that we may realise the
better all the nature of the country, we will not take the
pleasant road through the woods of Duncombe Park, but pass

on through the wide square of the little town of Helmsley, and
climb the hill till we see the black moors thrusting up their
heads on every side above the woods and fields. Sharp and
sudden these huge slopes sweep down into narrow valleys ; for
this, the eastward corner of the Hambleton Hills, is an intricate
network of deep hollows, fringed with woods and musical with
running streams. And down each one of these winding vales
there sings the fresh wind of the moors, keen and stimulating,
carrying the scents of gorse and heather into the denser air of
the low bottoms, so that each one of them is bright and breezy,
and the thick shadows flung across the streamlets by the woods
are continually shaken.

As the road drops down towards this broken country, a small
gate upon the left admits me to a little wood. I pull the bell,
and there comes to meet me one who takes a shilling, and
leads me through the trees out on what I conceive to be the
noblest stretch of turf in England. In full view of the valley
curving round beneath the hill in the direction whence I came,
far, broad and level, this glorious green sward extends along
the hillside, winding as the valley does, soft and springy to the
tread like the turf of a sea cliff, and sweet as that is with wild
thyme and vetches, and numberless small creeping flowers.
This green mead is bathed in the softest golden sunshine up to
the very borders of the heavy woods that bound it on the left,
while on the right a scrub of bushes falls with a swift descent
into the deep valley.

Over this fringe of coppice one looks down upon the narrow
meadows of the bottom, drowsing green and gold in the
shadow of the trees and hills, and, set among these sweet pastures like a lovely jewel, stand the grey ruins of the ancient
Abbey. It is late afternoon, and the valley brims up with
golden light, the old broken vaults and arches gleam, and over
the hill-top one or two sharp crumpled peaks thrust themselves
up against the sky, the broken summits of the Hambledons.

I doubt if all the hills and vales of England can show another

scene of such wild and solitary beauty. One may sit all day
upon the hillside even now, seeing no sight but the changing of
the shadows or the trooping of the deer over the wide hill
pastures ; hearing no sound but the murmurs of the wind and
water just as the monks heard them long ago. And if one sits
and ponders thus, suddenly it becomes clear how vast a courage
and how strong a faith must have been needed to set the first
walls of the Monastery in this lovely hollow, in an age when
the gaunt moors all around were haunted by outlaws, and lay
open to the raiding Scots, and when the bonds of society in
this northern land, shattered by successive invasions of the
Danes, had been torn up root and branch by the ruthless
vengeance of the Conqueror. There was worse than solitude
among these mountains then, and the perils which the monks
came out to face were exactly those which beset a colonist
to-day in a wild, unsettled land.

Well, they faced these perils—a poor handful of Cistercian
monks, coming with the blessing of St. Bernard to live the new
life of stern and abstinent labour among the lax monasticism of
the English Benedictines. They came to testify, and did it
nobly, in this lonely valley ; so that we have seen already how
the spark ran from their hearts to those of a few who dwelt in
luxury at York, and lit a fire in which tools were forged which
wrought a mighty work for the welfare of this country, as well
as for the profit of the Church of Rome. It was Archbishop
Turstin to whom St. Bernard sent them, and he commended
them to Walter Espec, who gave them land and some small
revenues with which they held their ground, we know not with
what suffering, though we can guess it was as bitter as the cold
and hunger which tortured the monks of Fountains only a few
years later.

Day by day they saw the sun break over the black moors or
heard the storm wind singing over the rough snow, while their
buildings rose fair and stately in the wilderness, till at length the
valley was no longer dark or silent ; and the lost traveller who

came stumbling over the highlands to the brow of the Rye Vales looked down on white-robed monks toiling actively upon their fields, or saw the darkness of the evening pierced by beams of warm light from the windows of the church, heard the sound of chanting on the still air, and pressed forward with renewed strength till he knocked at the fair gateway and was admitted by a brother, who fell on his knees, as was the rule with the

Rievaulx Abbey.

Cistercians, and thanked God for sending a weary stranger to rest within their gates.

The seed was sown by St. Bernard of Clairvaulx, the tillage came from the hands of nameless monks; but the plot of ground, without which the other labour would have been but fruitless, was given by the great baron, Walter Espec, an old man, full of days, but keen of wit, huge of stature, noted in that he never broke troth with a friend nor faith to his King. He had yet a splendid service to perform of which I shall say more presently; but it may be that as he watched the monks

of Rievaulx making the wilderness to blossom like a rose, that
thirst for peace, which had so strange an empire over all men in
his day, grew strong within him, for in the end he cast off his
harness and put on the white robes, and was carried to his rest
at length within the Abbey Church. There his dust lies among
the shapeless mounds to which the greater part of the noble building is reduced, but his memory is more lasting than the stone.

Come, let us go into the valley. A broken, winding path
descends through the steep woods into a lane which ends in a
tiny hamlet, built on the abbey precinct. Just beyond it are
the ruins, the nave no better than a string of mounds which no
one has cared to dig out ; the transepts fairly perfect, the lovely
choir lacking little but the springing of the roof to restore it to
its former state. Apparently there are few who love or care for
this exquisite fragment of a noble building. Overgrown with
nettles and briars, defiled by cows, the Abbey of Rievaulx
stands a bitter impeachment of our title to impugn carelessness in other nations towards their ancient monuments.

I would have every one who visits Rievaulx go down the hill
from the little hamlet, and, passing by the pretty rose-clad
cottages and the gardens full of stocks and peonies, cross the
river by an old stone bridge, just where a mill leat rushes down
to join the main channel of the stream. It is the bridle road
to Coxwold which runs up the hillside from this bridge ; and
after following it for some distance one may turn off by a gate
at a keeper's cottage on the left, and trudge up through a rough
lane ending in a wood, where the hillside is gashed with deep
valleys of fern and shady coppice. As one mounts upwards by
the rugged path, under the scrub of oaks and beeches, one is
drawn continually to stop and turn, so exquisite are the gradual
unfoldings of the valley depths. One moment it is no more
than the mill-house which one sees against the shoulder of the
green hill, the next turn brings in sight a corner of the grey
ruins gleaming over the fresh grass ; and a further climb throws
open the whole depth of the valley bottom, a sea of verdure

filled with golden light, so still that one can hear the river running over stones below, while the grey ruin stands up solemnly in the middle of the valley.

Just so, one thinks, so perfect and so beautiful, it may have looked on that still evening long ago when a monk who had travelled all day stood upon this hillside and gazed down into the valley. He had wearied of the strict rule of the abbey where he dwelt; had grown restive under the hard labour and the silence and the nightly penance in the church, and had slipped away ere dawn and gone out beyond the abbey bounds, which no monk might do, and sped away into the woods like a bird escaping from its cage. And so he wandered till the sun sank, and the taste of freedom grew bitter in his mouth; and at last, not knowing where he was, he came out on the hillside, and saw a fair abbey glowing in the evening sun, and heard the bell chiming for vespers, and went down and knocked at the gate with a beating heart, and, lo! it was his own Abbey of Rievaulx to which God had brought him, and his own home which received him back into its peace again.

I turn once more before losing sight of the old grey building, where so many lofty ideals lie crushed beneath the crumbling stone; and the memory comes back to me of an autumn day near six centuries ago, when this quiet valley resounded with the tramp of soldiery and the broken pomps of a hastily retreating army. For King Edward II., that weak and luckless monarch, had invaded Scotland, hoping to emulate the glories by which his father had bound the restless northern baronage to himself; but, lacking his father's wit, and it may be his father's courage also, had been driven back, and was retreating through this land with shame and danger. For the Scots, triumphant and merciless, were pressing hard upon his heels; and as the beaten King lay hidden in these hills at Rievaulx—so the Chronicle of Lanercost tells the tale—he could almost hear the din of shouts and slaughter which the kerns were wreaking on the fertile country, and could see

drifting black across the sky the smoke of homesteads which
it was his mission to protect. The King was of a timid heart,
and sent out the Count of Richmond, Don John of Brittany,
to feel for the enemy, which proved to be a very easy task, for
Don John had no sooner mounted a hill within the Abbey
precinct—it may have been this very one on which I stand—
than he saw the wild northern warriors upon him, swarming
with incredible activity out of the hollows of the hills. Don
John did his best to hold them in check as they came up the
narrow path, but he was overwhelmed; and the King had
scarce time to throw himself on horseback and spur down the
valley at full gallop, when the Scots were swarming with their
loud war-cries into the court-yard of the Abbey, and plundering
the baggage which he had dropped in his hurried flight.

So narrow was the escape of a feckless King, and such the
sufferings of the monks and farmers who dwelt even at such a
distance from the Scottish border as Rievaulx. For the restless
violence of that wild frontier overflowed like a seething cauldron,
and sent its devastation down on Yorkshire hardly less than on
any other of the six northern counties, which, indeed, were
bound together by this common peril into a sort of unity such
as was felt in no other group of English shires. In that debate-
able territory there was never any peace, nor was there ever
security that Yorkshire might not be raided on any winter's
night. It is somewhat strange that two centuries of union with
Scotland have wiped out so many memories of the never-ending
warfare of all the ages previous to those, leaving the recollection
of the border warfare only in those districts further north where
it was naturally most intense. However, all those bitter days
are now long past, and I am climbing up the hillside through a
wood which has not heard the shouts of battle for three centuries
or more ; but lies open, summer and winter, to the trooping of
the dun deer, who can

> ". . . Draw to the vale
> And leave the hilles hee,"

with little fear of being scared by man. Over the broken moor
they come in flocks, pausing an instant to watch the rare sight
of a stranger toiling upwards through the springing bracken
and the brown ling.   One moment only the leader stands
snuffing the air suspiciously ; the next he canters carelessly
away, followed by the whole herd, with a few shy backward
glances. The woods have dropped away, and the summit of
the hills is a brown waste of heather, crossed only by a few
tracks hardly worth the name of roads.   But it is not for the
moor alone that I have come this way, beautiful as that is in the
glowing of the evening sun, which catches every shoot of the
young bracken and makes it glow as if it lived. This must have
been the monks' track, for nothing more than the bulk of this
vast hill parted Rievaulx from its sister Abbey of Byland, and the
deer upon the hillside in old days must have been well used to
see the white cowled figures from one or other Abbey pacing slow
across the moor ; and on solemn days of feasting must have
witnessed their processions passing over the hill with banners and
with chanting, to take part in some great act of worship with their
brothers in the opposite valley.   Steeply and by winding levels
the road begins to drop when the hill is crossed, and it plunges
into a deep cutting filled with trees, whose topmost branches
are as yet beneath my feet, so steep and precipitous are the sides
of the rocky chasm through which the road descends.   It
passes onwards through the shadow of deep woods, and at last
emerges in a. broad and lovely valley, where the broken fragments of the Abbey lie little tended, and having lost within the
memory of living men a substantial portion of their buildings
from decay.

There is not much in the history of Byland Abbey which is
worth the effort of recollection.   William of Newburgh, author
of a dull though valuable chronicle, knew more about it than
most men, having indeed been born and bred upon the
charming hillslopes at the base of which the ancient abbey
stands ; yet his chief anecdote concerning it touches no one

among the saintly men who may be presumed to have dwelt
there, but falls on a poor sinner, one Bishop Wimund, who,
after gaining the undeserved affection of his flock in the Isle
of Man, took to ravaging the Scottish islands, under the vain
and insincere plea of being in very truth son of the Earl of
Moray.   In this rampaging career he met with singular success
but fell at last by the wiles of his enemies, who took him and
bound him, "and as both eyes were wicked, deprived him of
both. . . .   Afterwards he came to us at Byland, and

Byland Abbey.

quietly continued there many years till his death.   But he is
reported even there to have said that had he only the eye of a
sparrow his enemies should have little occasion to rejoice at
what they had done to him."

It was, I daresay, no fault of the monks of Byland that this
fierce old guest of theirs learnt so little charity within their
walls.   I make no doubt there was many a poignant scene in
cloister or refectory at Byland, when the blind old robber-bishop
lifted up his voice in tales of lust and rapine, while the simple

monks listened with a fearful joy, fascinated by the glance and
glitter of a fuller life than they had ever known, or crowded
away in terror at the imprecations of the maimed savage whose
thirst for vengeance tortured him even in old age.   Well, he
lies there now, resting at length beneath the green sward, over
which the shadows of the broken arches lie so thickly ; while

Coxwold.

I, if I would not lose the village of Coxwold in the coming
dusk, must turn away from abbeys, and follow in the footsteps
of the gentlest and the quaintest humourist who ever set forth
the coruscations of his wilful fancy in this our English tongue.
    " Gravity," said Yorick, " is an arrant scoundrel."   It is too
true ; yet that arrant scoundrel has entered into his kingdom
since Yorick's head was laid low in Bayswater Road, and does

now, indeed, possess the world. Responsibility comes posting
hard behind him, and deadens every quirk and fancy, turns
our minds to problems and our hearts to cares, lays on us the
burden of to-morrow, breaks the pipe and puts away the
tabor, so that this many a day we have not gone a-dancing
underneath the elm trees on a summer evening. It is so
much the greater reason why we should cherish the memory
of him who jested for us so incomparably ; and as I wander
up the street of Coxwold in the dusk, past the gabled house
where Laurence Sterne mocked the coming and the going of
the years, a certain sadness steals over me such as invades
a man who finds nothing but the scent of roses clinging to
a jar in which the dewy flowers once stood fresh and living.

Sterne's House, Coxwold.

CHAPTER VI

THE Cleveland hills, near the foot of which wild elevated region Helmsley stands, have always been regarded as difficult of access, and for all travellers, save him who goes on foot with knapsack deftly poised between his shoulders, they deserve their reputation fully.   For surely a country scored so deep by long, narrow, winding valleys is scarcely to be found elsewhere in England ; and be the keen breezes of the moorlands as invigorating as they may, the traveller who has carved out for himself a route through this wild land, will sometimes marvel at the penetration of the Romans, whose camps and villas are so few in Cleveland, comparatively with the rest of Yorkshire, as to testify that they were not fond of breakneck hills, even when from the summits they could gaze out over prospects very wild and lovely.   In fact, this rugged district, where a man may even now lose his way and perish on the moorside if he be not very wary on a winter's night, was regarded as a safe fastness by dwellers in the valleys in times much later than the Roman ; and as long as Scotch invasions harried the rich plains of Mowbray, the villagers used to drive their cattle into Cleveland, where they lay safely while the smoke went up from farms and cottages in the level meadows.

Now it is quite clear that men who design to visit a mountain fastness must not expect to do it without fatigue ; and it may

not be out of place to remark that the inevitable labours, or
delights, of going up hill and down hill in Cleveland are not
seldom increased to the degree of poignancy by the presence of
a very woful kind of clay, which, on small inducements of even
summer showers, makes a paste not to be regarded without awe
by those who go on wheels.

> " Cleveland in the clay,
> Bring two shoes, carry one away."

So sang one unknown in days long past ; and Cleveland is still
the same as when he came limping out of it on one stockinged
foot, composing his ill-tempered jingle in revenge.   Perhaps it
was he also who dealt that other metrical blow at the land
which had swallowed up his shoe, and declared, with a pleasant
indifference to any exactitude of computation,

> " Halton, Rudby, Entrepen,
> Far more rogues than honest men."

The bitterness of these unpolished versicles suggests identity
of authorship ; and, indeed, there can scarcely be more than
one poet, however rude, who has left Cleveland with no inclination to commemorate other qualities than its clay and its
rare lack of principles.   If only benefits and kindnesses impressed the hearts of poets as deeply as injuries score them,
what a memorable string of jingles we might have had, touching
now on the rough friendliness of the men of Cleveland, now
on their hospitality, and again on the sturdy independence
which makes their characters respected.

Of course, we shall never see Cleveland if we linger here in
Helmsley, talking of its qualities at length.   And yet the case
is one in which, as Sir Thomas Browne puts it in his pointed
way, "Festination may prove precipitation, and deliberating
delay may be a wise cunctation."   Never were any words spoken
so applicable to Cleveland, that wild land which gives up its
charms to no hasty traveller, but reserves them for such as

I

care to linger on its cliffs and moors, giving an ear to those fancies of the peasants which still preserve unto our own day the fiercer creeds of long-forgotten races. For time has stood still these many centuries in Cleveland; and while the world outside has submitted to the flood of advancing knowledge which has long since drowned and washed away the old, strange faiths brought to England by our pagan ancestors, or found here when they came—creeds how old we cannot even guess!—this rocky land, this half inaccessible boss of crag and moorland, has stood up like an islet out of the waves, keeping still its traditions, and speaking loudly in the ears of all who care to listen of ages which have left as little trace elsewhere as the shadow of the summer clouds.

But for the moment it is not of paganism that my thoughts are full. For when I turn eastwards out of Helmsley upon the road to Pickering, I have travelled scarce three miles before I see upon my left a sign-post notifying that the road which turns up across a ridge of moorland leads to Lastingham; and the name recalls so many memories of those great days of Saints and early Christians in Yorkshire, before the Danes ravaged the country into desolation, that I cannot choose but turn off from my road and plod up hill and down hill till I see the ancient village lying in a hollow and the old church rising above it on a little eminence. It is a fine and solitary situation which Cedd, the Man of God, chose for his monastery full twelve hundred years ago; and if there be some exaggeration in Bede's description of the site as hidden among "lofty and distant mountains," yet the hills do rise very sharply and with noble outlines on the west, while on the north and east they swell more slowly into purple moors, stretching wild and lonely and without one break through Glaisdale and Rosedale, and many another gash in the rugged cliff country, to within sight of the River Tees. As I stood and looked down on this ancient sacred spot, the copper-coloured clouds which had been gathering in the south and west drew heavily together, and

hung lurid over the little village ; in the northern sky there
were large watery spaces of pale green ; a wan light drifted
over the hills and woods, and before I reached the humble
village inn, thunder was crashing heavily around the hills,
and the sky was torn right and left by branching antlers of
forked lightning.   The summer air darkened till all aspect of
the day was gone ; and in this spreading blackness, lit by the
sudden lights that flashed from heaven, the strange old solitary
life of monks among the dipping moorland hills became more
real.   In this elemental storm Lastingham was of no age, but
bore the aspect which Cedd knew well when the storms of
twelve centuries ago broke and rolled in thunder round these
hills.

It is not easy for any man who lives to-day to form a picture in
his mind of the lives of these old monks.   But Bede and many
another writer will tell us of the strength and fervour of their
faith, of their communings with angels and demons, and have
set down many such a tale as that which is related of this very
house at Lastingham, where, in the latter days of the life of the
good Bishop Cedd, a monk named Ouini, who was working
outside the monastery, " heard the voice of persons singing
most sweetly and rejoicing, and appearing to descend to the
earth from heaven, which voice he said he first heard coming
from the south-east—that is, from the highest quarter of the
east—and that afterwards it gradually drew near him till it came
to the roof of the oratory where the Bishop was, and entering
the same filled the same and all round about it.   He listened
attentively to what he heard, and after about half an hour perceived the same song of joy to ascend from the roof of the said
oratory, and to return to heaven the same way it came with
inexpressible sweetness.   When he had stood some time
astonished the Bishop opened the window of the oratory, and
making a noise with his hand, as he often had been wont to
do, ordered him to come in to him.   He accordingly went
hastily in, and the Bishop said to him, ' Hasten to the church,

I 2

and cause these seven brethren to come hither, and do you come with them. When they were come . . . he added that the day of his death was at hand, ' For,' said he, ' that loving guest who was wont to visit our brethren has vouchsafed to come to me also this day, and to call me out of this world.' . . . When he had spoken thus much and more, he who had heard the heavenly song returned alone, and prostrating himself on the ground, said : ' I beseech you, father, may I be permitted to ask a question ? ' ' Ask what you will,' answered the Bishop. Then he added, ' I entreat you to tell me what song of joy was that which I heard of beings descending upon this oratory, and after some time returning to heaven ? ' The Bishop answered : ' If you heard the singing, and know of the coming of the heavenly company, I command you, in the name of our Lord, that you tell not the same to any one before my death. They truly were angelic spirits who came to call me to my heavenly reward, which I have always loved and longed after ; and they promised that they would return seven days hence and take me away with them,' which was accordingly fulfilled as had been said to him." So near was heaven to earth, and so wide its gates lay open, in the days when Bishop Cedd prayed and fasted at Lastingham.

But of the nature of the creed these monks enforced among their peasantry, coloured as it needs must be by the Paganism of the people, there are still some traces left. " When any dieth," says an old manuscript found by Ritson in the Cotton Library, containing an account of Cleveland, " certayne women sing a song to the dead body, recyting the journey that the partye deceased must goe. . . ," and this fiery and stern lyke wake dirge is, beyond all reasonable doubt, the song referred to :—

" This ae nighte, this ae nighte,
 Every nighte and alle ;
Fire and sleete and candle lighte,
 And Christe receive thy saule.

When thou from hence away are paste,
  Every nighte and alle ;
To Whinny Muir thou comes at laste,
  And Christe receive thy saule.

If ever thou gavest hosen and shoon,
  Every nighte and alle,
Sit thee down and put them on,
  And Christe receive thy saule.

If hosen and shoon thou ne'er gavest nane,
  Every nighte and alle,
The whinnes shall pricke thee to the bare bane,
  And Christe receive thy saule.

From Whinny Muir when thou mayst passe,
  Every nighte and alle,
To Brigg of Dread thou comes at last,
  And Christe receive thy saule.

         .   .   .   .

From Brigg of Dread na broader than a thread,
  Every nighte and alle,
To purgatory fire thou comes at last,
  And Christe receive thy saule.

If ever thou gavest meat or drinke,
  Every nighte and alle,
The fire shall never make thee shrinke,
  And Christe receive thy saule.

If meat or drink thou ne'er gavest nane,
  Every nighte and alle,
The fire will burn thee to the bare bane,
  And Christe receive thy saule.

This ae nighte, this ae nighte,
  Every nighte and alle,
Fire and frost and candle lighte,
  And Christe receive thy saule."

These splendid and memorable verses, throbbing with the
passionate faith of Christian conviction, yet lurid with the
sombre glow of Pagan fancies dying hard among these hills,

were surely chanted by many a band of mourners winding
down slowly from the moorland paths on Lastingham lying in
the hollow—men and women in whose minds there was a
guest-house for the wild Norse fancies of their ancestors, at
least as spacious as any they reserved for the new faiths taught
them by the monks.   The old creeds died hard, indeed they
are not dead to-day, though men have been slaying them for
eighteen hundred years ; and when I listen to the stories told
in a country such as Cleveland, or note in any work so ad-
mirable as that of Canon Atkinson the striking frequency with
which the Pagan world crops up in our midst, I feel like one
who wanders through some waste land of bog and rotting
vegetation, yet judges from the blackened stumps of trees
thrust up among the mouldering soil, that green woods waved
once upon that ground, and the wind sang through them
merrily.   Such are the Pagan creeds as we collect their relics
from the lives and actions of the peasants.   The blackened
stumps are there in strange profusion ; but the leaves are
dead, the sap has sunk, the beauty and the life have long
since ebbed away.

   I might dilate for many pages on this subject, but it is
enough to say that the traces of old superstition are still so
numerous in Cleveland as to suggest that in the days of the
monks at Lastingham it must have been a chief element in
their daily life.   The simple minds of men saw devils everywhere, and it was doubtless one of the principal functions of
the monks to exorcise them.   For such exorcisms there were
doubtless even then set forms ; and it may be that to some
lingering and corrupted memory of these solemn services of
prayer and conjuration we owe the strangely jangled charms of
wise men and witches in days much nearer to our own.

   I have before me a small and very curious book entitled
Flagellum Demonum, "The Scourge of Demons," published some
three centuries ago by a Franciscan monk who, I presume,
did but collect those services of exorcism which were traditional

in the unchanging Church which he served, and which may
well have been used in the dales of Cleveland in something
like the form here written down, even by the monks of
Lastingham and certainly by those of later foundations.   There
are many strange and terrible ceremonies set forth in this
work, many curses too awful to be read without a shudder.
But of all the services of conjuration, an essential part is the
following list of holy names, the crosses marking the points at
which the Sign of the Cross must be made on the forehead of
the penitent.

Hel + Heloym + Eheye + Thetragrammaton + Adonay
+ Saday + Sabaoth + Sother + Emanuel + Alpha + et

Castle Howard.

Omega + Primus et Novissimus + Principium et Finis
+ Agyos + Yschyros Otheos + Athanatos + Agla
+ Jehova + Homousion + Ya Messias + Esereheye
+ Christus Vincit + Christus Regnat + Christus Imperat
+ Increatus Pater + Increatus Filius + Increatus Spiritus
Sanctus + Per Signum Crucis De Inimicis Nostris
Libera Nos Deus Noster.

This is a strange medley of mystic names with phrases full of
sacred meaning, and we might well suppose that many a generation must have passed since men made any use of it.   But

there is a remarkable permanence in all beliefs or usages which have at any time stirred human minds at all deeply. Canon Atkinson has recorded the description of a very potent charm employed by a certain farmer to protect his stock from the witches who, as all men know, are powerful unto this day in Cleveland. It consisted of a half-sheet of note-paper, folded and sealed with three black seals, between each two of which was a hackle from a red cock's neck. On the paper was drawn a pentacle, the potent figure of all necromancers, in the spaces of which were inscribed the words "agla," "el," "on," "nalgah," "adonai," "sadai." Now out of these six words of awe, four will be found in the above extract from the monks' Book of Exorcisms, while the correspondence is made somewhat more remarkable by the circumstance that a cross is drawn above the word "nalgah"—possibly a corruption—just as crosses are marked in the monks' text to signify the holy sign. But this is not all. The farmer's charm is adorned with five texts, whereof three are identical with those used in the Book of Exorcisms in close association with the extract given above, viz., *Caro Verbum factum est, Jesu Christi Nazarenus Rex Judæorum*, and *Hoc in Vince.*

It is true that the charm contains one or two elements which I cannot identify in the Book of Exorcisms which was, however, only a part of a larger work wherein the other items may perhaps be found. At any rate, there are so many points in common between the charm and the exorcism as to suggest, strongly, that the one was taken from the other. It would surely be passing strange if the Cleveland farmer, or the wise man who advised him, had worked out of his own head a charm so similar to that written out for general use by the Franciscan friar. But if we take the other view, and maintain that at the dispersal of the monks, their mystical solemnities and their occult knowledge passed into the hands of ignorant men who forgot its vital meaning, and let it sink into nothing more than an out-lying swamp of that great bog of superstition which then and

now keeps many a charlatan from beggary, into what a strange
and ancient world does the permanence of this charm conduct
us !

I have lingered a thought too long at Lastingham, but it was the
fault of the great storm which weather-bound me.   At last the sky
is clearing, and the torn black clouds are driven far down in the
heavens, leaving a large dome of watery blue, out of which the
sun pours down hot and burning on the village.   I stroll up to
the church, which was indeed what brought me here, a fine
and interesting Early English building with a Norman apse, and
a crypt, or more properly a lower church, of such singular and
gloomy grandeur as drives out from the memory all things at
Lastingham except itself.   I do not venture to discuss the
question whether this dark and cavernous abode of God may
be old enough in truth to have seen St. Cedd kneeling at its
ancient altar.   It is enough for me that its rude and heavy
arches have caught the dreams and aspirations of more
generations of saints than I can count; and that in this
chamber full of shadows, this catacomb among the Cleveland
hills, past times return upon me strangely, so that I hear again the
Bishop opening his lattice at the sound of that sweet singing,
or catch the stern measures of the lyke wake dirge rising
or falling with the wind which sighs downwards from the
moors.

It is no part of my design to rend the hearts of those who
read this work ; and I say nothing therefore of the sorrows of
my ride to Pickering through Cleveland clay.   The sight of
the old town was as welcome as a desert well to a panting
camel ; and I called a halt to let the steaming country dry.

Now Pickering, a great headquarters of the House of Lancaster, and therefore redolent of all the associations of the old
bloody days, had also its share of joyousness, being in truth the
dominating point of a huge forest, very famous for its deer, and
therefore apt at all times to resound with horns and the cheerful baying of the hounds, and the jovial laughter of the

huntsmen trooping homewards from the chase. Good sportsmen, in the judgment of Gaston de Foix, who wrote a book
about them heaven knows how many centuries ago, lived long
and happily, and when they died all went to Paradise. I hope
with all my heart it is so ; but Gaston went on to add that bad
sportsmen would not go thither, and that wrings my withers.
Yet if right upon the one point he may very well have been
wrong upon the other. I calm my apprehensions therefore ;
and forgive him the anxiety in gratitude for the suggestion in .
another paragraph. "And when he is comen hoom he shall
doon of his shoon and his hosen and he shall wash his thighes
and his legs and peradventure all his body." Good cleanly
Gaston ! He must have wound his huntsman's horn in some
district not unlike the Cleveland clay.

A great forest is a great temptation. In these days morality,
that most changeable of sciences, has so far altered its bounds
that none but quite the lower classes ever think of poaching. I
rejoice in this striking progress of humanity, and I refer all who
wish to know how bad the old days were to the Coucher Book
of Pickering. In that shocking record are recorded the names
of those who took game unlawfully within the forest bounds,
with certain other details setting forth how hard the law could
strike at men who went to play without its sanction. But the
distressing part of the matter is that the transgressors were not
for the most part poor. They were the men of estate and
landed property ; they were the clergy, even the higher orders
of those holy men, the priors, the abbots, not to mention the
humbler parish priests, all of whom were demoralised by the
nearness of the greenwood, and the sight of the deer trooping
downwards from the hills. The Rector of Middelton, a mile
or so from Pickering, was desperately fond of coursing, and kept
four greyhounds on the borders of the forest. This was in the
year of grace 1328. Good heavens ! that I should dig up a
man's follies when he was dust six centuries ago ! Some years
earlier than this one Alan, huntsman of the Abbot of Whitby—

note how close we are coming to the dignitaries of the Church—
together with Thomas Nevill and some other wicked persons
who need not be named, took a hind in Ellerbeck; their dogs,
no less than seven in number, were the Abbot's dogs, and the
venison went to the Abbey.   This was on 8th March, 1294.
There is a deadly precision about the date which forbids us to
doubt the scandal.   They were all outlawed, I am glad to say;
and so were Robert Acklam, Geoffrey Lepington, John Duker,
and Geoffrey Acklam, with a few more who made up a pleasant
hunting party about the same time.   Somebody must have been
watching them all the day; for it is recorded that they took
three hinds in Simon Howe Moss with bows and arrows and
two gazehounds, one white and the other fawn-coloured, and
carried the game to Glycotes in Eskdale at Lithebeck, where
there is a sheepfold of the Abbot of Whitby—again this Abbot !
—and then went on to the house of Robert Acklam at Newton.
Well, they had a pleasant day no doubt; and within a short
time they had little else to do but hunt, for they followed Alan
the huntsman into outlawry and the green wood.

Page by page the Coucher Book records these sentences
of outlawry.   "To give the names of all," says the learned
editor, "would be to give the names of the gentry of North-
east York."   And indeed it is but too true that he does
not exaggerate.   They are all there, those names of weight and
mark which Yorkshiremen respect; so that one lays down the
Coucher Book with the thought that any man of family condemned by the Court of Woodmote, or the Court of Swainmote,
or by the Justices in Eyre, might at least console himself with
the reflection that he would find the best of company where he
was going.

Indeed the number of outlaws must have been very great in
Yorkshire; and as these wild moors which run from Pickering
to Whitby and the deep narrow winding valleys which intersect
them were constantly receiving recruits turned into them by the
wisdom of the law, it is not surprising to find the name of

Robin Hood, that prince of outlaws, recurring in this region. It may very well be that bold Robin found the dales of Sherwood, abutting as they did on more than one large town, and travelled by a populous highway, growing at times a trifle sultry ; and such a district as this high crest of North-east Yorkshire, this towering wilderness of moors and crags stretching from the very sea coast into lands so solitary that only the curlews knew their intricacies, must have offered an easy and inviting shelter from pursuit.   It is even yet a land in which a man might hide, as any one may ascertain to his cost who wanders from the beaten road ; and I know no reason compelling us to doubt that the deep red curving bay under the great cliffs of Ravenscar, with its little huddled town nestled together as if it strove to keep some secret of its bad old life from the stranger who comes in greater numbers year by year to that once solitary spot, may have some just title to the name of Robin Hood.   Perhaps it was his merry way of mixing up the rights of property which caused the little village to embark on that career of smuggling, if not worse, which all its natives own to with a cheerful smile.   It may have been immoral, they admit, but at least it was not dull.

But how I have strayed away from Pickering ! Let me get back across the moors to the old Lancastrian castle, which lies crumbling into a ruin, so picturesquely placed upon the hillside.   I have climbed up to the very highest point of the old fortress, where a few broken walls remain yet of the great keep which was once a landmark far and near across the Vale of Mowbray, over Slingsby, and Gilling, and many another stronghold as far as the hills where Castle Howard stands.   Far up into the Cleveland hills the red beacon must have flashed out from this summit in the times of Scotch invasion ; but now it is all dead, and the only watchmen are the kites and crows.   It is still a stormy afternoon, and a copper sky lours over the valley.   Away in the west a low swelling hill catches a gleam of sunlight, and the green fields flash quickly into gold.   But over the wide plain the sky is dark and heavy, and the grey haze makes the distance infinite. Below me I can see the battlemented wall sweeping round the hill, strengthened by square towers at due intervals. But all the strength is shattered ; here an ash and there an hawthorn has rooted itself among the stones, forcing them asunder, so that the soft growth of saplings does silently in a single season what not all the battering rams of the stoutest enemies could achieve. One

Pickering Castle.

small square tower is fairly perfect yet ; but if I look down on it and try to reconstruct the aspect of the place as the Second Richard saw it when he came riding up the hill a captive, wondering only whether it were here that the release would reach him from a world which had lost its savour, suddenly the outlines of the past are sent swimming into fragments like the reflections in a pool when a stone is cast into it, and I am called back rudely to the present unromantic age by the sight and sound of shunting trains just below the Castle wall. To

what purpose should I listen for whispers out of the fourteenth
century when the loud rattle of the nineteenth fills the air?
Peevishly I get upon my legs again, and, climbing down the
Castle hill, make my way into the church, which at least keeps
firm hold on the silence of the past, and which possesses a fine
Norman nave, several recumbent effigies of knights and ladies
whose identity is long since lost, and a series of remarkable
frescoes, which, when first discovered many years ago beneath
the plaster which had concealed them for I know not how
many centuries, were nicely whited over by order of the rector,
who held that a clean and snowy surface disposed his flock to
devotion much more certainly than any mass of ancient colour-

Castle Howard.

ing. Quite recently it has been discovered that frescoes are
not immoral ; and these very curious paintings are now open to
the inspection of the world at large.

The road from Pickering to Whitby opens from the lane
leading to the Castle, and many there must be who have stood
at the parting of the ways, hesitating whether they shall commit
themselves to this old coach road, or subside into the train
which goes racketing through the valley. I do not presume to
advise ; I only state my own experience. The way appeared
to go by gentle undulations along a ridge, and I said, "Go to,
it will be thus right into Whitby." I paid no heed to the
lowering of the sky, but started off at a good round pace, and

as I went cast a contemptuous thought behind me at the train, which even at that moment ran away screaming up the valley.

I had not gone far before the undulating ridge broke off sharply and let me down into the valley by a steep descent, followed by a sharper rise. The road became decidedly difficult ; the surface was by no means dry, and suddenly out of the still sky there swept a blast of chilly wind, there was a roll of thunder far down on the horizon, the sky darkened in a few minutes to an inky blackness, and almost without notice such a storm of rain hissed down upon the sodden earth as might send the stoutest of mankind pelting to the nearest shelter. For me there was no shelter on that accursed road. There would be some loss of dignity in recounting the state to which I was reduced, when the tyranny of that tempest was overpast, and the deluge subsided to a steady drizzle. Nor would it be fitting to relate in what temper I climbed the hills that lay before me, nor with what fond hope I looked out vainly for an inn. At length I saw a welcome signpost which informed me that I was no more than a mile and a half from Levisham station, and I shot off like a homing pigeon on the shocking byway to which the broken finger-board directed me. It led me through a meagre, miserable village, where the only sign of life proceeded from a tinkling blacksmith's shop. The man at work was civil but amused. He smiled largely as he stood in his doorway answering my questions. Yes, the station was straight on ; the road was easy to find, a bit hilly to be sure. I cut him rather short and plodded on. In one mile, I argued, the hills could not be intolerable.

Alas ! I did not know. My knowledge of the land of Cleveland is wider now. The road began to drop. It coiled a little so that I could not see its full iniquity, but trudged on gamely thinking I was near the bottom. I met a postman. He laughed and turned to watch me. I knew why presently, for I was on the brow of what could only by the grossest flattery be called a ravine. It was an abyss, and the road ran

straight down by a gradient which was even as the gradient of
a teacup. Down below me, in the very bowels of the earth,
was a pretty valley, winding among the steep shags of gorse
and ling that dropped precipitously to it on every side. I
could hear the gushing of a mill leat swollen by the rains, and
a small grey church stood midway in the narrow meadow which
occupied the valley bottom. The chilly wind blew up the
odours of damp woodland, and through the fresh shoots of
the springing bracken I could see the quick brown ears of
rabbits glancing on the further slope. Higher up the grey
rock cropped out, and from one of the grassy shelves, a
sheep, entangled in some mass of thorns, filled the whole
valley with its piteous bleating. I could have found it in my
heart to lament as noisily as he, and in good truth I hold that
he who takes a cycle by that road needs no less assistance than
a beam and pulleys. I looked back. The postman was still
watching me, and I could hear his odious chuckles as he
turned to climb the hill.

The rain had ceased and the narrow valley was deserted. I
paused a moment when I reached the bottom, watching how
the mill leat rushed out clear and sparkling from beneath the
wet blossoms of a hawthorn. A rather wild brown light fell
from the thunderous sky. The low church tower looked wan
and shadowy. The sheep upon the heights was bleating still.
The place had a strange aspect of solitude, of aloofness from
the world, which made its beauty rather eerie, so that when the
lightning began to play once more upon the hilltops, and an
occasional sharp crack of thunder rattled round the crags, the
sense of awe which it brought with it was but in keeping with
all the impressions of that lonely spot, and I climbed up the
steep and weary hill with a consciousness of pleasure in the
keener air which chased away the thick fancies begotten in the
valley bottom.

It was a rough, high ridge of waste pasture and shaggy moor,
adorned with a little village and the humblest of country inns.

The further valley was looking wildly beautiful, when the rough
road conducted me to the brow of the great hill above it.   It
was as deep as that out of which I had just climbed, but wider,
and set with exquisite woodlands all along both slopes.   There
was the fresh green of beeches and the ruddy growth of
budding sycamores, mingled with the darker foliage of firs and

Glen near Whitby.

ashes.   A few light wreaths of vapour were drawn across the
slopes, and from time to time a flash of lightning shot down
into the hollow, for the storm was growling still among the
crags.   Far away upon the right a towering hillside was all
scorched and black, while everywhere above the woodland lay
the dark green moors waiting till the breath of later summer
should kindle the warm purple flush upon their flanks, and the

K

noble colour leap like a flame from hill to hill, and make all glow with a splendour such as no king's palace ever boasted.

Such was the aspect of the deep main valley which cleaves Pickering Forest in twain, from the ancient town itself even up to the sea at Whitby; and you may go down between the folding of the hills, beneath scrub of oak and waving larches, and dark slopes of heather lit up by the fresh green shoots of springing bracken,—past Goathland, with its wild slope of moor, all ringing with the sound of waterfalls,—past Grosmont, past Sleights, until the river banks expand and the hills fall back, and you have reached a harbour full of clear green water, where one or two schooners are lying by the quay, and a couple of yachts are moored in midstream, while further off, above the old huddled red-roofed town, the rich mass of Abbey ruins stands out like fretwork against the grey sky.

Whitby.

CHAPTER VII

WHITBY AND THE NORTH-EASTERN COAST

It is a wild and windy morning, and as I climb out of the narrow streets of Whitby I see a gray tide breaking into white upon the long north beach, and a couple of fishing boats staggering along far out among the rough water. The wind comes in gusts, with an occasional short sob of rain, while over-head, through some gap in the torn clouds, a shaft of sunshine strikes downwards on the waves, and the gulls which sail across it gleam for a moment with flashing plumage, and are lost again in the grey, drifting haze. Round the base of the great cliff the

waves beat heavily with a low, deep tolling, which occupies all
the air, and brings into my mind the story of the abbey bells,
torn from the great tower on the cliff by some pirate, whose
ship, with all its company, was lost on Black Nab—but a little
way before me—as it ran down the coast with its ill-gotten
freight.   But the fishers plying up and down this coast hear the
bells pealing still on stormy days.   How should a man be free
from fancies when the sea beats under the hollow cliffs as it
does to-day ?   As I listen to its low, constant grinding, I almost
realise that strange conception of the ocean as a sentient thing,
which older writers found among the people on this coast.
" When the wind is down," says Camden, " and the water like
a level plain, it is no uncommon thing to hear at a distance a
kind of horrid groan, at which time the fishermen will not
venture out, supposing that the ocean is a huge monster, and on
those occasions expresses a violent craving to devour human
bodies,"   So it happens even in calm weather on this fabled
coast.

   I go toiling up a street of steps, and pause at last at the
weather-beaten church.   That ancient house of God, which
stands out so finely in the sight of mariners, is not on the very
summit of the cliff.   There is a short further ascent to an open
wind-swept space, where I can see an ancient cross surrounded
by stone steps, and beyond it the blackened splendour of the
abbey ruins, a seaward monastery, courting that exposure to
the elements which monks almost invariably shunned.   Looking
downwards I can see the spray flying white and vivid round the
lighthouse on the pier head.   The north beach is one long line
of grey breakers, lit up by rare gleams of fitful sunlight.   The
harbour runs inland like a deep gash among the lofty hills, and
on either side of the tossing water red-tiled houses nestle cosily
in the shelter of the hollow.

   Such was the ancient town of Whitby, and such is all that a
stranger tries to see who visits it to-day.   For it was the rule in
ancient times to build in sheltered spots, and the care with which

the townsmen hugged the hollow makes more striking the
conduct of the monks or nuns who built the great abbey on
the heights, where it was scourged in turn by every wind that
God sent out of heaven.   Fountains stands in a valley as
fertile as a little Eden.   Rievaulx was placed among the
foldings of deep and lovely hills.   Kirkstall commanded the
rich water meadows of the Aire.   But Whitby cast aside all
such soft luxury and loveliness, and placed itself where its lights
would beam far out to sea, and testify its mission to men who
went to and fro upon those lonely waters.

What was it that induced the first builders to choose this
site ?—a ridge so noble and so far seen that the abbey, ruined
and shattered as it is, must ever be one of the chief grandeurs
of the English coast, ranking with Tintagel and St. Michael's
Mount, and its own nearer neighbour, Scarborough ; or, perhaps, related more closely still to that old monastery of
Lindisfarne on Holy Island, further north, or the smaller
Farne Island, where St. Cuthbert built him an hermitage, and
dwelt with no other comrades than the storms and sea-birds,
working miracles which may be read in Bede.   There are
some writers who maintain that Whitby was never populous
until late Tudor days, till when none but the very smallest
town grew up in the hollow underneath the abbey.   I do not
believe it.   I go up and down the Yorkshire coast, noting the
singular scarcity of harbours north of the great inlet of the
Humber.   Bridlington is an open roadstead, Scarborough a
tiny artificial port, Robin Hood's Bay a paltry fishing village.
Others there are none ; and will any one say that in this vast
and wealthy county, so prolific both in the stuff for trade and
in men of wit and courage sufficient to turn it to profit, the
value and importance of this deep shelter for shipping among
the Cleveland hills can have been overlooked in any age of
history ?   Twenty centuries ago bold sailors were roaming the
North Sea.   Are we to suppose that they used other harbours,

but not Whitby? The Danish settlements are thick and close
in Cleveland. What would those bold seamen prize half so
much as a commodious harbour for their pirate boats? In
truth, it is not upon the English coasts that we need look for
any safe and defensible harbour, however small, which has not
from the very earliest times given shelter to shipping, and
gathered round itself the dwellings of the sailors and the
stores which satisfy their needs; and if one must speculate
about the age of Whitby town, I say I hold that it was there,
red-roofed and sheltered, long before the black magnificence
of the rich arches was reared up as we see them now, and
that seamen came and went from Whitby when a much lowlier
abbey stood upon the height, when monks and nuns dwelt
together on the windy cliff and the Abbess Hilda ruled them
both impartially.

I doubt whether any large part of the good Hilda's
authority was admitted by the sailors. Those who go down to
the sea in ships are the same in all ages of the world's
history, good, honest fellows, with no disinclination to other
people's goods, when they can be had without undue trouble.
It will be noticed throughout history that morality has ap-
proached all seaports from the land. Now the land approaches
to Whitby in old days were particularly arduous, and morality
is not an eager traveller. A thick darkness shrouds the
actions of the Whitby sailors, and whenever it is broken by a
ray of light, those brave men appear rather as sufferers than
as malefactors. As thus, in the early days of the government
of Lord Protector Cromwell, one Denton, who enjoyed a
considerable notoriety upon these coasts, and was captain of
a ketch armed with one piece of ordnance and about twenty
men—a modest equipage for a pirate—robbed a Whitby ship
of no less than two hundred firkins of butter! Pirates cannot be too particular, I know; but surely this greasy cargo
must have been an embarrassment to Denton. We are not

told what fight the Whitby ship showed against these twenty
men ; but probably Denton was such a terrible fellow that he
overawed all opposition.   At any rate, he did well along the
Yorkshire coast.   About the same time he picked up a good
ship called the *Amity*, of Scarborough, somewhere between
Scarborough and Filey, and held the crew to ransom ; and his
exploits were piling up a fortune for him rapidly when he
met with a sad accident on hailing a ship owned by Mr. Wig-
gone of Whitby, and was taken prisoner by unsympathetic
men, and carried off to York Castle.   This was in February,
1650-1, and in gaol poor Denton languished until June,
though not without distractions and the pleasures of society,
for his gaolers allowed him from time to time to dine with
some of the many people in York who recognised his virtues
and respected his character.   One summer evening he went to
dine with Captain Thornton ; and after dinner, being probably
a thought confused, took the wrong turning, and instead of
getting back to his cell again, found himself at Walmgate Bar,
where somebody was waiting with horses, and insisted on his
mounting, and I think he must have ridden to the coast, for
he certainly did not return to York.

Now this piracy was dignified by the name of warfare ; for
the pirates as a body were on the side of the banished king, and
there were many who when they could no longer operate on
land carried their swords to sea and did what they could to
harass the commerce of the winning side.   It is therefore open
to any one to maintain that the only piracy upon the Yorkshire
coast was inspired by a lofty motive ; but for my part I believe
rather that the passions of the cavaliers caught up the
system which they found existing, and that Whitby, if only it
would speak, might tell us many a tale of rovers upon the sea
and of wealth unlawfully acquired.   For it is admitted generally
that there were plenty of outlaws within the bounds of Yorkshire, and we have warrant for believing that they liked upon

occasion to mix a dash of sea life with their forest plunderings
What says the old ballad, speaking of Robin Hood?

> " When the lily leaf and the eglantine
> Doth bud and spring with a merry cheer,
> This outlaw was weary of the wood side,
> And chasing of the fallow deere."

It is true he went to Scarborough; but we know well he
came to Whitby also, where he was in high favour with the
abbot, and used to amuse him after dinner with displays
of archery. What brought him to Whitby? The desire to
enjoy a higher atmosphere? By no means; he tells us the
real reason : —

> " The fishermen more money have
> Than any merchants, two or three."

There lies the secret of Robin's visits to Whitby and other parts
of this lofty coast. There was more money in the pockets of
the fishermen than in the purses of the fat traders who rode
through Sherwood. I wonder how it came there. Was the
price of fish so high in old days, and the market so good that
fortunes could be made by catching it equal to or greater than
those obtainable in trade? Surely this cannot be the sole
explanation? There were, it is true, on most lonely coasts
certain modes of growing rich much faster than by fishing.
But we have leaned long enough on the wording of a ballad. I
really know nothing of the practices of the Whitby fishers; and
what I may suspect is certainly not evidence.

The storms of eight hundred winters beating up this bleak
sea coast, and the blasts scouring over the hillsides from the
wild fells inland, have blackened the arches of Whitby Abbey
with a rare magnificence. Dark and intricate, stained here and
there with brown, the mouldings and the tracery have the fine
colour of some worn sea cliff, on which the light never changes
without revealing some fresh beauty.

It is said that the very sea birds stooped upon the abbey as they winged their way ashore to do homage to St. Hilda ; and indeed that pious lady might have felt herself slighted if they had paid her less respect, for the crows, and indeed all the fowls of the air, showed a singular deference to St. Cuthbert upon Farne Island, and it rarely happened in the old days of faith that one saint was content with less reverence than was rendered

Whitby Abbey.

to another.   Perhaps the birds were conscious of a certain curiosity to see what was going on at Whitby in this mixed brotherhood of monks and nuns ; for the winged creation has always had a reputation for repeating scandal, and those who dwelt at neighbour monasteries were glad enough to hear it.

As I climb out upon the windy common which surrounds the

broken arches of the abbey, the season remembers that it is
summer, the grey clouds part, and a flood of soft and vivid
sunlight falls upon the ancient cross and casts deep shadows in
the precinct of the ruin. Far away on the north beach the sea
spray is torn from the rough breakers into a sort of mist, which
drifts along the sand, shot through by sunlight in a radiant
cloud, mysterious and fanciful, such as might well stimulate a
man's imagination till he dreamt of visions and saw saints
appearing on that shore which in old days was so lonely.

It is difficult not to talk of saints when one stands beside the
ruins of this abbey. Yet I do not know that those who dwell
in Whitby town to-day are distinguished by godliness above
their fellow men. And, indeed, it will be noticed that the
abbey is still left a good deal to itself, standing free from
modern houses, as if there were some tradition in the town that
a rather trying moral atmosphere existed on the cliff top, and
that it was pleasanter living in the hollow, where by no means
everybody was unnaturally good. Thus the town, being what
it always has been, and the abbey standing empty of its saintly
occupants, the visitor of to-day is likely to carry off, stored up
in his recollection, as many tales of witches and of fairies as of
St. Hilda, or any other of the holy men and women who dwelt
there in old times. I have said much of saints already upon
this desultory journey. Let us talk of witches now, notwithstanding that we are in much the same difficulty as that in
which Corporal Trim found himself when asked suddenly to
talk about white bears. "'Didst thou ever see a white bear?'
cried Mr. Shandy, turning his head round to Trim, who stood
at the back of his chair. 'No; an' please your honour,'
replied the corporal. 'But thou couldst discourse about one,
Trim,' said my father, 'in case of need?' 'How is it
possible, brother,' quoth my Uncle Toby, 'if the corporal
never saw one?' . . ." It is a difficulty truly. Now, I have
never seen a witch, but really there are so many in the Cleveland district, of which Whitby is by far the most considerable

town, that it would be absurd to stay my pen because my
personal experiences have been less rich than those of other
men. Why, the very streets and shops of Whitby are often full
of spirits, and not very many years have gone by since a man of
Guisborough, entering a shop in this old fishy town, saw his
own wraith standing there unoccupied. He called it a "waff."
Now, it is unlucky in the highest degree to meet one's own
double ; in fact, it is commonly regarded as a sign of early
death. There is but one path of safety ; you must address it
boldly. The Guisborough man was well aware of this, and
went up without hesitation to the waff. "What's thou doing
here ? " he said roughly; "what's thou doing here ? thou's after
no good, I'll go bail. Get thy ways yom, wi' thee, get thy
ways yom," whereupon the waff slunk off abashed, and the
evil design with which it came there was brought happily to
nought.

But waffs, however interesting, are not witches, and I must
not let the manifold superstitions of Cleveland tempt me from
my text. " For my part," said Sir Thomas Browne valiantly, " I
have ever believed, and do now know that there be witches."
I have no desire to be thought wiser than the silver-tongued
physician of Norwich, and if I had, I should find it hard to
resist the mass of evidence which is extant in Cleveland. Canon
Atkinson has collected much of it with a loving hand. "Not
believe in witches, saidst 'ee'? Wheea, ah kens well there's
eleven in G—— at this present tahm ! Neea, neea, it will na
dee to be wivout my witchwood ! " So said an excellent old
woman who, in pulling out her purse, had pulled out also her
witchwood, and was much concerned on discovering her loss.
Probably there are some people so ignorant as not to know
what witchwood is, or what use to make of it. Such igno-
ramuses would do well to sit at Canon Atkinson's feet rather
than at mine ; but as *Forty Years in a Moorland Parish*—
that delightful manual of wit and wisdom which no Yorkshire
topographer can henceforth ignore—may not be on the shelves

of every one who reads this book, I will draw upon its learning sufficiently to explain the point.

Witchwood must be cut from the rowan tree, and from a tree, moreover, which the cutter had not only never seen before, but of whose existence he had no knowledge. It must be cut from such a tree upon St. Helen's day, and with a household knife, and must not be carried home by the same route on which the searcher had gone out. Witchwood is thus, in the language of the economists, difficult of attainment ; and it has also value in use, otherwise how would the witches be kept out of dairies and kitchens, where they might work much mischief? A piece of witchwood laid upon the lintel of the door is a sure protection, and it is of no less service in a cow-byre, where it is indeed even more needed, since everybody knows how apt witches are to draw the milk of cows. Of course, there are other ways of protecting cows ; and one such was discovered near Wakefield—another district where witches always have been rampant. An old cow-byre was taken down, and in a hole over every cow's head was a paper bearing the following scrap of odd Latinity :—

> " Omnes Spiritones landent Dominum,
> Habentu Mosa et Prophetores,
> Excugat Deus et dissipentur,
> Manu segas amori,
> Fiat. Fiat. Fiat."

It is a natural tendency with men who deal in tales of super-stition to believe those gleaned within the districts they know best to be peculiar to it alone ; and thus it is a somewhat un-pleasant shock, uprooting partially one's faith in human kind, to discover that many of these tales are flourishing hardily not only elsewhere in England, but even far beyond the seas and in lands of ancestry widely different from our own. I should not have taken this occasion to make an observation, which is after all not very original or recondite, had it not been that the persistency with which some of these tales are claimed as being

purely Yorkshire becomes exasperating. Take the Farndale
story of Hob, the demon who worried a certain farmer so
much that he resolved on flitting. Early in the morning as he
was on his way with his household goods in a cart, a neighbour
meeting him said, "Ah! I see thou's flitting." "Ay," cried
Hob out of the churn, "Ay, we'se flitting." On which the
farmer, seeing he could not rid himself of Hob, turned back to
his old abode. Now this tale is repeated in almost every book
on Yorkshire which has been written, no doubt with perfect
justice, since it is indeed a story current in the north, if not
quite peculiar to Yorkshire. But while Canon Atkinson has
produced the Danish counterpart of the tale, I may add that it
is current also in far distant Apulia, where Hob passes under
the name of "Il Lauro." "The Lauro," says Miss Ross, in
her *Land of Manfred*, "is most capricious. To some who ask
him for money he gives a sackful of broken potsherds; to
others who ask for sand he gives old coins. He took a particular dislike to a cousin of the old shepherd's, sitting on her
chest at night and giving her terrible dreams. At last she was
so worried by the Lauro that she determined to leave her
house. All the household goods and chattels were on the
cart; nothing was left but an old broom, and when the good-
wife went to fetch it, the Lauro suddenly appeared saying,
'I'll take that. Let's be off to the new house.'" What is this
but the tale of Farndale Hob? And since it is equally un-
likely that Yorkshire taught it to Apulia, or Apulia to Yorkshire, we are started on a vein of inquiry more fitted for the
learned pages of some work on folklore than for those of such
a rambling chronicle as mine.

Well, I have lingered long enough upon the headland; let
us go down and see the port. There is not much of interest
in the town itself, save a knot of narrow, winding streets, in
whose individual buildings one may search vainly for any
beauty or even quaintness of design. It is only when one
reaches the water's edge that the magic of the place reasserts

itself; for as the cliff comes in sight again, the houses appear
only as a blur of colour, and it is the ruin dominating the
whole scene to which all eyes are drawn.   One is always conscious of it; and as I walk along the quay, out upon the pier
which juts eastwards underneath the town, it is not the lighthouse, nor the great range of cliffs which occupy my thoughts,
nor the large empty harbour, nor even the great crowd of
fishing boats, Scotch, Cornish, and East Anglian, which make
such a merry spectacle when they run out into the rough water
on a breezy morning—it is the abbey, still the abbey, the work
of men whose life was done and their ideals ground into dust
full ten generations ago.

   If anything could rid me of this prepossession it would be
the beauty of the scene which lies spread out before me at the
end of the pier.   For the sun is breaking through the heavy
tent of clouds on every side, and blue sky is chasing gray all
down the heavens.   The sea, which has been brown and sullen,
is changing colour every moment, so that great heaving swells of
vast extent have caught the softest tints of green, while beyond
it is all gray and silver.   I look out northwards along the sands
to the further side of a wide bay terminated by three lofty
headlands all in shadow; but at their junction with the land
the sun catches the green fields in the dip, and glows there
sweetly.   As far as I can see, on every side there is a rough
sea tossing into sparkles, brushed by myriads of sea-birds,
glancing up the rocks in vivid flashes, driven along the sands
in 'that singular translucent mist which I have already mentioned, and which, as it eddies and rolls along the northern
sands, takes now one shape and now another as rapidly as the
changes which one watches in the glowing embers on a winter's
night.

   Such is Whitby, a seaport of some consequence, though it
has lost the chief portion of that whaling trade which the sturdy
Yorkshiremen of the last century pursued with relish in its
danger.   It was doubtless the spirit and tradition of those

great voyages among the ice which animated Captain Cook, as it did many another brave sailor of whom the world knows

Whitby Harbour.

nothing, and sent him from the huckster's shop at Staithes to a renown as great as that of Torres and Magellan. He is the

true hero of this coast in modern times, and as I climb out of
Whitby by the hilly road which passes northwards, his great
adventures and his piteous fate serve to amuse my memory
until I find myself running out upon the shore at the hamlet of
Sand's End.   There are a few neat cottages upon the landward
side, and the beach is broken into terraces or platforms by low
shelves of rock cropping out amid the sand.   I turn for a last
view of Whitby.   The lighthouse at the entrance of the harbour
is clearly visible, and a reef of low rocks is just left uncovered
by the tide, which whips over them in spray driven by the gusts
of a sharp northern wind.

It is from this pleasant village of Sand's End that the
judicious will diverge to see Mulgrave Castle and the lovely
woods which surround it.   But I have far to go ere night, and
indeed when I call to mind the great distances of the West
Riding, the valleys and the waterfalls which lie before me, and
the sweet air of the moorlands which I have to climb, I feel
that I have delayed too long within this land of Cleveland, and
must hurry onward with what speed I may.   But it is a weary
road, and hills lie before me which are too steep to be made
pleasant even by the sight of sea-birds soaring round the grey
cliff-tops ; while ere long the road runs inland, as it often does
in this part of Yorkshire, where the railways have usurped the
coast, and I have consequently nothing else to think of than
the stories and traditions of this country, where gnomes and
fairies have continued their pranks unchecked almost to the
present day.

There was one such in those very Mulgrave Woods, which I
have but this moment left behind me.   Her name was Jeanie ;
she may be there still for aught I know, but few will go to look
for her when they hear what befell one who desired her ac-
quaintance many years ago.   He was a farmer in this neighbourhood, and he rode up on horseback to her dwelling, calling her
by name.   I do not know whether he omitted any title of
respect, or whether it was merely the unauthorised attention

which enraged the irritable Jeanie. But the fact is that she rushed out in a towering passion and flew at the unlucky

The Coast Road to Whitby.

farmer with a wand. He spurred his horse and avoided her blow, but she gave him chase, and gained upon him for all

L

the fleetness of his horse ; so shuddering and pursued the luckless farmer galloped to a brook, which he leapt in the very nick of time. For Jeanie was upon him, and as the horse rose to the leap, her wand descended on his back, cutting him in two, so that Jeanie retained his hind-quarters on her side the water, while the farmer with the head and forelegs fell on the safe side of the flowing stream, which fairies cannot cross. It was a narrow escape, and one may understand why it is that when the clashing of the bittles which Jeanie and her fellow bogles use in washing their linen at Claymore Well is heard echoing down the dales, the peasants will not interfere nor attempt to see what the demons are about.

The subject of bogles is a tempting one, and I would fain linger on it in this region where they are so numerous. One famous member of the clan dwells at Runswick, whither I am going as fast as the hilly road permits, or rather he did dwell there until men quarrying for jet tore down the cliffs and destroyed the hole in which he used to lurk, reviled because he was fond of drowning people, yet loved because he cured them of the whooping-cough. Runswick is still what it always has been, a mere fishing village.

> " Souther, wind, souther,
> And blow father home to mother ; "

so the children used to chant while dancing on the cliff-top ; and though they have grown too wise to do it in these days of Board schools, that is not because their hearts are set less eagerly on the changes of the sea, or the prospects of the fishing grounds. The houses are dotted here and there on the high broken ground which sweeps down in fine undulations to the shore, where two or three small boats lie hauled up on the beach, and a few low shelves of blackened rock jut out into the receding water. Cloud and sunshine sweeping over red rock and grey sea, the heavy blows of a caulking hammer resounding from a hillock just above the beach, the cries of children

playing near the water's edge—such are the memories which I
retain of Runswick Bay, a pleasant solitary spot unto this hour,

Runswick Bay.

and one which somewhat stirs the imagination by the very
aloofness from the outer world which distinguishes it yet.

It is no long journey from Runswick to Staithes; and my

wonder as to the conditions of life in these solitary hamlets in
old days outlasts the undulations of the way, so that when I
come down the bare road underneath the railway, and find
myself standing on the brow of the hill above the cramped and
fishy town, I am still pondering whether it can indeed have
been fish alone which amused the people. Even mermen, such
as were caught at Skinningrove, a trifle further up the coast,
cannot have done much to relieve the monotony of nets and
lines.   Human nature will break out and find excitement.   As
for the town, it has feared to climb the hill ; and so, as it
expanded—if indeed it contains more houses now than the first
builders planted there—it has crushed itself more and more
tightly into the hollow of the last slopes near the sea.   Thus
it follows that when you are within twenty yards of the town
you might jump upon it from the summit of the hill ; and as
you go down you plunge into a winding street of plain and
ugly houses which precipitates you at last upon a small beach
of shingle, walled in by two fine and lofty cliffs, having more
beauty of outline than is common on this coast, where the
precipices are for the most part of such a crumbling stone that
only their sheer height makes them imposing.

    There is much quaintness, though little beauty, in this cramped
cleft of houses, where Captain Cook began his career by
stealing a shilling from his master's till, and running off to sea.
It was a slender equipment for so great a journey ; but probably
the till contained no more.   I lament the theft as I climb the
hill, and take up my long journey towards Guisborough ; but
indeed I discover in my heart a certain sympathy for the erring
lad who did so nobly afterwards.   Staithes is certainly a place
of most portentous dulness.   Its attractions have been over-
rated.   There are half a hundred fishing villages upon the
English coast of equal quaintness and of far more beauty ; and
as I run on through the bare unlovely country, I am well content to leave the remainder of the Yorkshire coast unseen.
Flamborough is a great and noble headland : Scarborough

a crag of wondrous grandeur : Whitby in sheer beauty may vie
with any port in England. But the true loveliness of Yorkshire

Staithes.

does not lie upon her coast.   In that she can be outmatched.
It is in river scenery that she is peerless ; and that is why I am

now hastening westwards, towards the pretty town of Guisborough, beneath the noble cone of Roseberry Topping.

I should be something less than the good Shandean, which
I proclaim myself to be, if I could pass the town of Guisborough without allusion to the terrific curse which Doctor Slop
was inveigled by Mr. Shandy into levelling at his unfortunate
man-servant Obadiah ; and as I am tired of describing scenery,
while my readers will have to submit to many pages of ecstatics

Near Guisborough.

before we part beneath the slag heaps which adorn the neigh
bourhood of Sheffield, I will leave all pretty Guisborough to
Mr. Pennell to describe, and recall the circumstances which
supplied Mr. Shandy with the original of this awful imprecation.

It must have occurred to many of those who read Tristram
Shandy that the unadorned wit of a humble parish priest could
scarcely have contrived, without assistance, to put together a
curse so strangely detailed and so comprehensive. The doubt

is warranted. The curse was the composition of a greater man
—one far more used to cursing, and who, moreover, had
received at least the shell of it from immemorial ancestors, all
experts in the pleasing exercise of appealing to the powers of
heaven to punish those whom earthly terrors could not reach.
There was a certain Sir Thomas Chaloner of Guisborough,
who, while travelling in Italy, visited by special permission the
alum works, from which the Pope of that day drew a substantial
revenue; and pondering on the nature of the processes, he
began to recollect that on his own estate at home he had all
the materials for the lucrative manufacture which was so
profitable to the pontiff. He was wise enough to keep his
thoughts locked up in his bosom until he found an opportunity of secret converse with some one or two of the Pope's
workmen, whom he tempted by large offers to accompany
him to England. It fell out as he had anticipated, and ere
long the Pope heard that a large trade in alum was growing
up in Cleveland by the energy of Sir Thomas Chaloner whom
he had befriended, and of his own workmen whom Sir
Thomas had stolen from him. The outrage was intolerable.
Had Sir Thomas been within reach, the Pope would have
settled the matter for himself, in some one of the time,
honoured ways by which Popes rid themselves of men who had
offended them. But since the ocean roared between them,
nothing remained but to send a blighting curse across the
sea, and the Pope started off in this way : " By the authority of
God Almighty, the Father, Son, and Holy Ghost, and of the
Holy Canons and of the undefiled Virgin Mary, the Mother
and Patroness of Our Saviour, and of all the Celestial Virtues,
Angels, Archangels, Thrones, Dominions, Powers, Cherubim
and Seraphim, and of the Holy Patriarchs and Prophets, and of
all the Holy Innocents who, in the sight of the Holy Lamb, are
found worthy to sing the new song ; of the Holy Martyrs and
Holy Confessors, and of the Holy Virgins, and of all the Saints,
together with all the Holy and Elect of God, we excommunicate

and anathematise you, Thomas Chaloner, &c., &c., &c., from the thresholds of the Holy Church. . . . and as fire is quenched by water, so let their light be quenched for evermore, unless they repent and make satisfaction for their crime. . . . May they be cursed wheresoever they are, whether in the house or in the field, in the highway or in the path, in the wood or in

Guisborough Abbey

the water, in the market or in the church ; may they be cursed in living or in dying, in eating and in drinking, in hungering and in thirsting, in fasting and in sleeping, in slumbering and in working, and in resting, in sweating and in blood-letting ; may they be cursed in all the faculties of their bodies, inwardly and outwardly, may they be cursed in the hair of their

head, and in their brain, in the crown of their head and in their
temples, in their forehead and in their ears, in their eyebrows
and in their cheeks, in their jawbones and in their nostrils. . ."
Upon my word I weary of this anatomical category of organs,
and will leave any one who lists to complete it for himself.

Such was the curse launched from the holy stool of St. Peter
at the audacious Englishman who dared to make alum. It did
no particular harm to any one, and serves merely as an amusing

Saltburn

relic of the savage spirit brought to the performance of their
sacred duties by the successors of St. Peter.

It is growing dark, and the long journey is nearly over. This
long while my road has been dropping out of the hill country,
and entering on that vast plain which, as I have said already,
occupies the whole of central Yorkshire, and to me, remembering
through what wild, undulating country I have come, the importance of the towns lying in the centre of this level strath becomes

plain, as by a sudden flash, and I comprehend why the musters of knights and yeomen assembled to repel the Scots were gathered so often at Northallerton, and why the raiders passed so frequently by this level route into the heart of Yorkshire, avoiding as long as they might those hills on either hand through which the conduct of even light-armed troops must have been a matter of some difficulty, while an army encumbered with booty would fall an easy prey to any bold attack.

On the Greta.

CHAPTER VIII

NORTHALLERTON, CATTERICK, GRETA BRIDGE, AND BARNARD CASTLE

I OFTEN think that much abused person, the rapid traveller, might if he would make a telling answer to his critics. For how inaccurate, he might say loftily, is the impression gained of the

individuality of a people or the aspects of a country by those
who only creep around it, devoting weeks of indolence to the
study of a single district! For grant that in their gropings among
minute and long forgotten things they have indeed found some
of note and interest, that from the heap of motley rubbish
they have raked together they can in truth extract some one or
two pearls of price. Grant that their loitering is no excuse for
idleness, that they have noted flowers I have missed, plucked
fruits which I left hanging on the tree, heard songs of which I
only caught the echo, and listened to the multitudinous murmuring of the sea which did but glance up green and azure at
me as I hurried by. Let them rejoice in their knowledge of a
single furrow; let them loiter down one hedgerow and believe
it is the universe. I leap over it and go my way, out into the
laughing world, over the green fields and away through the
sunny country, noting how the shadows chase each other across
the grass, with careless heart and eyes wide open, catching now
a glimpse of hill country, and now a scrap of valley land, eating
my early breakfast by the sea and munching my bread and
cheese for lunch in a roadside tavern many a mile inland, till
all my heart and body are a-throb with the joy of wandering and
of rapid motion, and my fancy stimulated by the change of
scene shows me in quick flashes how the joints and struts of the
whole land are dovetailed in together, and what manner of
beings it has brought forth to help on its destiny in the life of
man.

Heaven help me! I have blundered into an apologia, a
thing I never dreamt of doing, and one which I abhor in others.
But let it stand, for indeed if such a thing is ever excusable, it
is to be forgiven in me at the present moment, when having
come down out of the highlands upon the level plain which is
the heart of Yorkshire, I look round to see what I have done on
this one section of my journey, and what I have in mind to do
upon the other. Here is the time to stand and think, to repent
of acts of haste and carelessness, and resolve to commit no more.

I know my failings. I have many mentors. One man grieves
because I did not notice that this church was Saxon, while
another murmurs that only by poring over Domesday Book at
every stopping place, could I make my journey profitable. " It
is mere levity not to deviate to see these camps," shouts one ;
while another adds that if I do not mean to talk about the
grave-mounds on a certain moor, I had better stay in the south.
For all these faults, and many more unmentioned, I do
grieve and am duly sorry. Heaven made me so that at certain
times I would rather wander across the hills without a definite
purpose in my mind, swallowing the wind and basking in the
sunshine, than turn aside to speculate on the wildest fancy of
the most learned antiquary, or the ugliest building of the most
ancient man. And that is why this book is not a guide ; and
now let me get upon my way, for the western hills are wide, and
the dales run up for many a mile into their recesses, and the
becks that leap down their rocky sides are so many and full
that the whole land is musical with running water, so that its
rivers and its falls give it a character of wondrous beauty, over
which we will not hasten, but will leave ourselves full time to
linger where we will.

And, therefore, passing out of this old town of Northallerton,
and crossing the level, fruitful country, where the great battle
was decided, and which lies smiling now as if it had never seen
the Scotch and English banners hurtling together in most
deadly strife, I ride down over Swale till I reach the grand old
highway which the Yorkshiremen call Leeming Lane, an
obvious old Roman road, cutting straight as an arrow through
the country towards Catterick, and undulating by gentle rises
and declines as far as one can see in either direction. A
Roman road it was, as I have said, for this is part of Watling
Street, by which the Roman legions marched northwards,
whether they were bound for Newcastle or for Carlisle. The
two roads diverge at Scotch Corner, where I shall pause
presently ; but in the meantime, as I run on over the smooth

and velvet surface of this ancient way, I cannot choose but
remember that it was notable much nearer our own times, and
that its fine, broad reaches saw the gallops of as many a team
of fine horses as ever made the coaches spin on any road in
England. Not all the coaches for the north ran upon this
splendid road, for some turned eastwards from Boroughbridge
and went north through Topcliffe, Northallerton, and Yarm.
But there was enough traffic throughout all the days of
coaching to maintain two fine old inns, now, alas, turned
into goodly farms ; and the "Telegraph," a very famous coach,
ran this way from Leeds to Newcastle, up to the outbreak of
that sad fondness for machines which made the British public
love the smut and soots of the iron way better than the clean
dust of the old high-roads.

Never did any highway proclaim its old lost consequence
more plainly than does Leeming Lane. Not the nine miles
between Doncaster and Bawtry, which I take to belong by
undoubted right to the nobility of roads, the primæval
aristocracy of travelling ways, lost and swamped amid a crowd
of paltry modern imitations, can show a nobler stretch of wide
grass borders, or a fairer surface than this lane which follows
where the Romans trod, themselves in all likelihood adapters of
an even older highway which may have followed in this track
since the very earliest days when men began to pass from south
to north within this land of Britain. One cannot fail to be
conscious of some reverence for that which is so very ancient,
some respect for the shadows of all the countless hosts which
have passed this way on their long-forgotten business. And
as I ride on through the summer morning, running now under
the deep shade of elms, now out into the sunlight, and always
tasting the sweet scent of hawthorn and wild roses in the
hedges, it seems to me that the very goodliness of the farms
and villages, their spacious outbuildings, and the ordered roomy
comfort of the houses, leads me back to ages which are not our
own, so that I almost look to see stage wagons toiling along the

level road with high-pitched tilts, and wagoner plodding beside
them on his stout, white pony, or to behold a packman casting
off his bale of goods by a roadside tavern, while from all the
village doors the women pour out eagerly to get first sample of
his wares.

But they are gone. All that old life has passed away, and
the road is sleepy and deserted. I run into the old town of
Catterick—I call it town designedly, for how can one insult
with the name of village a place at once so ancient and still
so dignified in its decay ? What sights it saw, this old place
which was once so sportive, when all the gentry of the county
of broad acres met those of the surrounding shires on the
racecourse, long disused, or when some chaise spattered all
over with mud dashed up to the door of the "Angel" or the
"Golden Lion," disgorging some couple of insane young
persons on their way to Gretna Green, while the cry, "First
pair out," woke the sleepy post-boys in the old inn yard, and
the housemaids ran to the door and giggled and wished that
some one would run off with them. Ah, gay old life ! It is
dulness, sleepy dulness which afflicts us now, and old towns
like Catterick are a standing protest against our anæmic
modern ways, a mute and pathetic appeal for the restoration of
the old, full-blooded, noisy, rattling life of fighting cocks and
runaway marriages. There, let me get on my way, or the
spirit of old times will lead me too to hire a chaise for Gretna,
and carry off a chambermaid, forgetting that the useful blacksmith is dead, and his register will hold no more names.

I go on past that fine old inn the "George," which still
adorns the very ancient bridge a mile beyond the town of
Catterick. It is the Swale across which the road is carried at
this point, a river which even there is full of beauty, and which
inclines me to turn westwards to the great old town of Richmond, not so far away ; for the fact is that the shadow of
that vast stronghold of the Earls of Brittany dominates this
country, of which it was the feudal centre, and of which it still

remains the grandest ruin, and the most hoary centre of tradition. But my route lies onwards; and with reluctance I pass by the pleasant road which turns off at the river's bank, solacing myself as I go on with the pleasant memory of old Jenkins. I suppose that most men have some knowledge of this worthy, though I fear he is apt to be confused with another patriarch who gave his name to pills. Jenkins lived before the days of pills. He was born in 1501, and died in 1670—if any one believes this to be a lie, I really do not care—so that he reached the respectable age of 169 years. Any person interested in English history may take down his books and work out the events which Jenkins must have seen or heard of. I only mean to say of him by way of pointing the curiosity of his great age, that towards the end of his long life, a certain lawyer who was in search of evidence of the kind that lingers only in the minds of very aged people, journeyed to Bolton on Swale, where the patriarch resided, and seeing a white-haired, feeble man sitting in the garden of the cottage pointed out to him, began to tell his tale. The old man heard him out, and then said feebly, " I dunnaw nowt aboot 't. Tha'd best see my feyther in t' hoose." Marvelling that one so old should have a father to refer to, the lawyer went inside, and found there cowering over the fire a poor, palsied creature absolutely broken down with years, whose toothless jaws mumbled out with difficulty that his memory was not very good, but that his father had a grand. one ; and that he was outside in the yard chopping wood Marvelling still more the lawyer went out behind the house, where he found a hale and ruddy old fellow chopping logs with vigour that would have done credit to his great- great-great-grandson. He put down his axe and greeted the visitor courteously. He remembered all about the matter in hand, and gave the necessary evidence with all kinds of confirmatory circumstances, which won the cause. Not long afterwards, he died, leaving at this, the very gate of Swaledale, a flavour

of the marvellous, which we shall find abundantly maintained
when the moment comes to enter that deep and winding gorge
which the most rapid of the Yorkshire rivers has hollowed out
among the hills.

These agreeable reminiscences of old Jenkins have brought
me to Scotch Corner, where the coaches for Carlisle turned off
from the main north road to traverse the exposed and lonely
way through Bowes and across Stainmoor, sacred for many a
century to outlaws, for whom alone it is a proper habitation.
I shall not go out upon that dreary waste, but I jog along
the ancient road for some eight miles yet, passing on the left
the village called Gilling, which was the centre of this country
before the Norman earls built the great castle at Richmond.
Behind Gilling rises the lofty wooded ridge which bounds the
valley of the Swale, and the hollow on this side is fertile and
pleasant. There is not much else to see upon the road, till
after some eight miles it begins to trend downwards, a wide
fertile country opens in advance, bounded by blue lines of
moorland, and suddenly, before one realises that any scenery of
more than common interest is at hand, the road has run out
upon a small steep bridge, under which a brown shallow river
splashes onwards over boulders, past green meadows full of
grazing cattle, and under overhanging thickets of beech and
sycamore. It is the Greta. Brignall banks are but just out
of sight. Rokeby stands upon my right, hidden by stately
trees. Mortham Tower is but a little way down stream, and
that way also lies that fairy scene which most of us have gazed
on upon Turner's canvass, not without some beating of the
heart, some qualm of doubt whether such loveliness is indeed
revealed to any save to those rare souls who are worthy to
receive "the light that never was on sea or land." Let this
remain among the questions which each man prefers to resolve
according to his own judgment. I will not describe the meeting of the Greta and the Tees.

M

Indeed, when having rested and refreshed myself at the "Morritts' Arms," I sally out to stroll along the noble meadows by the bank of the small noisy stream, watching the wagtails

Bridge on the Greta.

flying in and out beneath the bank, and the shadows driven quickly by the wind across the great trees and the wide lawns of the park beyond, I find myself little disposed to describe

once more in my own words those scenes which I learnt to
love long years ago in the work of the great master, Walter
Scott. I stroll onwards up the hill by a path that leads away
a little from the river, and goes by an exquisite wood all
carpeted with wild garlic, and a few late primroses lingering
where the cool shade is thickest, till at length I come upon an
old house surrounded by a wall which was built clearly for
defence, and gathered round a tower which is a castle keep in
miniature. This is Mortham Tower, and the place is worth
visiting on every ground. In fact it is one of the old border
peels, and speaks eloquently of the days of Scotch invasion.
Indeed the ancient house of Rokeby on the lower meadows
by the river was burnt by the Scots in a foray after Bannockburn, at which time this ancient stronghold was doubtless
besieged and perhaps defended with success by reason of its
greater strength.

So here, too, fell the strokes of border warfare, full sixty
miles from the debatable land, and the chosen haunts of those
Armstrongs and Johnstones whose restless turbulence drew so
bitter a toll of life and happiness from every district they could
reach.

> " Lord God, is not this a pitiful case,
>   That men dare not drive their goods to the fell,
>   But limmer thieves drive them away,
>   That fears neither heaven nor hell ? "

So sang one too sick and sore at heart to make good verse ;
and, indeed, it is only those ballad writers who caught up the
cries of anguish floating in the air and crystallised them in a
form which defies all time, it is those nameless bards alone
who can tell us what the border warfare meant. It is all so
long ago that nothing but a confused din of slaughter and the
clash of arms floats down the centuries, save when out of the
stanzas nursed in the hearts of the people there rings a cry of
woe so utter and of desolation so supreme as awes even the
careless listener of to-day, and teaches him in one brief moment

M 2

all that history, in its dignified narration, can never tell
him.

> " My love he built me a bonny bower,
>   And clad it all with lily flower,
>   A brawer bower ye ne'er did see
>   Than my true love he built for me.
>
>   .   .   .   .   .
>
> " He slew my knight, to me sae dear,
>   He slew my knight and poined his gear.
>   My servants all for life did flee,
>   And left me in extremitie.
>
> " I sewed his sheet, making my mane ;
>   I watched the corpse, myself alane ;
>   I watched his body night and day,
>   No living creature came that way.
>
> " I took his body on my back,
>   And whiles I went and whiles I sat,
>   I digged a grave and laid him in,
>   And happed him with the sod sae green.
>
> " But think na ye my heart was sair
>   When I laid the moul on his yellow hair ?
>   Oh ! think na ye my heart was wae,
>   When I turned about away to gae ? "

In those few lines, so potent still to touch the heart, lies the
whole bitterness of the border warfare.   And if that sea of
cruelty and troubles surged up more rarely into Yorkshire than
into its neighbour counties of the north, yet there was no land
on that side of the Humber where the people dwelt in safety,
and this rich valley of the Tees was never likely to escape.

This old house, therefore, which now stands mute and
desolate, has many tales to tell ; and amongst them all we
ought not to forget the memory of that great family which
gave its name to the estate and made it illustrious with a
grandeur which clings about it yet.   Rokeby was a name of
power throughout this country in early Plantagenet times,
and ever after, till the civil wars ruined the house, like many

another which had owned a heritage as notable, and left the
head of the family burdened with debts, yet surrounded by a
group of sons and nephews in whom he might yet hope to see
the glory of his family restored.

Now, these boys had an uncle, one Ralph Rokeby the
younger, of Lincoln's Inn, who held the post of Secretary to
the Council of the North, and to him it was of very dear concern that they should grow up to an honourable future.   So he,
desiring to leave nothing untried which might secure that end,
left behind him a memoir in which human love for the lads is

Rokeby.

so blended with solicitude that they should not fall short of
the honourable conduct of their ancestors, that one cannot
read it without sympathy for the good Secretary in his hopes
that the boys whose growth he watched might again lead the
name of Rokeby upwards, and plant it firmly in a future as far
distant as that long past it had adorned.

" Mine owne good boyes," the Secretary begins, "mine owne
good boyes and best beloved cosyns, seeing that in these our
times honest behaviour and faire conditions are soe far gone to
decay . . . I have, therefore, thought good to help you forward
to desire and by good and commendable meanes to deserve

honour or honestie, the faire and goode rewarde of virtue . . .
to fear and abhorr shame and dishonour as the gates of hell
. . . and now, good boyes, let my advice sinke into your hearts,
when the vessel for the first season has taken the taste therof,
for the most part it keepeth a very long time the savour. . . .
You shold continually in all your doings have in remembrance
that—thankes be to God—you are gentlemen, who, how they
must be qualified, and in what comeliness behave themselves, read Solomon's Proverbs, the Book of Wisedome,
Ecclesiastes, Ecclesiasticus, Tully's Book of Offices, Count
Balthazar Castiglio of the Courtier." The choice of literature
is notable. I do not know how many of these works a parent
of to-day would put upon his boy's bookshelf. One at least
among them, and that not the least useful, might be searched
for long enough in English bookshops, though rightly popular
in the days when Mr. Secretary Rokeby wrote. But the boys
were not to rely only on their literature, however aptly chosen.
They were trained to remember what their fathers were.
"Thomas Rokeby, Lord Justice of Ireland . . . being con-
trolled that he was served in wooden cups, answered that these
homely cups paye truelye for that they conteyne. I had rather
drinke out of these cups and paye gold and silver than drink
out of gold and make wooden payments. Oh, my good boyes,
forgett not this golden speech, and be ashamed while you live
once to make soe worthy a gentleman groane in his grave at
any your misdemeanours."

Thus impressively did the Secretary try to teach "mine owne
good boyes" how to value what he had learnt to prize. I know
not if the attempt was more successful than any other of the
kind ; yet I would fain think that the lads must have paid some
heed to words so wise spoken with so great affection. And
having spoken out his heart in brief the Secretary was careful
not to bore them, but strewed his homily with anecdotes, and
even wove into it the ballad of the felon sowe which "Raph of
Rokeby, with full good will," gave to the fryers of Richmond.

I must give some extracts from this ballad in another chapter.
In fact I will pick up the felon sowe on my way back to Richmond, and make the journey which proved perilous enough to

The Greta River.

poor Fryer Middleton, who was sent to fetch her.   For the
moment my face is set in the other direction ; and when I
can get away from Mortham and from Rokeby it is towards

Barnard·Castle and the high fells of Teesdale that I shall set my course.

Reluctantly I turn away from the old border fortress, and leave the high banks and sloping woodlands all aglow in the rich reflections of the afternoon sunlight, and the Greta chattering down its stony bed to meet the louder waters of the Tees chafing in their rocky channel. The whole country is lit up with a golden gleaming—the hilly path, the wide park, the ancient trees, over all there falls a mellow radiance which is more beautiful than words can tell. And so I left this little fairyland and came out once more upon the road, that very highway, let us not forget, which Nicholas Nickleby, followed by poor Smike, trudged sturdily along, when, having beaten Squeers the schoolmaster and carried off his drudge, he set out manfully to seek his luck once more in a world which up to that moment had treated him but scurvily. Poor, lonely wanderers! They are not the least pathetic among the many memories and shadows on this ancient road.

I have spoken more than once of witchcraft and of occult practices upon the living. Now here at Greta Bridge not many years ago was found a pair of tablets which illustrate so luridly the manner in which the hate of families found vent, that I cannot pass it by unnoticed. Two leaden plates were dug out from a heap of stones on Gatherley Moor. They were carved with planetary signs and with the following inscriptions :—

"I doe make this that James Phillip, John Phillip his son, Christopher Phillip and Thomas Phillip, his sons, shall flee Richmondshire, and nothing prosper with any of them in Richmondshire." And on the other was this even more comprehensive aspiration : "I doe make this that the father, James Phillip, John Phillip, Arthur Phillip, and all the issue of them shall come presently to utter beggary, and nothing joy or prosper with them in Richmondshire."

This family of Phillip was one of property and standing. In

the early days of Queen Elizabeth they held an estate at Brignall, up the stream, and the owner of the land was James, who is given the place of honour in the evil wish recorded on the tablets.   John Phillip, who made the spell, appears to be the representative of an elder branch, which had by some means been dispossessed by a younger one ; and failing other remedies he took this dark way of avenging himself.   It is easy to smile at the folly that supposes a few scratches on a plate of lead have any power to control events.   But is there any one who would not feel some qualm of horror on discovering that a curse so awful had been levelled at himself?   It is perhaps a mere coincidence that the fate invoked by John Phillip did indeed descend upon the family he cursed.   All the male descendants named upon the plates died without issue ; and the name of Phillip ceased to be known in Richmondshire.

   I do not want to exaggerate the significance of this grim story of the past.   I daresay it may be true enough that such curses were of very rare occurrence.   Yet the inscription of planetary signs upon the plates suggests that they were made after a pattern which a man would not discover for himself ; that they were in fact the work of some practitioner in magic, whose trade it was to gratify bad men with hopes of vengeance dealt out by powers against which no human foresight might contend. Possibly there may be many tablets such as these not far below that kindly veil of springing grass and future harvest which hides so many ugly things.   Strange tragedies must have been played out in a lonely district where passions flamed so hotly and the superstitious northern fancy fed on solitude, on the whispers of the wind sighing downwards from the fells and the rushing sound of rivers at their flood.   Here is none of the great silence of the midlands ; but in the air there is a perpetual course of sound, now a summer trickling, now a winter spate, now a zephyr charged with scent of roses, now a bitter gale scattering dead boughs, wind and water always lifting up their voices in the wilderness, so that a man left alone with his own imaginings on

the summit of the fells might well hear in that close network of
noises which overspread the land articulate speeches levelled at
himself.

It is well known to those who dwell upon the banks of the
Tees that the loud sounding river, in whose gorge the depth of
water varies wonderfully, is inhabited by a malicious sprite,
with long green tresses and an insatiable desire for human life.
The children of the district know Peg Powler well, and many
an urchin lingering behind the rest has run screaming after his
companions at some fancied turmoil of the water betokening
the rising of the sprite.   There are vague tales of men beguiled
to lonely places in the stream, and drowned beyond all hope of
rescue ; and how then should little children save themselves but
by flight ?   Far down from the higher reaches of the Tees, out
of the region of the great waterfalls whither we are tending,
there are borne masses of white foam, whirling here and there
upon the river eddies ; and these, too, bear the name of the
sprite, being called " Peg Powler's suds."   Peg has her cousins
in other Yorkshire rivers, as we shall see later ; and, indeed, in
a land where rivers are so many, and so very wild and beautiful,
it could hardly be but that the fears and fancies of mankind
should centre round them, and gift them with sentient passions
like their own.

I run out of Greta Bridge beside the woods of Rokeby, and
their cool shade follows me, dappling the road with brown and
gold for a mile or more, till the way falls and rises and falls again
without any striking width of prospect, and so at last runs out
suddenly upon a bank, where I can hear the river chafing over
terraces and boulders far below among the woods ; while on the
hillside rising on the left, swept clear of trees, there stands a
group of buildings, of which one only sees at first that it is half
farm, half ruin.   Presently one perceives that the great empty
window, all whose tracery is gone save four upright dividing
shafts, has nothing in common with the barns and stables
which surround it ;   and on looking further the eye is

caught by the foliated arches of two or three windows in a
fragment of old wall, which must be presumed to have inter-
fered but little with the operations of herding and sheep-shearing,
otherwise it would doubtless have shared the fate of the rest
of the desecrated building, where the heirs of Rokeby and Fitzhugh, and many another noble house, were laid to rest in trust
that posterity would pay the dead respect. That trust was

Eggleston Abbey.

repaid by an outbreak of wild fanaticism which worked irrepar-
able ruin, but which did less harm than the centuries of neglect
and carelessness which have gradually robbed us stone by stone
of the most beautiful and interesting buildings in this country.
Who made it necessary to let rough farmers work their will
among these priceless treasures, quarrying their stones for gate-
posts, and tearing down screens and altars to mend rents in

their own houses? We speak sometimes indignantly of the barbarism of the past. Would it not become us well, ere condemning other generations, to see that cattle are not defiling those enclosures which were counted holy through many centuries? It is surely no great act of reparation that now, at least, the poor shattered remnants of what was once so beautiful should be dug out and cleared of brambles and rank growth of nettles, and placed in such a state that men who care about their beauty, and are interested in their history—there really are such people after all these years—may be able to guess the nature of that vanished grandeur without having their thoughts called off at every turn by the noise and interruption of a farmer's daily business?

I turn aside and stand upon the Abbey Bridge, a modern structure replacing one built by the monks, which in the early days when it was designed may have ranked as a considerable feat of engineering, so deep and precipitous are the cliffs across which it is flung, and so impetuous the boiling of the river in the rocky bed below. Standing here in the warm afternoon I can see Eggleston Abbey through a screen of trees, which trick me easily into forgetting all its desolation. Before me and beneath there lies at any rate a scene whose extraordinary beauty has not changed at all. I spoke of deep cliffs, and they are there, but hidden. For the dense growth of beech trees spreads its sunny shelter far beyond the limits of the rock which root them ; so that all the shelves and reefs that border the brown waterway are lying in deep shadow, broken now and then by a flicker of little dapples that runs along the worn and fretted stone whenever a light wind stirs the trees. But if the rock terraces are in shadow the channel of brown moorland water is alive with light. Sweeping now into deep pools whose level surface is just marked by the force of the current flowing underneath, or rippled by a fish which rises lazily at the fat flies buzzing along just out of reach ; now broken suddenly into streaks of brown and vivid foam, flashing and

quivering like jewels as the water flies and scatters over sharp
juts of stone and the rough irregularities of the shelving bottom ;
there is no yard of the long vista down which I am gazing that
has not a special and peculiar beauty.   Here in this northern
land the trees have not yet their full summer leaf.   The ashes
are still feathery.   The sycamores splash the woods with red.

Eggleston Abbey from the River.

The oaks have here and there a vivid mellow gold, which I
can follow in the sunlight far away down stream, where the
fretting of the water is too distant to be seen as more than
a bright sparkling underneath the trees which shade the Dairy
Bridge and the confluence of the Greta and the Tees.

There are few river scenes in this country worthy to be
matched with that which is disclosed from the Abbey Bridge,

bursting suddenly as it does upon the sight of every traveller,
whether he come from Greta Bridge or Barnard Castle. It is
the direct road to the latter famous town which most men follow
from this spot, climbing the hill among thick woods and coming
out at once upon the open ridge. But this is a mistake. For
when the river is left behind that road has no interest at all,
and it enters Barnard Castle through the unimposing outskirts
of the town. I choose the better part, and loiter onwards by
the bank of the river on the Yorkshire side, dropping down
between the Abbey and a group of cottages, where early roses
bloom pink and scarlet in the gardens, and a child carrying a
pitcher to the river stops and gazes at me as if I were a wild
man of the woods. At the foot of the hill a footbridge is
thrown over the mouth of a stream which runs out of a lovely
glen, while carts splash through the shallow sparkling water.
The valley is famous in its way. Scott calls it . . . No, I
will not succumb to a temptation I have resisted for so long. Let
others search and see how the great wizard speaks of Thorsgill,
if, like many a tourist in this region, they have " Rokeby " in
their pockets ; or, if not, let them more wisely wander up the
glen alone, and use their own eyes in admiration of its
elms and ash trees, and its pretty chattering beck. For
my part I have no time to loiter here. The clamour of the
river calls me on, and I follow up a hill, and over a steep ridge,
till the road, rough and untravelled, drops sharply to the river,
opening before my eyes the ancient town of Barnard Castle,
and a prospect which grows in grandeur as I approach the
bottom of the valley. For the rock of Barnard Castle
has not the sheer height of Richmond, and is the more dependent on being seen from the proper aspect. I reach the
foot at last, and cross the Tees by a high-pitched ancient bridge,
whence the town looks feudal, old beyond all modern computa-
tions, while on the crag the shattered towers of what was once
a strong and noble fortress rise in melancholy ruin.

CHAPTER IX

IF any one desires to interrupt me at this point with the remark that I had no right to come to Barnard Castle, which is not in Yorkshire, but in Durham, I shall submit patiently to the rebuke, and answer only that the circumstance was not unknown to me. But when, I ask, did I ever promise to rein in my caprice, if she chooses to go cantering off outside my title page? Who cares for county borders? They were fixed for the most part by persons possessing neither taste nor judgment, and if I can improve on them I will. The unity of Yorkshire, the rotundity of my theme, demand a town of note and mark in this remote north-western corner of the county. Here is such a town, and shall I hesitate because stupid people in the past have declared that it is in Durham? There is a verity of romance and a verity of fact. I care not under which head I become entitled to Barnard Castle ; and as a last word to my captious reader, I protest that he may account himself more fortunate than I expect if he be not carried into other counties before he gets out of the chariot to which my wandering fancy has been yoked.

I sometimes think that when one is so lucky as to discover a point of view from which an ancient town retains its mediæval aspect, or any trace thereof, it would be the part of wisdom not to pry any further, but to go away at once. Had

I turned after looking upward from the bridge at the quaint
houses rising out of the brown, rushing river, at the Castle
Crag, and the massive remnant of old keep which crowns the
eminence, I should have had a fairer memory of Barnard
Castle than the somewhat grimy, squalid, aspect of the town has
given me. For while, as I said, it looks feudal from below,
recalling, in some dim way, those hill forts surrounded by the
houses of the retainers, which may still be seen unchanged in
other and less settled countries, I am bound to admit that the
whole illusion vanishes when one passes through the streets,
marked visibly with the mean and unimaginative shops and
buildings which distinguish most English country towns, however ancient. One house, indeed, there is which has some
beauty and distinction; its style has been carefully avoided
by all subsequent builders. A memory of Dickens clings about
the " King's Head " Inn, and draws many a traveller to that
roomy hostelry. Of the town itself not much else is to be said.
It bears an evil reputation in the north—I have vainly sought
to know why, for something piquant, doubtless, underlies the
taunt which schoolboys used to fling at each other—and,
perhaps, do still—" A coward, a coward of Barney Castle."
Cowardice neither was, nor is, common in the north. What
reproach can it be that fell upon the town in days so long forgotten that it lingers only as a childish taunt ? One smiles at it,
yet there is in truth something terrible in this long tradition of
disgrace. Something happened, some heart failed in a sudden
danger, perhaps but for a moment. The heart is dust, who
shall say how many centuries ago ? But the reproach is living.
Is there no statute of limitations for a popular tradition ? " In
my own village of Edmundbyars," says Mr. Featherstonhaugh,
" I stopped to listen to two viragos abusing each other. When
vocabulary and breath were almost exhausted, what appeared
the most pungent and irritating epithets were ' Barney Castle '
and ' Bewcastle.' "

Well, let us go and see the Castle, which, broken as it is, has

still nobility enough to be impressive in itself, apart from all the
striking memories which gather round it.   Many a winter storm
has sent great fragments of masonry dropping from the old
untended walls, and sent them crashing down the precipitous
incline towards the river bed, carrying with them, often enough,
half a house, or the whole structure of some stable, as is told
tearfully by those who occupy the dwellings underneath the

Barnard Castle.

shadow of the vast old fortress.   But not three centuries of
neglect can destroy utterly the work of Norman builders ; and
as I walk round the inner ward, watching the swallows skim
in and out among the roofless guard rooms, while the air is
filled by the singing of the river, just as in those days when
men at arms and pages paced the courtway, and whispered
secretly of the great stake which their masters set upon the

N

turn of fortune, I can still cheat myself into seeing once more the whole motley crowd of mediæval knightly life—the squires and ladies riding home from hawking, the monks, the pilgrims, the passing travellers in search of shelter, the packmen guarding their wares with difficulty from the greed of the rough soldiery— all these shadows of the past start up unbidden as I wander round the walls which Barnard de Balliol built in the centre of his fair heritage of the Forests of Teesdale and Marwood, with the lordships of Middleton in Teesdale, and Gainford, and all their royal franchises, liberties, and immunities—that noble heritage, I say, which William Rufus had given to his ancestors some eighty years before.

So there the Balliols lay and grew continually greater, till at last they dreamed of royalty, and into this old courtyard there came the glamour of a throne.   For John de Balliol married with Dervorguill, heiress of the Constable of Scotland, whose mother was eldest of three daughters alone remaining in the younger branch of the royal house.   So that when the elder branch died out, the Lord of Barnard Castle was next in descent to that crown which the northern barons coquetted with as often as they quarelled with their own liege lord at Westminster, and with which, indeed, at many periods they had relations scarcely less intimate.   For in those days the frontier of the kingdoms was uncertain, and the feudal rights and titles of the two kings crossed and recrossed it in a very intricate mesh of rival obligations ; so that the most single- minded of the baronage might well doubt on some occasions whether his duty ought to be rendered north or south of the Tweed, and would incline one way or the other at the bidding of a clear self-interest.   Thus a Teesdale baron, who was also Lord of Galloway, and who carried in his veins the blood of Scottish Kings, was no foreigner in Scotland, and it was not incongruous that he should aspire to the crown.

How the lesser barons of the north must have flocked to pay their court to Balliol when the sunshine of this prospect

[*To face page* 178

"*The Return from Hawking.*"

broke on Barnard Castle ! How thick the pennons of Fitzhugh, and Bowes, and Mowbray, must have crowded down the narrow causeways, with those of many another noble house, all suppliant for the favour of him who might be King. The very pages must have cocked their caps a trifle higher, and added a few more tones of insolence to the swagger of their bearing when fancy showed them the broad fiefs of Scotland lying at their master's feet. For a while the house of Balliol was like a rosy cloud that catches the full splendour of the dawn. But a grey day followed. The support of England set John Balliol upon the throne he coveted, but it was given on conditions too hard for his compliance, and turned into hostility which brought the puppet king to ruin and a prison. That was not the end of the pretensions of his family, and, indeed, all the world knows the great story of the contests of Bruce and Balliol, both Yorkshire barons, for the Scottish Crown, and how England supported one or the other as pleased her best, and how great gain came to Scotland from the spirit and patriotism which that bitter struggle brought to life. But it was the end of the story so far as Barnard Castle is concerned ; for the English King gave the confiscated fortress to Guy Beauchamp, Earl of Warwick, from whom it passed to the Nevilles, and so became again a centre whence on more than one occasion the interests of Kingdoms were directed, and plots discussed which ended in tragedies among the bitterest in history.

Ah, if these old castles could but tell their stories ! What wondrous things should we not hear then of the turbulent Nevilles, and of Crookbacked Richard, who got this castle by his wife, Anne Neville, and concerning whom there will be more to say when we reach that great stronghold at Middle-ham, where he chiefly dwelt when visiting the north, which he loved and which loved him. But these are very ancient days into which I have wandered. It was the singing of the river which beguiled me, filling the air with a steady murmur which touches I know not what cord of fancy, making the past seem

far less distant and the old days real again.   It is time to move
onwards up the valley, where very noble sights are waiting ; but
before I go, I climb up to the ramparts and sit down on the
warm stone, whence I can look out upon the river and the
summer woods below, and across a wide and memorable prospect
of broken sunny country, dropping gradually towards the east,
but on the west rising into those great hills which culminate
in Mickelfell and Crossfell, and the high ridge of Burnhope
moors.

Reluctantly I turn away ; and, as the road to Middleton is
both long and hilly, I think it well to quaff a tankard before
setting out.   There is but one other occupant in the smoking
room of the " King's Head."   I greet him with the accustomed
Yorkshire toast, "'Ere's to thee, may thee want nowt, me
nother, nor nobody."   And as the bottom of my tankard
tilts up slowly, he bows solemnly and drains his own in
acknowledgment of the courtesy.   So I part with Barnard
Castle on the best of terms ; and run on past Lartington and
Cotherstone under great fells and bare rough heights till I
cross the River Lune at Romaldkirk, and in a little further the
old town of Middleton is seen lying in a well-wooded hollow,
out of which—having made the easy discovery that there is, in
fact, nothing to see there—I pass by a road that mounts and
mounts.   The sky has grown a little sad since I left Barnard
Castle, and a gusty wind sighs across my way, blowing at times
with considerable force.   The country has now all the aspect
of the high dales, wide, grassy slopes, dropping into the broad
valley from lofty moorland ridges, which, as I see them on this
stormy afternoon, are swathed in angry shadows and obscured
by driving mists.   Wild, sudden lights fly along the hill crests
from a sun which is not seen ; a white cottage high upon the
down catches the reflection and gleams out vividly, while the
lower slopes are dark and sullen.

Still the road goes on mounting, and presently it makes a
sudden turn which brings the river into sight, and gives a fine

backward glimpse of broken foaming water sweeping under a
lofty precipice crowned with a few firs, gaunt and black against
the skyline. Shelf by shelf the river bed drops in little terraces,
over each of which the brown water pours with gathering force,
making a long line of rapids, white and foamy, washing the base
of the cliff in little whirlpools, and filling the quiet air with
noisy sound. Such is the character of all the upper course of
this most lovely river, a constant spouting of cascades ; and what
is seen beneath this dark cliff is but a miniature rehearsal of the
effects which rise to grandeur at High Force and Cauldron Snout.

The road grows wilder as it continues to ascend. What few
trees the dale can boast are on the Durham side ; the Yorkshire slopes can show nothing but rough pasture and mere
wastes of ling and heather; the northward limits of the great wilderness of Stainmore, which for many a generation bred nothing
but the fiercest outlaws known within the limits of the north,
which is a large thing to say. Over those heights came the road
from Westmoreland ; and many a traveller in old days had
cause to dread the lonely passage over Stainmore. Indeed, as
I ride onwards watching those grim heights, a tale comes into
my mind which illustrates so strangely the wild life of that most
solitary district, that I set it down in full as I find it in the
collections of the Folklore Society, to whose discriminating
labours all topographers owe so great a debt of gratitude.

" Wild and varied as I know the superstitions of my native
county to be, I must plead guilty to some astonishment at
finding among them what Brand calls the foreign superstition of
the Hand of Glory, once firmly believed in many parts of
France, Germany and Spain. Sir Walter Scott brings it forward
as a foreign charm. It is the German adventurer Dousterswivel who is conversant with it, and who describes it." But
here we may break off a moment to remark that the clever
rascal Dousterswivel does not describe it with sufficient accuracy
or give the receipt so fully as to enable the unskilled practitioner to set to work without some further guidance ; wherefore

the curious would do well to pay the more attention to this
note. "The Hand of Glory is the hand of a man who has been
hung, and is prepared in the following manner. Wrap the hand
in a piece of winding sheet, drawing it tight to squeeze out the
little blood that may remain. Then place it in an earthenware
vessel with salt, saltpetre and long pepper, all carefully and
thoroughly powdered. Let it remain a fortnight in this pickle,
then expose it to the sun in the dog-days until it is completely
parched, or if the sun be not powerful enough, dry it in an oven
heated with vervain and fern. Next make a candle with the
fat of a hung man, virgin wax and Lapland sesame. The Hand
of Glory is used to hold this candle when it is lighted. Wherever one goes with this contrivance, those it approaches are
rendered incapable of motion as though they were dead."

There! Now any one can make this so useful Hand of
Glory for himself! So let us proceed to see how it was used on
Stainmore. "One evening, between the years 1790 and 1800,
a traveller dressed in woman's clothes arrived at the old Spital
Inn on Bowes Moor. The traveller begged to stay all night,
but had to go away so early in the morning that if a mouthful
of food were set ready for breakfast there was no need the
family should be disturbed by her departure. The people of the
house, however, arranged that a servant-maid should sit up till
the stranger was out of the premises, and then went to bed
themselves. The girl lay down for a nap on the long settle by the
fire ; but before she shut her eyes she took a good look at the
traveller, who was sitting on the opposite side of the hearth, and
espied a pair of man's trousers peeping out from under the gown.

"All inclination for sleep was now gone ; however, with
great self-command she feigned it, closed her eyes, and even
began to snore. On this the traveller got up, pulled out of his
pocket a dead man's hand, fitted a candle to it, lighted the
candle and passed hand and candle several times before the
girl's face, saying as he did so : 'Let those who are asleep be
asleep, and let those who are awake be awake.' This done, he

placed the light on the table, opened the outer door, went
down two or three of the steps which led from the house to the
road and began to whistle for his companions.   The girl now
jumped up, rushed behind the ruffian and pushed him down
the steps.   She then shut the door, locked it, and ran upstairs
to try and wake the family, but without success.   Calling,
shouting and shaking were all in vain.   The poor girl was in
despair, for she heard the traveller and his comrades outside the
house.   Suddenly she remembered the Hand of Glory, ran
downstairs again, seized a bowl of skimmed milk and threw it
over the hand and candle, after which she went upstairs again,
and woke the sleepers without any difficulty.   The landlord's
son went to the window and asked the men what they wanted.
They answered that if the dead man's hand were but given to
them they would go away quietly and do no harm to any one.
This was refused, and the landlord's son fired among them.
The shot must have taken effect, for in the morning stains of
blood were traced to a considerable distance."

Such is the tale of the Hand of Glory used on Stainmore—a
tale which is remarkable not only as comprising a superstition
rarely· met with, but also as throwing a flood of light on
the conditions of life on these wild uplands, which lay almost
beyond the reach of the law, slowfooted as she ever is and
infected with the love of ease.   Indeed, not only here, but all
through the dales and moors of the West Riding, there are
told dismal tales of murder, pointing to the days when travellers
who carried things of value bore their lives also in their
saddlebags, and had to take the risk of losing them like any
other article of merchandise.

That this was the reputation of Stainmore in very early
times may be seen from the records of the sanctuary of
St. Cuthbert at Durham, to which I have already referred in
proof of the warm-hearted friendliness which existed between
that holy man and such dwellers in this part of Yorkshire as
were prompted by their feelings to rob and slay.   Thus, on

the 10th October, 1487, Adam Ewbank rang the bell of the sanctuary and claimed protection from the penalty of having slain a man on Stainmoor. It would be easy to multiply such cases. The men of Dent, far away towards the head of Wharfedale, seem to have had an evil aptitude for offences which needed the intervention of the saint. Doubtless they skulked across the moors this way, avoiding trodden paths and settled country till they were in sight of the bounds whence their pursuers could not snatch them. And as I have referred again to this matter of the sanctuary, I may as well mention a curious case which shows how unreservedly the monks sheltered even those criminals whom they must have most abhorred. In February, 1485, "James Manfeeld, late of Wyclif, gentleman, in his own person came to the Cathedral Church of Durham, and there, having rung the bells, urgently sought the franchise of the Church and the liberty of St. Cuthbert for having, near the village of Ovington in Ebor, together with others, attacked Dom. Roland Mebburn, Capellanum, Rector of Wyclif, and struck him in the body with one'le wallych bill (*sic*), and given him a mortal wound of ·which he died." If ever any man were turned away from the mercy of the Saint, it would surely have been the author of this atrocious murder ; yet he was received like others, and sat, I presume, in the refectory among other fugitives who must surely have shrunk away from the wretched man on whose hands there lay the blood of a servant of the Church.

Wyclif and Ovington are but a little way down stream from Barnard Castle ; and the learned editor of the Sanctuary Book of Durham remembered that in his childhood the ghost of a priest used to walk in a field between those two pretty villages, clad in a gown of rustling silk. So long does the tradition of a crime linger in solitary spots !

But that is an old story now, and in these days the only living things which go in dread about the hills of Richmondshire are grouse, for which the Teesdale moors are famous.

How those birds must dread the flowering of the heather! At
last I come to a little roadside inn, of no great outward seeming,
but worthy of full confidence, as many a traveller can testify
who has arrived there wet and cheerless. Opposite the inn is
a little wood, a wood of firs entered by a white gate which I

High Force.

am inclined to open, if only to discover for myself what is the
cause of the great roar of falling water which occupies the air
with a thousand times more power than I have heard yet from
the river, noisy as it has been all the way from Middleton.
But even as I turn to open the wicket I discover, with all the

shock of a quick surprise, that the fall is there, before my eyes. Over the wood I see it, placed more beautifully than the most cunning artist could devise. Upon the sky line there is a green hill scarred with patches of black ling, and sweeping downwards with a fine abrupt descent until it meets a jutting shoulder of the moor which cuts across it; while from their intersection there sweeps out the wide brawling river, flashing gloriously in a sudden burst of sunlight, and sparkling on for some half mile till suddenly it meets a lofty precipice of scarred grey limestone, forces itself with a quick contraction into a channel scarce ten yards wide, and plunges over in one grand leap of turbulent brown foamy water into a dark pool not less than sixty feet below, while the scattered broken spray of that great descent blows out like smoke from behind a screen of jutting elm trees.

Yorkshire, that land of rivers and of rivulets, has many water-falls, and not a few which are of memorable beauty. Hardraw is loftier and more exquisite; Aysgarth has a charm of form which persuades one to forgive its lack of height. But neither can approach the grandeur of the mighty leap which carries Tees over this huge precipice; and High Force remains without a rival, the glory of Yorkshire and of Northern England. An hour after I had absorbed my first impression, I opened the white wicket and strolled down among the fir trees. A shower had fallen and the raindrops glittered on the heavy spreading boughs. There was an exquisite freshness in the air that blew down from the great moorlands, keen and stimulating, and full of summer scents; while from time to time the fragrance of wild hyacinths came down the woodland path, for on this high ground spring flowers linger, and even primroses had not vanished from the open spaces where the fir trees fell away and left the wild flowers free to grow and spread.

A sharp descent brought me to a rustic bridge thrown over a small stream which rattled down between high banks, and the path, sweeping round towards the left, came out upon the river

A NORTHERN EVENING 187

bank, but high above the water, which was scarce seen through
a fringe of trees and bushes, while the sound of its harsh
brawling was drowned by the thunder of the fall. The path
was overarched with beeches and dwarf oaks, while the wood
stretched exquisitely up the hill upon my right, carpeted with
moss and brown droppings from the boughs, broken here and
there by a grey scar of jutting limestone. Across the river I
saw through chance openings of the trees, a towering cliff, and
at its foot a stretch of broken stony grass land, for the stream
swept close beneath the path which I was following, and in a
moment more a sudden gust of wind sent a whiff of spray
across my path, and I was in full sight of the brown fall and
the deep pool which receives it.

The mighty volume of the water which falls into that chasm
of brown and wavering lights is for the most part carried under
by the force of its descent ; so that the basin beaten into foam
and whirlpools where the water drops, yet washes gently round
the base of the vast limestone buttress through which the river
ate its way above, and in which it has carved out little caverns
down below. The peat-stained water comes down in every
shade of yellow ; the face of cloven rock, half hidden by the
drifting spray, has given root to moss and lichen ; the dark fir
trees topping the ravine, the rustic paths and steps dropping to
the water's edge, the indescribable fresh scent of falling water
mingled with the odour of wet woods, and the keen air of the
northern evening—all these combined to stamp the picture of
High Force upon my mind in colours which are still so bright
that they return upon my memory unbidden, tempting me northwards with that strange attraction which even men of the south
country feel who have once opened their hearts to the music
of the rivers and the wind sighing down from the distant moors.

It is not very long ago since I congratulated myself on the
advantages of rapid travelling. I meant what I said at the
time. I am sure I must have done so, but now my mood has
changed, and I am all for sauntering. The truth is, since I

struck the Tees at Dairy Bridge, I have learned to love its
rapid flashing course, its pretty wilful wanderings through
moor and meadow, its petulant splashings over little rapids,
its sparkles and its eddies, and all the wanton carelessness
which sends it gushing here and there up to the very brink
of the great fall over which it rolls in thunder, and goes on
sobered for a mile or so till it emerges from the dark ravine,
and forgets the terror of that mighty plunge, and frolics on
as gaily as before. And, indeed, I should ask nothing better
than to follow on up stream till I pass beneath Falcon Clints,
that sheer range of Basalt Cliffs, which skirts the road, and
come by Caldron Snout, where the river plunges in a short
half mile down a series of inclines three times the height of
High Force ; though, lacking sheer descent, they are to be judged
as rapids rather than as waterfalls, and have but little of the
grandeur of that noble cataract : and so climbing the hills
where Tees subsides to a mere trickle in the heather, I should
gaze out over the great Alps of Cumberland and Westmorland,
magnificent beyond anything in Yorkshire. Yet it is as well
that I have not time to prolong my wanderings in this direction, and must turn away down stream, for in Yorkshire dales
one is apt to loose all sense of grandeur if one remembers the
elevations of a true mountain country ; and it would be easy
to destroy the admiration of these wild moors which, while my
eye has no other standard, I can count quite satisfying.

So I travel back lightheartedly down the valley, swallowing
the keen air which makes it good to live, and warmed by
the sunlight, which is bright enough in the valley now, though
the great shadows which sweep downward from the hills and
chase each other over the hollow, promise wet jackets for those
who stray too far from shelter. One by one the remembered
landmarks glance by me in the sunny morning, and it is still
far on the pleasant side of noon when I see the ruined pinnacles of Barnard Castle standing black against the sky, while
a long streamer of white cloud floats steady like a pennon from

the very summit of the keep, bringing back into my mind again
that gallant, hopeless "rising of the north," when "all the
flower of Northumberland" came to seize this ancient stronghold, and I go on humming to myself :—

> Lord Westmorland his ancyent raisde,
>   The dun bull he rays'd on hye,
> And three dogs with golden collars
>   Were there set out most royallie.
>
> Erle Percy there his ancyent spread
>   The half moone shining all so faire ;
> The Nortons ancyent had the crosse,
>   And the five wounds our Lord did bear.

I protest I had forgotten this rising of the north, so rash and
headstrong in its inception, and so tragic in its consequences,
the last blow struck by the great feudal lords of the north
country on behalf of the old religion which was slipping from
men's hearts, and on behalf also of their own power which was
being undermined by the advancement of new men to the
high places of the realm. It was in the first winter of those
twenty which Mary Stuart spent a prisoner in England that the
turbulent began to gather round her name ; and Sir George
Bowes, one of the few men of great family whose heart was
wholly with the Government, reported day by day, in letters
which are still extant, his observations of the growing agitation
round him. He was in command of Barnard Castle ; and as
that stronghold lay upon the road from Raby, where the
Nevilles chiefly dwelt, to Topcliffe, which was a favourite seat
of the Percies, Sir George saw all the comings and the goings
between those two noble plotters, and knew more about all the
stages of the insurrection than any other man.

In November, 1569, he wrote to the Earl of Sussex at York :
" I have certaine advertysements that all reteyners and household servants appertening to the Erle of Westmorland, with
the most part of all others, his tennants, beying furnished with
armour and weapons of his Lordship of Raby, in their war-

like apparel, repaired to Bransepeth yesterday. . . . Ther is great fear upon these doings newly grown in these parts." On the 8th he reports that Northumberland himself had passed through on his way to Topcliffe, and on the 10th he has more decided news to send. "This day in the afternoon the Erle of Northumberland, armed in a previe cote under a Spanish jerkyn, beying open so that the cote might be seen, and a stele cappe, covered with grene velvet, is returned to Bransepeth, with VIII. with him all armed with previe cotes and dagges; and in another company returned to Bransepeth Francis Norton and divers of his brethren. . . . And in the third companye returned Markenfield, and in this companye thirty horse, all armed in corselets under jerkyns. . . . Marvelous fear aryseth in these parts, for they passe in troppes, armed and unarmed, so fast up and down the contrethe, that no man dare well stir anywhere."

How picturesque are these notes of the gathering of the forces for the great rising! Bowes had no troops with which he could venture to restore order ; and his part was merely that of a spectator, yet of one who saw the gibbet dangling in the background ready for many a one of those who rode by so gaily in their Spanish jerkyns and caps of green velvet. On 17th November the whole host marched by Barnard Castle in open rebellion, and Bowes reported that the Earls would lie that night at Northallerton or Ripon, that they had promised to attack him on their return, but " I trust, by Goddes helpe, the old adage in them shall be verified, 'God sendeth an evyll-willed cow with short hornes.' "

In truth, the horns of those who directed this unwieldly enterprise were not long enough to be very dangerous. Bowes had taken the measure of the leaders accurately. They celebrated Mass at Ripon and elsewhere; they marched to Tadcaster, and then, with marked infirmity of purpose, changed their design and marched back to Durham, where they laid siege to Bowes in Barnard Castle.

Bowes was a good soldier, and made a stout defence, but he had to deal with mutiny and treachery within the walls, as well as with an overpowering force without. He says himself, " I found the people in the castle in continuall mutinye, seaking not only by great numbers to leape the walls and run to the rebels, but also by all menes to betray the place and all in ytt to the rebels. So far as in one day and nighte two hundred and twenty-six men leapyd over the walls, and opened the gates and went to the enemy ; of which number," he adds, gleefully, "thirty-five broke their necks, legges, or arms, in the leapyng."

Of course the rebels took the castle, but, while they lay besieging it, the army of the south was gathering at Doncaster, and when Sussex marched out of that ancient town, the Earls, not waiting for the attack, dismissed their infantry and fled with their horsemen into the wild country of the border. It was all over then. Nothing remained but to hunt down the fugitives and hang them. It is a ghastly tale. Bowes was Provost-Marshal, a stern and pitiless avenger of the Queen's wrongs and his own. How pitiful and futile it all is ! What noble lives and what far-stretching family traditions were broken and wasted in this rising, when the very life and spirit of the north went down in ruin and utter destruction.

I shall refer again to the closing scenes of this rebellion, so closely interwoven with the family history of the north. For the present I may not loiter any more. Did I not promise to drive the "felon sowe" from Rokeby with me towards Richmond ; and do not all men know—or, if not, it is full time they did—how troublesome that most wanton daughter of many wicked pigs proved to men who are far holier than I, and commanded spiritual resources to which I can lay no claim ?

It is not unknown to many that there was a Friary at Richmond. Ere nightfall we shall see the very goodly tower, which alone remains of all the buildings. They were Grey Friars who dwelt there, well known throughout this country, much respected and, perhaps, like other ecclesiastics, a little feared ; so that

most of the surrounding gentry took occasion to make them
gifts from time to time, and Ralph of Rokeby, having a sow
which he did not want, courteously and kindly presented her
to the friars, and notified to them that they might come and
fetch her when they pleased.

Now, this sow had certain defects of character, besides being
quite unusually large. The ballad writer says of her :

> She was more than other three
> The griseliest beast that ever might be,
>   Her head was great and grey ;
> She was bredd in Rokeby Wood,
> Ther was few that thither yood,
>   That came on live away.

I know of one just like her. But more of that hereafter. Now
these being the qualities of the felon sowe, it was only natural
that her owner should have thought her very suitable to be
presented to somebody else ; and thus we read :—

> Ralph of Rokeby, with full good will,
> The fryers of Richmond gave her till
>   Full wele to gar them fare ;
> Fryer Middleton by his name,
> He was sent to fetch her hame
>   That med him since full sare.

Everybody must respect a cheerful giver, and we need not
grudge to a man of such generosity the satisfaction which,
knowing the habits of his sow, he doubtless derived from
watching secretly the reception which she gave the friars.
Somebody must have been looking on, or how should we know
what passed? Well, Friar Middleton brought with him Peter
Dale and Brian Metcalfe of Bear in Wensleydale, and they all
came smiling cheerfully, going " at ther will," as the poet puts
it, till they came to Greta Bridge.

> These three men went at ther will,
> This wicked sowe while they came till,
>   Liggand under a tree.

> Rug and rustic was her haire,
> She raise up with a felon feare
> To fight against the three.

Now, in this first round, the sow, being, perhaps, taken by
surprise, had chosen her ground incautiously, so that after a
short skirmish she backed suddenly into a kiln, in the astonishment of which mishap she permitted her enemies to noose her
and haul her out and set off on their homeward way, in the
cheerful trust that nothing now remained except to make the
sausages. But the sow was revolving other plans, and did but
go softly till she thought the proper moment had arrived. It
came at the foot of a little hill, and then the friars saw the
sow in her true colours. I do hope Ralph, the cheerful giver,
was not too far off to see all this.

> And there she made them such a fray,
> As if they shod live untill domesday
> They colde it never forget.
>   .   .   .   .   .   .
> She chasèd them both to and fro,
> The wight men never were soe woe
> Their measure was not meete.

But Peter Dale was not dismayed. He perceived that the
difficulty, and the whole outrageous behaviour of the sow, must
proceed from the fact that she had not observed their cloth,
and took them to be hinds, not friars. For did not even the
crows on Lindisfarn obey St. Cuthbert? Should, then, a
grovelling sow disdain a friar of Richmond. Not so. Peter
stood firm.

> He seigned him with crosse and creed,
> Tooke forth a booke, began to read
> Of Saint John and his gospell.

Unhappily the sow was baser than he thought, and persisted
in sinning against the light.

> The sowe she wold no Latin heare,
> But rudely rushed at the freare
> That blenked all his blee.

O

I do not know where Peter went when the sow ran at him with such ferocity ; but I conceive he was either on the safe side of the hedge, or perched in a tree when he made the following pitiful lament :—

> He said, alas, that I was freare,
> And I shal be tug'd in sunder here,
>   Hard is my destinie ;
> Wist my brethren in this houre
> That I were set in sike a stoure
>   Yett wold they pray for me.

While Peter chanted this doleful lay from some safe refuge, the sow was busy settling accounts with his friends.

> This wicked beast that wrought the woe
> Tooke the rope from the other two,
>   And then they fled all three.
> They fledd away by Watling Streete,
> They had no succour but their feete,
>   It was the more pitye.

So they went, and the sow trotted back triumphantly to Greta side. Ralph, the cheerful giver, saw her coming, and judged from the bit of rope still hanging from her neck that there had been some trouble. The ballad writer admits as much as that ; but as I have suggested already, I suspect Ralph of having watched the whole.

I am sorry I have not space to tell what happened when the friars got back to Richmond with their woeful tale ; but as most of my readers may have sympathy enough with a bonny fighter to desire to know the end of the sow, I will quote a few more lines which give the tragic close of so much strength and truculence.

> The warden waged on the morn
> Two boldest men thas ever was born
>   I weyne or ever shall be.

Gilbert Griffin was the name of the doughtier of these two heroes. The sow showed him no respect, but ran at him with

no less ferocity than she had exhibited towards Peter Dale.
But Gilbert put his trust not at all in Latin, but rather in his own
good thews, and they achieved the better result.

> Then Gilbert greeved was so sare,
> That he rave off both hide and haire,
>   The flesh came from the bone.
> All with force he feld her there,
> And wanne her worthily in warre,
>   And haud her, him alone.
>
> And kest her on a horse soe high,
> In two panniers well made of tree,
>   And to Richmond anonne
> He brought her. When they sawe her come,
> They sang merily *Te Deum*,
>   The fryers, every one.

Happy friars to get their sausages at last! Thrice happy
Peter Dale, to behold his enemy going into the frying-pan and
stew-pot! This pleasant story has beguiled the long, dull
course of Watling Street. Already I have turned out of the
long, main road into the pretty village of Gilling ; and now
there lies before me the steep ascent of the ridge which hems
in Swaledale—a pretty road, passing by the woods of Aske, that
famous house whose very name recalls one of the most tragic
of north country stories, and which in later days has won
a happier repute as the home of true sportsmen and kindly
gentlemen.

O 2

Road to Richmond.

CHAPTER X

RICHMOND AND EASBY

It is once more a stormy evening; and as the grey clouds darken down over the gate of Swaledale, I find myself upon the castle bank at Richmond, following a path which curves around the foundations of the ancient Breton fortress, just where the masons set them on the solid rock, and gripped it tight with bonds which seem as if they must outlast the world. High over my head the old walls rise firm and solid still, their worn grey outlines broken by splashes of yellow gillyflower, and by jutting ivy bushes, where the nesting birds fly in and out beyond the reach of any enemies not having wings. Far down below me on the left the Swale rushes over boulders with a pleasant splashing; and following its course with my eye against the stream, I see three arches of a grey stone bridge flung across

the waterway, and beyond it woods falling rapidly on either side
and fringing all the banks up to the point where the river seems
to issue from the hills, which close down grandly with already a
suggestion of those stern and lofty ridges which gain for this river
valley the character of the wildest among all the Yorkshire dales.

It is a matter of much concern to me that I can nowhere get
a distant view of Richmond Castle.   Turner did it ; and many

Richmond Castle from the River.

people know the grand result.   For my part, I searched vainly
for a point whence I could see the full outline of this very noble
building at any distance ; and having at last relinquished the
attempt, I have come to sit upon the castle bank, and
consider the place as Providence and the Norman builders
have made it, which is much more sensible than climbing
feverishly up hill and down hill to discover whether Turner
told the truth.

For some reason the castle walk is deserted. Perhaps the Richmond people are at dinner. Perhaps they distrust that watery sun which, shamed and beaten by his enemies, is just now dropping down towards the wet woods, while a fresh wind steals out of the foldings of the hills, and stirs the hanging ivy by my head. It comes down from the moor, that little wind ; it has the scents of gorse and standing pools among the heather, and I know not what sweet smelling things which I shall find for myself to-morrow when I follow up the river past the woods and out on the bare downs, where the hills close sharply round the narrow valley, and the sheep call and answer to each other from the opposite heights. Just so it blew, I suppose on many an evening when the Bretons dwelt here in the fortress above my head, with all their followers from across the sea, who descended on Richmond in such a cloud, as the old song tells us, keeping alive old grudges as is usual with songsters,

> " Each came out of Brittany,
> With his wife Tiffany,
> And his maid Manfras,
> And his dog Hardigras."

It would surely have been more blameworthy if they had come without their wives, since come they must. It was William the Conqueror who brought them, so old is the grievance ; for he gave Richmondshire to Alan of Brittany, and though that fair inheritance was confiscated as often as the English kings differed from their Breton cousins on any point of consequence, yet it was always restored again, and many a generation went by before Hardigras ceased to bark about the hilly streets of Richmond, or Tiffany to scold in her harsh Breton tongue up and down the courtyards of the castle.

But it is very necessary in things historical to begin at the beginning ; and I have the less excuse for having wandered off to Bretons since there lies somewhere within arms-reach of me, that is to say, in the bowels of the castle rock, a much more notable and famòus person, to wit King Arthur, and not he alone but all his knights. Let no one interrupt me with foolish tales of Glastonbury, or of a Cornish chough which flies around the shattered walls of Old Tintagel waiting the awakening of Merlin, the enchanter, and the word of power which will set the blameless king once more in human shape upon the throne of

Richmond Castle.

England. These tales are very good for the West Country, and when we go there we will believe them. Here at Richmond it is well known that Arthur and his knights lie sleeping in a cave at the base of this great rock ; and many a boy has spent his summer afternoons in wandering by the river's edge in the hope that he might find the winding entrance, long since lost and forgotten by the world, and look upon the sleeping knights who sought the grail and tilted in the forest, and sinned and suffered for it so many centuries ago.

One man did find that entrance. Long ago, I do not know how long, there dwelt a poor butt in Richmond, a rather loutish fellow, who was not much use to any one, but who, like other ne'er-do-weels had perhaps his dreams and fancies, little though they might profit him in those prosaic days, when cobbling would have served him better. His name was Potter Thompson ; and one day, having quarrelled with his wife, Potter was wandering about the base of the castle rock, in some wonder why he did not choose some deep pool in the river and drown himself, when he noticed an opening in the cliff which seemed to penetrate a long way, and he went into it with a sort of idle curiosity.

The passage widened out as he advanced, and it was not dark ; for a faint light shone upon the rock walls which must come, he thought, from crevices open to the day. But when he groped a little further, and the light grew brighter steadily, he thought he might have reached a guard-room of the castle by some old forgotten postern ; and he went on boldly, for if that were so, he might get a sum of money in exchange for the secret. At last he turned a corner suddenly and stood at the entrance of a lofty cavern, which stretched away so far on either hand that even the bright light of the lamp hanging in an old cresset from the ceiling could not scatter the thick shadows, nor reveal the limits of the cavern. Underneath the lamp there stood a stone table, on which were laid a gigantic sword and such a horn as Potter Thompson had never seen before, rich and wonderful with gold and ivory. Now this was what Potter saw in the first moment ; in the next he distinguished huge figures of knights in armour lying asleep on the floor of the cavern, and among them one who bore on his helmet a crown of gold, and lay breathing gently in his slumber as if he dreamt of none but sweet and pleasant things.

So Potter Thompson, the poor fool, stood and held his breath and watched them, while his heart beat heavily and his scared wits told him he was looking on a sight that never living man had seen before. There lay King Arthur and his knights, sleeping, as he had known they would be found, waiting for the hour when England called for them. And as he watched that

Richmond

strange and noble sight the desire grew eager in him to carry off some proof that he had indeed beheld it ; and he stole on tip-toe to the table, and laid hand upon the sword and horn and lifted them, and was stealing back towards the gloomy passage which had brought him thither when the dark vault rang with a clash of steel, and a knight turned over in his sleep and raised himself upon his arm, and fear seized on Potter Thompson, and he dropped the horn and sword and fled.   But as he went a loud voice mocked him, crying at his back :—

> " Potter, Potter Thompson !
> If thou hads't either drawn
> The sword, or blown the horn,
> Thou'ds't been the luckiest man
> That ever yet was born."

So Potter Thompson went, and lost his fortune because his heart failed him.   Rarely does a second chance come to a man who cannot grasp the first, and Potter never found again the winding passage which had led him into the bowels of the mountain.   It is a long sleep which the blameless king has slept since Potter saw him ; but no one doubts that he lies there dreaming still.   Some day the busy world that spins so rapidly will have leisure to remember him ; England will demand her hero king, and in that hour it will need no Potter Thompson to penetrate the hill and wake him.

I suppose it is no more than natural that in the neighbourhood of so great a fortress men should find their imagination somewhat stirred by the knowledge that in the course of ages many passages and chambers have been walled up, blocked or forgotten.   There are few great buildings in the north to which some such story does not cling, some tale of buried treasure watched by enchanted powers.   I shall have one notable story of the kind to tell when I reach Kirkstall Abbey ; but here at Richmond such traditions are the more inevitable because there are said to be in truth passages leading from the castle underneath the river, and one too which strikes off down the stream in the direction of Easby Abbey.   Once long ago—who ever tries to date these stories?—some soldiers quartered in the castle resolved to test the truth of the old tale that this latter passage ran to Easby.   They were wise men ; their campaigns had taught them prudence ; for they perceived the dangers there might be in creeping through a long closed passage, blocked at least in part by fallen masonry, and doubtless

[To face page 203.

"Selected a small Drummer Boy."

reeking with mephitic vapours.   So they resolved to run those
risks vicariously, and selected a small drummer-boy, such a boy
as could be replaced with little trouble to the regiment, and
who, moreover, could creep through almost any crevice larger
than a mousehole.

Perhaps the boy was glad enough to go, eager like any
other urchin to make discoveries, and having his head full of
King Arthur, whom he might very well find and win the
fortune that Potter Thompson had let slip.   So he went boldly
enough into the dark vault, carrying his drum before him, and
when the prudent soldiers who had sent him stood and heard
the last echo of his drumming die away beneath the ground,
they went up again to the castle courtyard, where they heard it
plainly coming from below.   And so the muffled rolling of the
drum, played by the stout-hearted little lad below, led the
soldiers out of the castle gate and through the steep streets of
the ancient town, sounding fainter and more distant, till at last
when the men stood upon a spot outside the Grammar School,
which any child in Richmond will point out, the drumming
ceased.   It did not die away and become inaudible by degrees.
It stopped suddenly, as if the lad had ceased playing ; and
listen as they might, they never heard him beat again.

I know not, nor can any one tell me, what it was that stopped
the poor child's drumming.   Perhaps he found King Arthur
and lies there sleeping with him at this hour.   Perhaps . . . but
why speculate on what remains a mystery? Yet there are those
who say that if you stand upon this spot at night, when the
streets are quiet and the lights are out, and only the loud
singing of the river fills the air, you may hear, very faint and
distant, the long rolling of a drum, some signal, surely, from
the child who lies forgotten in dark caverns of the earth, some
appeal to those who go about in fresh air and see the clear
skies of the upper world.

While I sit upon this castle bank, telling myself these strange
old stories, the evening sun has broken through the clouds

again, and sent a flood of gold light down upon the woods,
filling the bend of the river where it issues from the hills with
a yellow haze which clings to the plantations, and reveals their
colouring, and flashes warm and soft from the broken water.
Presently the glow has reached the bridge, which it touches
with a flush that quivers on the stone till the whole of the
parapet and arches are enveloped in the gleaming. Then the
western sky turns rosy, and flecks of gold appear upon it, and
the river catches the reflections and casts them back so that all
the waterway is full of colour. I had thought of going up to
see the castle, but on such an evening who could give his mind
to machicolations or stone curtains? The valley looks like
fairyland. I will wander down to Easby, where at every step
I can look back and see the great castle and the strange old
hilly town all reddened by the sunset.

A winding lane leads me down the flank of the steep rock
past the handsome church, till I have almost reached the
river's bed, when it turns up through a wood and crosses the
fine cliff, running high above the river, which is heard rushing
noisily below, and is seen flashing through the cool shade of
elms and beeches. On this still evening the wood is beset by
birds—thrushes singing nobly on the highest boughs of the tall
trees, remembering their fullest notes in these first days of
summer, while from every bush and shrub that clings to the
rough surface of the cliff there comes a constant chirping, which
is both melodious and cheerful. Presently the path leads out
of these brown shades, and runs beside wide water-meadows
where the hills fall back to a little distance from the stream
leaving lawns of exquisite fresh grass, broken by woods, all wet
with raindrops and glowing in the sunset, while through the
clear air there rings the whistle of a blackbird, rejoicing somewhere in the warmth and light.

These are the meadows of St. Agatha, or rather I should say
they were her property, for many a day has gone by since any
one in Richmond has cared a jot for St. Agatha or for her

canons, whose white robes used to flit so often up and down
the river banks, but who went away for ever so long ago.   But
here is their old abbey, still not quite destroyed ; its grey walls
running down so close to the little belt of shingle over which
the river washes that there is no more than space for a path
between the two, and when Swale is in flood, and the snows
are melting on the highlands above Reeth and Muker, the old

Easby Abbey, Richmond.

canons must have heard the water on many a night lapping
round the walls themselves, and threatening to sag through
into their halls and cloisters.   For Swale, which ripples down
its stony bed so brown and cool this summer evening, is a
turbid raging torrent on some days of winter, when the black
clouds break, and the first breath of spring frees the courses of
the becks, and each one leaps down tumultuous and angry to

lash still further the turmoil of the swollen river in the valley, and the storm wind coming out of the west piles the waters up on their course down stream.

But it is not the power of the waters which has wasted the Abbey of St. Agatha. Neither storms nor years would have torn away the vaulting, or cast down the massive pillars of the church, had not man, prompt to ruin his own noblest works, shattered the whole structure without compunction. Nothing but the eye and knowledge of an expert, trained in all the lore of monkish life, can trace out among these broken walls the locality of the great chambers which were once so full of busy life, the Frater house, the Refectory, the Abbot's dwelling, all silent, grass-grown and deserted, while in the centre of the enclosure the visitor looks out wondering over a vast expanse of grass, almost bare of masonry, which by gradual reasoning he perceives to be the church. Here, where one grey stone crops up out of the fresh turf, must have been the springing of the arches at the entrance of the choir ; and a few steps further on, shorn of all the pomp of stone and heraldry which marked them, lies undoubtedly the dust of many a knight of that great family of Scrope which gave to England freely generation after generation warriors and statesmen who take rank among the noblest in our history. "Above the choir," said the Abbot of Easby, nearly two hundred years before the Dissolution, above the choir it was that Sir Henry Le Scrope lay buried "under high stones, and upon the stone a knight graven of stone and painted with the arms azure, a bend or, while near him lay Sir William Le Scrope on a high tomb all armed, and many others of their lineage were buried under flat stones, and upon the same stones are flatly graven their images for sculptures with the arms."

Now this evidence was given on a great occasion ; and as it is useless to look for any of the tombs the worthy Abbot named, the green grass having covered over more desecration than one cares to talk of, I think it will be well to say very

briefly what all the pother was about, since by dwelling on this
tale for the little while we loiter round these beautiful old ruins,
we shall get some true idea of the greatness of the Scropes,
who still provide the noblest memory among these dales, and
whose castle must set the idlest visitor wondering who it was
that built it.

I feel almost apologetic for the credit of the Scropes when I
say the whole coil was about a coat of arms.   Of course, in
these days we know better than to worry about such a trifle.
Any one who wants a coat of arms takes down "Burke's Manual"
and selects the first that strikes his fancy. Public opinion smiles
indulgently, while the College of Arms shrugs its shoulders and
goes to sleep again.   I hope no one will despise the Scropes
too much because they cared for their coat armour as much as
for the honour of their wives.   William le Scrope, in one of
the French wars, was for killing a prisoner whom he found
accoutred in his bearings.

It was, I think, on one of the Scotch expeditions in the reign
of Richard II., that Sir Richard le Scrope found a Cheshire
knight, named Grosvenor, bearing the shield, "azure, a bend
or," which he and all his forefathers had carried into the
thickest press of every battle for more years than any one of them
could count.   Now, it happened that but a little time before, a
Cornish knight, named Carminow, had fought in France under
this same shield, and when challenged by the Scrope had been
able to show so long a title, stretching back, as the record says,
to the days of King Arthur, that the heralds had no choice but
to leave both Carminow and Scrope in possession of the shield.
But when Grosvenor, an unknown knight—for the days were
yet far distant when the heirs of this knight would beget a
dukedom—when this fresh claimant started up with no long
record of great services behind him, Scrope summoned all the
noblest of the land to testify that these were indeed his ancient
bearings, and that he, not Grosvenor, had carried them to
honour in the past.

So there came old John of Gaunt, "time-honoured
Lancaster," followed by Henry Plantagenet, the Earl of Derby,
and gave witness that the arms were Scrope's, and that of
Grosvenor he knew nothing. Behind them came Lord Poynings
and Sir Thomas Percy, Sir Hugh Hastings, and Sir Thomas
Erpingham, weighed down with honours, he who afterwards
commanded the archers at Agincourt, and gained honour in
every employment which he took. They were followed by Lord
Scales, and Courtenay, Earl of Devonshire, in whose veins there
ran the blood royal of the House of France,—all having seen
the golden bend on the azure field borne high in battle by the
Scrope. And then came Sir John Sully, that old and noble
warrior, whose years were then past one hundred, and had
seen Sir Henry le Scrope bear those arms at Halidon Hill,
when the English bowmen broke the Regent Douglas three and
fifty years before, and had seen Sir William bear them, too, at
Cressy and at Poictiers, and had fought side by side with Sir
Richard in the sea fight of Espagnols-sur-Mer and at Najara,
and knew no other bearings of the Scropes in all these fights,
and many more, save those which were now unjustly claimed by
Grosvenor, whom he did not know. And when these, and
vast numbers more, had stated what they knew from service
in the field, there came forward the Abbot of Selby, who said
the arms were on the south aisle of his church, in a glass
window, at the altar of St. John the Baptist, and had been
there "since building of the church, which is beyond
memory. And the Abbot of Rievaulx had ancient charters
sealed with those same arms, while the Abbot of Jervaulx
said the arms were in divers places in his abbey, in glass
windows and in paintings. The Abbot of Byland said they
were painted in divers places in his abbey, and the Abbot
of Roche said they had been painted in a glass window in the
north part of his church beyond the time of memory. The
Abbot of Coverham said that Sir Geoffrey le Scrope was
interred in the body of his church before the high cross in a

lofty tomb with the effigy of a knight, while other witnesses
testified that the arms were painted in the priories of Gisburgh,
Wartre, Lanercost, Newburgh, Bridlington, and Watton.

Such was the fame and so wide the power of the Scropes in
those old days. Nobody, I suppose, credits the monks of all
these abbeys with having blazoned the Scrope arms in their
churches out of love. Monks received favours. They did not
confer them, save in return for good hard value ; and the family
which could enrich so many different foundations must have
been powerful indeed. Grosvenor gave way before this weight
of evidence ; and his arms were altered to "azure, a garb or,"
which device the ducal family of Westminster yet bears,—while
the line of Scrope has perished off the earth.

I shall have more to say about the Scropes when we reach
their castle in the heart of Wensleydale. It is enough for the
moment to know that this roofless abbey, this church with
never a wall, holds the relics of many members of that house,
who were respected by the monks of Easby as founder's
kin, though that was in truth by purchase only—much in the
same way as the major-general in "The Pirates of Penzance"
obtained his ancestors. Over the hills from Bolton must have
come many a long funeral train, led by the white canons of St.
Agatha, winding down the long dale till it reached this ancient
house of God, where for many a day the canons sang "messe,
placebo, and dirige, and messe of requiem," both for the soul
of the last comer into the haven of their church, and for those
of his ancestors who had attained that port before him, while
in the great castle away across the hills other Scropes, looking
forward to the future of their house, foresaw no time when that
splendid refuge should not be open to receive their dust.

Well, it is the birds who sing "placebo" now, above the
lost tombs of the Scropes ; and out of the Abbot's Elm, which
spreads its great branches still above the spot where many a
monk has drowsed away the summer day, there comes a perfect
witchery of sound, such a fluting of liquid and melodious notes
as sets my idle fancy wondering whether it is, indeed, a bird

P

which sings so nobly, or if it may be that some echoes of the
long silent music that used to float up from the windows of
the church are lingering still among the broken arches.   I turn
away from the great empty space which was a church.   The
ragged shadows of the broken transept slant steadily across
the grass, they lie thick and heavy in the Frater house ; and
presently, when the heavy tolling of the curfew from the old
tower of Trinity in Richmond shall boom across the valley, the
lights will be already out in the Abbey of St. Agatha, and the
night, which hides all ravages, will have folded round the ruined
home of many warriors and saints.

As I wander back through the river meadows towards Richmond, I feel an impulse of gratitude to those who have kept
the Abbey of St. Agatha so reverently.   It is not always so in
Yorkshire, or, indeed, elsewhere.

I think that no one who comes down out of the wood that
covers Easby Cliff, well though he may know all the banks of
Swale, can fail to pause a moment in sheer wonder at the
magnificence with which the great square keep rises over
the red-roofed houses and the broken outer walls of the old
fortress ; while, if he be a stranger, and see for the first time
that lofty crag and the stern buildings that surmount it, he must
surely recognise that he has here to do with something nobler
far than the ruins he has seen elsewhere in Yorkshire, that it is,
indeed, the dwelling of a reigning family that confronts him,
rather than of a noble, however powerful.   Many a banner
which could summon followers sufficient for a little army was .
borne proudly to its tributary station in the great hall of Scolland.   The blood-red fesse of Marmion fluttered there, and
the chevronnels which were the ensign of Fitzhugh, and the
gold and azure of Fitzrandolph of Middleham.   There, too,
were the shields of Fitzalan and Fitzrobert, and many another
owner of a vast estate, all rendering feudal service to the great
Duke of Brittany, who was also Earl of Richmond, and owner
of the fairest territory in the whole north country.   How many
of those who read " King John " remember that this was the

heritage of Constance, whose ill-fortune forced from her that
dignified lament, "Here I and sorrow sit," and of her son, that
little Arthur, whose eyes Hubert was ordered to burn out,
and who met with so piteous an end? But if I stay here
sentimentalising about such very old stories I shall be too late
to see the curfew rung—I say see advisedly, for there is no
difficulty in hearing it from any part of Richmond, and if it
were not that I want to see what effect it has upon the people
in the market-place, I should not trouble myself to hurry up
the steep street as I do, until I emerge breathless and flushed
upon the wide, sloping, hilly place, paved with atrocious cobbles, on one side of which the ancient church of Trinity displays
proudly its tower and its tobacconist.

The Richmond people point proudly to this last possession
as unique; and, indeed, I think it is. I do not recall any other
church which has its own tobacconist cuddled comfortably up
in its very bosom. At some distant period—possibly that con-
vivial age when churchwardens, dropping all austerities, gave
their name to long clay pipes—Trinity Church yawned asunder
in its very middle, and took in the tobacconist. There he is
to this very hour, wedged in between the body of the building
and the tower, a true prop of the establishment, and to connect
himself with that great institution by ties of office, as well as
by those of bricks and mortar, the excellent tobacconist either
does or did ring the curfew at morn and even; while, as the
tolling in the morning is fixed by ancient custom for the silly
hour of six, when none but foolish people are astir, he has the
bell-rope brought out of the tower down beside his bed, and,
waking up, rings lustily and goes to sleep again. Dear tobacconist, from the bosom of the church! How close these little
touches of humanity bring thee to my heart!

The square is almost empty. The few honest citizens who
stand about in knots are, I presume, waiting only till the
"gathering bell" booms out from the tower to break off their
gossip and go home to bed. Eight sounds from the steeple.
At the fourth stroke a little old man comes scurrying round the

P 2

corner and rushes into the belfry door.   He has hardly whisked
his body out of sight when the last stroke sounds, and on that
instant the sonorous clanging of the curfew peals out over the
old town, a little wild and unsteady at the first, as if the guiding
intelligence that grasped the rope was a trifle out of breath,
but settling down to a deep, solemn note, which resounds
over the empty market-place, and strikes upon my ear with all
the lost significance of past days.   But the worthy citizens of
Richmond heed it not one whit.   Their talk, their very jests
go on unbroken, without even a glance at the belfry.   Not one
evinces the least desire to go home to bed ; and even a party of
small children playing hopscotch treat the mediæval admonition
with true modern contempt.

The last stroke of the curfew dies away ; and once more I
can hear the rushing of the river.   Since there seems to be no
compulsion to go to bed, I turn out of the market-place, and
stroll up to the town of Greyfriars, whither Friar Middleton
brought home the piteous tale of his discomfiture by the felon
sow of Rokeby, and where, not much afterwards, he had the
joy of seeing her turned into sausages and brawn.   Very nobly
the rich perpendicular tower rises against the night sky, but of
all the other buildings, the church, the cloister, the offices
erected by this order sworn to poverty and a life of mendicance,
there remains no more trace than they themselves could have
shown of the realisation of their vows.

"A frere ther was," says Chaucer, "a wantown and a
merye," and he goes on to say of him that—

> " He knew the taverns well in every town,
>   And everych hostiler and tappestere.
>
>   .   .   .   .   .
>
>   He was the beste beggere in his hous,
>   For though a widewe had nocht oo schoo,
>   So pleasant was his in principio,
>   Yet wolde he have a ferthing or he went."

Such were the friars as Chaucer knew them—half knaves,
half wandering minstrels, haunting the taverns, carrying the

news and gossip of the day from town to town, and dropping it
distorted as they pleased at lonely houses, where no other
rumours ever came from the outer world ; terrible enemies for
any Government, able to set whispers running like a flame all
over England, and to stir secretly an agitation which could not
be either checked or traced, because it burrowed underground.
Such was their action when the report arose that the poor King
Richard was not really slain at Pontefract, but was living still
in Scotland ; and if we could now trace out the secret history
of the devoted risings which disturbed the first years of the
House of Lancaster, we should surely find that from Richmond,
and many another friary of the Franciscans, came those wild
rumours and those disturbing fancies that brought to the block
the great Archbishop Scrope, with others far too noble to have
spent their lives on shadows.

Yet the Franciscans suffered too ; for if they were mischievous
they knew how to die, and eleven of them suffered the penalties
of treason for this very matter.   And when the Dissolution
came, and the dreaded visitors arrived proffering the new oath
of faith in the monarch as supreme head of the church, the
friars of Richmond stood fast in their allegiance, and as a
penalty were driven into the world without those scanty
pensions given to ecclesiastics who foreswore themselves.
Therefore there is honour to their credit as well as mischief ;
and if the two be mixed, what is that other than the mingled
thread that twines in every one of us ?

Ah, strange old Richmond ! how many ghosts go about its
hilly streets !   The moon is up, the pinnacles of the old Friary
Tower are marked out in shadow on the silvered roadway.   I
go back through the market-place, and turn down the hill for
one more sight across the noisy river.   The hills are dark, the
woods are scarcely seen, one twinkling light comes from the
old castle wall, the broken water of the river seethes and
flashes like a living thing, and the cataract below the castle is
all of frosted silver.

Approach to Richmond.

CHAPTER XI

SWALEDALE AND THE PASS OF BUTTERTUBS

AH, strange old hilly Richmond ! True centre of the romance and feudal grandeur of northern England ! How firm a hold she lays on the imagination, and how loudly she calls us in these happier days to recollect the husbandry of strength and skill with which the first growths of English life were tended, or all the legacy of chivalry and greatness handed down to us by those who occupied these walls. It is not here, in sight of the great squared keep, that one can lose the sense of unity with old past days, nor forget one's sympathy with the passionate hot life which was so very human, which blazed so fiercely and fought so nobly, and passed away at last with such a cry for mercy as one may see even now on a battered tomb at Eggleston :—

> " Jesu, for thi passion sere,
> Have mercy on the sinful here."

But it is time to shake off all these fancies and turn my back
on the Castle Crag, and see what Swaledale looks like on this
bright windy morning, which sends vast shadows flying quickly
over hills and river, so that the water, which is black one
moment, in the next is flashing brown and foamy in the sunlight, while the woods turn from dark to golden and from gold
again to dark so suddenly that the whole valley seems alive and
quivering with light and motion.   I ride on through the valley,
following one of the loveliest of roads, of which, indeed, I should
say much, were it not that I have lingered so long already on
the lower reaches of the Swale, and must hurry forward to the
higher valley and the noble Pass of Buttertubs.   And so I let
the woods go by with their brown and dappled shadows, and
ride past the shallows, where the gravel sparkles brightly under
the quick-flowing water, and the rapids where the river makes
such a merry splashing that it seems to strive against the
rustling of the woods, which shall add the most to the great
murmuring sound that fills the valley, till the trees grow thin
and fall away from the river, and the hills sweep down with
great bare flanks of pasture scarred with patches of brown moor
and ling, between which the sheep stray up and down cropping
the short sweet grass, while here and there the sunlight flashes
on the white and silver of a beck tumbling from the heights,
leaping from point to point of the outcropping rock.   And so I
come at last in sight of the old square-towered church of
Grinton, set beside the stream at a spot where dale and river
both divide, Swaledale throwing out an arm which takes the
name of Arkengarthdale, from the tributary stream that winds
among the narrow pastures left below the rugged range of hills.
There is an old stone bridge, in the shadow of whose buttresses
the trout lurk idly on these summer mornings ; and from that
spot it is but a little distance to the sloping irregular expanse of
green round which is built, in a somewhat purposeless way, the
little town of Reeth.
    I am sorry that in this solitary townlet I could find nothing

worthy of comment save a pig. Pigs, as Friar Middleton knew
to his cost, are not in all cases beneath the dignity even of
verse ; and it would be mere folly to conceive my own poor
prose too lofty to concern itself with them. Besides, there may ·
be those who give no credit to the tale of the Felon Sow, but
read it with a shrug of wonder at my ready faith in the prowess
of a beast which usually frightens only rather small boys. If such
there be, I beg them to go to Reeth, where they will find in
the piggery of the " Buck Inn " a beast which will restore their
faith in Friar Middleton and me, in addition to curdling their
own blood with fear, if it be let out into the yard for their
greater admiration, as the too kindly owner did when I
beheld it.

I do not mean to dwell on this incident, nor to comment on
what occurred when this large and fearsome beast, "rug and
rusty," like her prototype, began to sniff about the yard. I
prefer to let the whole matter pass. Life is too short to tell the
tale of our defeats ; and how I fled from the field of any battle
is nobody's business but my own. Let me get on to the aspect
of the hills, which indeed occupy all one's thoughts at Reeth,
and stamp themselves upon my memory so clear and lucent
that I can see no other pictures when I turn my recollections
backward to that spot.

Around Reeth the hills close in a sort of amphitheatre, open
only to the west. On all sides the ground drops swiftly from
the brown scarred moors into the width of three fields of pasture, with one more beside the river in the narrow bottom,
where the water courses brown and swift, while here and there
a patch of gravel sparkles brightly in the sunlight. Never was
any light more soft and bright and beautiful than that which
bathed the slopes of the high dale on this June morning. For
the aspect of the day had changed ; the conquering sun had
driven the white clouds down to the very borders of the sky,
and left them piled there in great masses, save when one
escaping floated suddenly up over the blue vault and sent a

Muker.

flying shadow far across the hills, and was caught and chased by the eager wind and forced back to its prison with the rest. So the shadows slept upon the hill-tops, while the lower moors were in fresh bright sunshine ; for the keen delightful wind was blowing low, sweet with the odours of hawthorn and the scent of flowing water, while here and there the slopes were all aglow with campion and forget-me-not and a thousand other flowers. By Gunnerside the road crosses a brown beck flashing down-ward from the highlands, and so turns to the other bank of the river, which brawls along beneath a lofty cliff rising sheer out of the broken rapids ; and a little further on the air is shaken once more by the musical splash of falling water ; and there high up on the ridge, where cloud shadows lie, and sheep and cows are grazing over the grassy fells, a brook flings itself down some sixty feet ; while far below, where the dell is filled with trees, it makes a second headlong leap, and so comes out beside the buildings of a little farm, bringing with it the sparkle of clear mountain air and the breath and odour of the moors.

Through such sights and sounds I loitered up the dale. Now at a point where the swift water had swept in close beneath an overhanging bank, leaving on the other side a wide expanse of gravel, dry and whitened by the sun, a quick flash of silver shot across the river bed, and the next moment it flashed again a little higher up, doubling to and fro along the surface of the water and gleaming brilliantly. A great white bird, not unlike a gull, was fishing in the stream ; and presently I saw its mate sitting on a spit of sand, and the two soared off together up the stream, now lost among its windings, now flashing into sight, till they passed away beyond my vision into the deep recesses of the hills that look towards Keld. But always when I think of Swaledale, and see again the river winding through its narrow flats and the cloud shadows sweeping over the great hills, there rises into the middle of the picture the glorious flashing of the wings of those two fisher birds, adding I know not what that is cool and exquisite and fresh.

As I trudge on up the valley, the aspect of the little farms, each nestling in its hollow of the hills, calls back to memory the day when I gained a friend in such another farm, not here, and yet not far from here ; and the tale may serve as an instance of that simple hospitality which is common still among the dales.

I was weather-bound one day in early summer at a town a little west of this.   Late in the afternoon, tired of watching the heavy showers blow past the windows, I started on my way ; but the walk was wet and cheerless, and I was not sorry when a cart stopped by my side and the driver offered me a lift.   I looked at him.   He had a face of exceptional kindness, such as invited instant confidence even from a surly dweller in great cities ; and I got into the cart and sat beside the tall old farmer with a sudden feeling that something warm and friendly had risen up out of the cold rain and clinging mist which were beating once again across the road.

In his slow way the old man insinuated many questions as to my journeys, and finding out at last that I was expected nowhere, his face broadened into a large smile, and he said, " Then tha'll come hoam wi' me " with such an obvious delight in having found an unexpected guest that I had no mind to make excuses ; and we drove away off the main road which I had been following, as friendly a pair of comrades as any in the north country.

He was a Quaker, the old man told me, and he had much to say about the decadence of that once numerous body of simple, upright men among the dales.   The ancient meeting-houses rarely, on any first day, held more than a handful of worshippers, though he remembers them crowded.   Presently we passed the meeting-house of his own village, a grey old building on the hillside, bearing an early seventeenth-century date above its little porch, and looking down the long valley through which we had come something in the manner of a sentinel set to watch. Almost in the bottom of the valley lay the old man's farm ; and

as we uncurled ourselves, cold and rather stiff, from our seats in
the market cart, the house door opened, letting out a glow of light
and warmth from a ruddy kitchen fire ; and in the doorway,
backed up by the bright reflections from pots and pans which
shone like mirrors, stood a little rosy-cheeked old woman, clad
in the grey shawl and spotless cap which still, in solitary places,
proclaim the Quaker.   The aged collie, who had risen slowly
with a toothless bark of welcome, sniffed suspiciously about
my heels ; but the old woman beamed, and when her husband
brought me up, saying, " This is a friend, and he's coom to stay
t' neet wi' us," she held out her hand and shook mine warmly,
saying, " Thou art very welcome, friend ; " and so took me in, a
stranger, out of the wet evening into the warmth and light of
her cheerful home.

Dear, kindly people ! I can still see the little parlour lighted
up, the great chair in which the farmer always sat drawn over
to the hearth, and another smaller one set close by the arm.
There, after a few vain efforts to ensconce me in the seat of
honour, the old man placed himself with the comfortable action
of a man who, after hard toil, finds himself resting in a familiar
spot ; and by his elbow sat his old wife knitting.   " She likes to
sit there while I read," he said, with a half suspicion that the
propinquity might need some explanation to a stranger.   As for
the little Quakeress, she looked up and smiled without speaking,
for it was not her habit to talk much.

So they sat all the evening in the little dimly-lighted room, while
my host talked to me of the things which were next his heart.
And so I see them still in my memory, sitting side by side in
absolute content, a pair of happy, placid people, for whom life
held no difficulties any more, and who had no wishes save to
enjoy the evening of their days together.   There were long
tracts of silence, during which the old man lay back in his
chair, and his wife looked up smiling as often as she caught my
eye ; and in the end a supper of milk and cheese was brought
in, and I went to rest in a room where the old mahogany four-

poster was polished like a mirror, where the sheets smelt of
lavender, and a lilac bush beneath the lattice window filled the
room with sweetness all the night.

In Swaledale it is always the sound of falling water which
call back one's wandering thoughts.   I have paused to rest
beside a little stream of wondrous beauty.   Across the field,
where two or three ashes grew together in a clump, I first saw
it gleaming silver in the shadow ; and a little lower down it ran

Butter-tubs Pass.

beneath a bridge in the prettiest cascade imaginable.   The fall
was of trifling height, no more than three or four feet ; but
the water shot over it in a curve so full and copious, and fell
into so brown a pool below, between banks so cool and mossy,
that there was more delight in watching it than one finds in
many a stream of far greater volume.   A large ash tree drooped
over the little fall, and on a grass bank just beside the bridge
a few sprays of forget-me-not twinkled azure in the shadow.   The
very splashing of the water seemed to reduce the growing heat,

and I loitered on the bridge, glancing unwillingly at the high moors over which my road must go to Hawes.

For I am drawing near the boundary of Yorkshire, and ere long shall find myself in Westmorland unless I turn. There is but one way to turn, and that a sad one, namely, over the road of Butter-tubs, misnamed a pass. For may one justly give that name to a stony track which spares you nothing save a few yards of the very highest summit? The road of Butter-tubs climbs and climbs with a deadly steepness which one might pardon were it possible to boast of having attained any height, when, breathless and exhausted, one lies full length upon the heather at the top. But great Shunnor Fell is little more than a poor two thousand feet, and Lovely Seat, which faces it, is even less. Why, then, can one not get up without all this pother? I am told it is a very ancient byway; and that may be true, for it is certainly decrepit, and is not likely to be restored to health by any such desultory sprinklings of sharp-pointed stones as I found strewn about its surface, unless by persuasion or by force more travellers can be induced to cut their boots upon them than are disposed to use the road at present. In sober truth I met nothing but a sheep, until, coming out upon the very summit, I turned a sudden corner of the rock, and found reclining in the cleft a battered grey old shepherd, musing through the afternoon upon God knows what, while his pipe sent up a blue curl of steady smoke, and his collie stood at bay and snarled at me a few yards further on upon the path. The fellow looked at me with a half humorous smile. Had he spoken, I should have lit a pipe and sat down beside him, glad to chat with any one upon that lonely height. But he offered me no greeting ; and I went on past the growling collie, while all the thin air of the vast solitude was pierced by the pitiful crying of a lamb somewhere in the valley bottom far below ; and, presently, looking backward on my path, I saw the shepherd plunging down the side of the ravine in search of it.

A little way before I reached the summit of the pass—before,

that is to say, I had risen high enough to see the wide mountain
country which lay beyond the green fells over which I was
climbing, I found by the wayside the first of those circular

The Butter-tubs.

chasms in the limestone which gave the pass its name of
Butter-tubs.   Cool, dark, and cavernous, they are deep, black
pits, walled by very strangely splintered limestone, standing
now in crumpled pillars towering out of the sheer depth, now

breaking into fantastic shapes of every kind, with here and there a flowering alder, or a mountain ash growing out of a crevice, or some sweet white flower straying fearlessly down into the abyss. Into the largest of the Butter-tubs there trickles down a little stream, sobbing quietly enough as it oozes out of the long grass and struggles through the boggy patch between the slope and the descent ; but plunging down the dark chasm with a kind of startled cry which sounds eerie in the great silence of the fells, and so drips out of sight among the shining liverwort, and falls in spray into the bowels of the earth.

There is something in the sight of this small stream tumbling out of the cheerful sunlight, away from the green hillside into unknown caverns of the earth, which fascinates me. Then the Butter-tubs are not mere shallow rents in the crust of the great hills, but the mouths of some vast subterranean hollows, huge un-trodden chambers in the heart of the fell which I had thought so solid. I look askance at them as I go by, marvelling to note how near the gaping mouths lie to the roadway, whence a man following this pass by dusk or dark might easily stray off the rarely trodden path, and know no more until he found him-self lying somewhere in those caverns into which the stream descends. That man must have little dread of solitude who would come this way in winter, when the early night may catch him on the hillside. Pedlars travelling out of Westmor-land, or hawking their wares up Swaledale and down Wensley-dale, must many a time have been benighted among these fells —poor, weary men, with valuable packs ! Was there never any shepherd lurking on these crags who would enrich himself by a sudden blow ? Tales of lost pedlars wander all around the Yorkshire dales, where for so many centuries every housewife was dependent on their coming, and every child watched through the dull days of winter for the playfellow who could crack a droll jest, tell a merry story, or sing a ballad with as much readiness as the strolling minstrels of older days, whose modern representative he had some claim to be.

There is no smoke without fire ; and when I hear so many
tales of pedlars who vanished on the moors, I know that here,
as elsewhere, human nature has been acting after its predatory
kind.   Sometimes the story speaks of a sudden gunshot, or of
a few bones dug up, or found bleaching on the moor, years
afterwards ; while, as if to suggest that life and death among
these wildernesses ran in no other channels eighteen centuries
ago, there was found on Fremington Hagg, above Reeth, the
pack of some travelling Roman artisan, whose silver-plated
horse harness and the other gew-gaws which he hawked from
camp to camp may now be seen in the York Museum.

I suppose there will be some who, not knowing much about
the matter, will declare that the suggestions I have thrown out
are a slander on the people of the dales.   To confuse any such
objectors and to establish my good faith, I will draw on a queer
storehouse of forgotten tragedies, published by the Surtees
Society, which contains one tale at least which is very much to
the present point.   In December, 1666, the depositions of
James Hutchinson were taken at York Castle, respecting certain
events which had occurred upon the moor between his home
just over the border of Westmorland and the town of Askrigg
which lies away below me in the valley of the Ure.   " In spring
was two year he went from his own house with one Thos.
Whiteheele to seek for two young horses on the moor ; and
being parted, he heard a voice cry out, ' Murder,' and did verily
believe he heard the sound of a blow given and two other men's
voices, and after a little while he saw a horse with a riding
saddle on his back coming towards him, and a man following
him on foot ; whom he asked if he saw not two staggs, and he
said, ' Noe.' Then this informant said unto him, ' You have sure
been fighting, for you are all bloody,' though he saw no blood
on him, and that man replied, ' Noe.' . . . And this informant
went into a place called Hollow Mill, and looked down into the
gill and saw two men standing together with their backs towards
him, and something lying on the ground as if it were cloathes,

Q

and saw Whitcheele, and told him what he had seen and
heard, ... and at the latter end of summer they went unto
the moors to seek their staggs again ; and coming near to the
place where they saw the two men bearing something, they
began to look about, and in a water hole to their thinking they
saw the ribs of a man sticking in the bray, which when they had
moved with a staffe fell into the water and swome, and then this
informant did conceive there was the corpse and head of a man
with hair on it. . . ." Pah ! that is quite enough of this
ghastly story. Few people, I imagine, will care to pursue the
matter ; and fewer still will venture to declare, in the teeth of
such plain depositions, that there is exaggeration in the wild
rumours of the fate which overtook lost pedlars on the moor.

Upon my life I am sorry for the pedlars, but if people will
carry precious packs in lonely places . . . and really this hillside, which I thought I had surmounted, is too steep to leave
me any expansive sympathy for others, however luckless. If I
carried a pack, I should certainly hurl it down the deepest of
the Butter-tubs ; even my unladen back creaks and remonstrates
against the unnatural steepness of this most vile and stony road.
Each green ridge attained reveals another ; till at length there
projects above the grassy slopes something blue and sulphurous
and distant which is clearly no part of Shunnor fell ; and quicken-
ing my pace, I find I have reached the top ; and standing in
the clear air and sunshine underneath the noisy larks which
mount and mount even from that high ground as eagerly as
from any cornfield in the valley, I see spread out before me a
vast hill country, a wilderness of blue ridges and of shadowy
summits, basking in the steady light of the afternoon, and
stretching infinitely far into the west, with alternation of
crumpled hollows and wide open valleys gashing the mountain
sides, where my eye loses itself in mazes of green pasture land.
There stand the huge flanks of Ingleborough, that flat-topped
table mountain on whose plateau old nations in forgotten days
kept watch and refuge ; and there too is the elongated ridge of

Whernside, and the hump of Pen-y-gant among a crowd of other summits less well-known, but notable and fine. It is a wild and lonely scene. Far as the sight stretches, the great slopes lie very bare; and even grazing animals are few,—here a couple of horses, there a flock of geese.

Such is the aspect of the head of Wensleydale to-day, though good roads have traversed it for full three generations; and, as I look down on the wide green valley, the white steam-cloud of a train travels slowly up the sunlit fields. Before the roads came, or the iron horse began to scatter news and strangers indiscriminately, how solitary must the life have been within these highlands! Was it not here that two brothers, escaping from the rout of Charles Edward's army in the '45, took refuge, in security that the arm of law would not reach them; and planted Scotch firs at the gate of their house, that any other wanderers of their own faith who came that way might know that men loyal to a lost cause dwelt there? And across the valley it is but a little way to Dent, of which place in old days the monks of St. Cuthbert at Durham held so sad an estimation. For they were turbulent men who dwelt at Dent, a law unto themselves, as any one of us might be who found no other law that pleased him; they were men who were a thought too ready with their knives, and they looked to St. Cuthbert of Durham to get them out of all their troubles. Not in vain did they trust to the loving kindness of the Saint, who, in his un-washen days at Lindisfarn, had learnt to sympathise with all the failings of humanity. So many a lad of Dent scuttered over these hills and cast himself upon St. Cuthbert's breast, while his pursuers stood and gnashed their teeth at the outer limits of the sanctuary.

Dear days of old, when guilt was washed away so lightly, and merry England was studded with refuges for the erring! But it were well to curtail these pleasing backward glances, and get down out of the mountains, for the way is long and winding, and Hawes, the first town where I can rest, is yet a great way off. Besides, it is not really easy to go down hill, though many people think it is ; and when the steep path slips and slides with loose stones at every step, the descent is hard and painful. But it is done at last, and when the moor is left behind, and I come down into the first trough of the valley, just where the undergrowth of woods appears in refreshing contrast with the bare uplands through which I have been climbing, I turn aside by a few white cottages, and find a mountain stream no more than three feet wide, tumbling noisily over little ledges in the rock, and washing swiftly up among the ferns which overhang its bed and the long grass which grows between them. Up the banks, and down to the margin of the beck, there grows a host of bluebells, and the sunshine dropping down in dapples through the trees that almost meet overhead finds out golden patches in the waterway and sets them gleaming. A flagged path goes beside this pretty beck, a cool refuge from the glaring sun ; and as I loiter onwards in the fragrant shadow, I find here and there a little bridge flung across the stream where some inducement lies to idleness, some still, brown pool out of which the water clatters with renewed impetuosity, or a small cascade over which it roars with sudden force, while the valley, which at first was shallow, deepens continually, the trees grow higher, and the moor is lost to sight. So the little stream brawls down the wood, gathering volume as its channel drops, and casting off its pretty wilfulness more and more, till at last it collects itself into one smooth, gleaming shoot, and leaps down six and ninety feet into a black pool below.

There is something in the aspect of this great cliff, this sudden stair breaking the monotony of the steady slope from the highlands to the level of the Ure, which is singularly strik-ing and impressive. Conceive a precipice of lofty, blackened stone, curving round in a wide amphitheatre, absolutely sheer ; and at its midmost point a slender stream shooting out into mid air, far away from the face of the cliff, a tangled column of fretted spray, broken at first into the semblance of filagree

Venetian glass, intricate and silvery, but disintegrating as it
falls, till at last it scatters into nothing more than a cloud of
spray blown into the black pool, which lies waiting for it among
large boulders at the foot of the descent.

This is Hardraw Force, and its beauty lies at the mercy of
time. For there was doubtless once a day—dear heaven, how
often have the leaves budded and fallen since then ! Perhaps
it was even before the first Roman pedlar came across the hills !
—there was a time, I say, when this beck at Hardraw did not
shoot out into mid air as it does now ; but finding the face of
the cliff at the very moment when it touched the edge, splashed
and struggled down the surface of the rock, tumbling from
ledge to ledge perhaps with beauty, but certainly without its
present grandeur.   Now, while the top of the cliff is of hard
limestone, its face is of softer stone, and as the moorland water
bit and bit upon this shale, tearing away and dissolving now
one fragment, now another, the rock dropped back from the
level of the shelf above, so that now the fall is projected far in
front of the precipice, and touches nothing till it attains the
bottom. Yet in course of years, or centuries, the whole process
will begin again ; the stability of the shelf will be endangered ;
some day it will crash down among the boulders in the lower
valley, and the stream, like a creeper seeking for support, will
once more help itself down the black face of the rock.

When I climb down to the foot of the fall I find a rather
gloomy valley, through which the stream courses on under dark
limestone scars, topped by heavy firs, through which the slant-
ing sunshine of late afternoon hardly finds its way.   The roar
of the fall rolls through the deep hollow : and as I turn I can
still see its silvery column, quivering and scintillating with quick
lights and flashes, which put odd thoughts into a man's head if
he sit and watch it, and let the monotonous voice of its descent
touch his fancy, as it surely will.   But the afternoon is gone
already, and the growing clearness of the hills warns me that I
have but little time to loiter.   And so I pass through the gate

Hardraw Force.

at the bottom of the gorge and go down into a lane which conducts me quickly through a tiny village towards a field path
cutting over level meadows, where the Ure meanders with a
slow, steady course, differing strangely from the mountain freshness of the Swale, or the loud rushing of the Tees over its
stony bottom. Here, upon these wide water meadows, from
which the hills fall away on every side, there is the silence and
the fruitfulness of a lush midland county : and the gold light
of the westering sun touches nothing swift or animated, but
only the forms of red grazing cattle, and the slow stream slipping on between the fields. At a little distance over the grass
and the silent river lies the town of Hawes—it looks better
when one is not very near—and beyond the dull grey houses
rise the long range of rounded hills which, pierced by Bishop-
dale and Coverdale, and a dozen other glens, each rich with its
own separate and striking beauty, part the valley of the Ure,
this famous Wensleydale, from the lesser Nidderdale and the
green Craven Hills.

To me, after so long wandering over rough mountain country,
all this soft fertility is as pleasing as the sight of palmtrees to an
Arab in the desert. For there is still the sense of solitude,
and aloofness from the world. Thoughts, habits, and manners
have yet their own decided stamp in Wensleydale, and one may
still hear the herdsman counting his sheep with those old
numerals which he applies to nothing else, and which may be
the last trace of Celtic speech lingering in his mind, so open to
traditional impressions and so impervious to change. *Yain*,
tain, eddero, peddero, pitts, so one who told me heard the shepherds counting in a fold on the hillside near Askrigg, a little
lower down the dale ; and having thus reached five, the hind
went on : *Tayter, later, overro, coverro, disc*; and then, as the
eleventh sheep slipped, frightened and bleating through his
rough hands, he shouted out *Yain disc*, and so on up to fifteen,
which he called *Bumfitt*, while sixteen was *bumfitt yain* and
twenty *jiggit*.

So strangely does the speech of days immensely ancient cling to the tongue of a man who knows only English, and who, if questioned, would deny stoutly that he was speaking any other than the language heard all about him in the present day. I think it may have been in those forgotten times when all men among these hills spoke as the shepherd did beside the hurdles of his fold, that an old man came wandering down from the western hills, even as I came to-day, and stood weary and wanting shelter in these fields. It must have been nearly as long ago as I suggest ; for there were only meadows where we see the town of Hawes, while on the hills which now stand bare and swept by every storm, there rose the towers and gate-ways of a noble city, populous and proud, drawing vast riches from the fertile valley. The old man toiled up the steep road to the gate of the town, never doubting that in the midst of so much wealth there would be many who recognized that kind-ness to poor travellers is the first as it is the simplest of all virtues. But the people of the city had forgotten to be simple, and had taken into their hearts the lust of riches, and despised the traveller who wandered wearily about the streets, meeting only scoffs from those who might have helped him, till he came to a wretched cottage where a man, scarcely less destitute than himself, took him in and sheltered him, and gave him what he could. So the next morning, when the first rosy light was breaking in the sky far down the vale, and the dust lay thick in the streets of the wicked city, the old traveller rose up, and standing high on the hillside, called out loudly :—

> " Simmer water rise, Simmer water sink,
> And swallow all the town,
> Save yon little house
> Where they gave me meat and drink."

And as he spoke there blew a great wind out of the moun-tains, and after it, heaped up and foaming wildly, came the floods, sapping and levelling first one tower, then another, and washing over the ruin with resistless waves, till the last house crashed down into the conquering tide, and the whole of that great city lay beneath the water.

So it lies yet unto this hour ; and when Simmer water on some still summer evening is unruffled by any breeze, there are those who say that beneath its glassy surface they can see the drowned houses and the minarets which used to gleam so brightly in the setting sun.   I do not know what the truth may be.   It is all so long ago ; and I think the people who refused their hospitality must have been of another race than those who dwell in Wensleydale to-day.   Or is it that they, too, might forget their sturdy welcome to the stranger did they but grow as rich as the men who built the city on the hill !   Heaven keep them from the heaped up riches ; and to go no further than the facts which are existing, I may remark that they are so little apt in Wensleydale to leave a stranger wandering alone, that to this day in Bainbridge, when the hills are darkening, and the traveller following the moorland tracks, fears to stray off the half-seen trodden way, and plunge in some morass, or lose himself among the waste of fern and heather, they blow a horn within the village, so that the hoarse blast floating up from the valley may guide the stranger into shelter and security.

Wensley.

CHAPTER XII

WENSLEYDALE

I DO not know why Wensleydale should be the only one
among the Yorkshire dales which does not take its title from
its river. Intrusive little Wensley, at the opening of the valley,
hath eaten up the credit of the whole—a rank injustice which I
will revenge on the vainglorious townlet by saying little of it
in this my desultory chronicle. "He hath got possession of
another man's house," said sturdy old Sir John Gayer, when
King William, he of Holland, came and asked to see Stoke
Poges Manor House, and Lady Gayer went on her knees before
her lord to gain admission for the usurper waiting in his carriage
at the gate. "He hath got possession of another man's house,
and he shall not come into mine." So Dutch William knocked
in vain, just as pretty Wensley shall sue fruitlessly for admission
to my garden, where silver bells and cockle shells await those
who have not stolen other people's credit.

I must give way, however, to this insolence of usurpation. I
cannot speak of Jorvaulx as the monks did, or be the only
man in England who will talk of Yoredale. Yet what is there
which gives beauty to this wide open valley if it be not the river
flashing over Aysgarth Falls, or stealing through the holms of
Middleham? The hills and villages may be the blood and
bones of Wensleydale, but the river is its soul; and as I turn
my memory back on what I found there it is the river,
always the river which leaps first into sight, the rush of

Askrigg.

its falling waters which makes all my quiet study musical,
and the sweet clear light of early morning turning all the hillside above Aysgarth into "sovran gold."

Wise men rise betimes on a summer morning in Wensleydale,
and there were still a few light mists in the hollow of the river
as I came along the bare road which runs from Hawes by
Buttersett to where Bainbridge lies under the great slopes of
Addlebrough. It is a little town, not wholly destitute of
charm; but it is not near the hour for horn blowing, and how-

ever pleased I might feel to see the lights of Bainbridge after toiling along uncertain paths in twilight on the moor, the spot does not interest me much in this clear sunshine. I am more delighted in identifying Garland Hill, beyond the river, up which a kind old lady, long since dust, set many generations of mankind toiling frantically. For having in her walks abroad noticed that a part of the declivity was particularly steep, it struck her that it would be charmingly comic to see a number of young men panting up it for a prize. Doubtless the fancy served her for much solitary laughing while she lived, and on her deathbed she worked it out into a really very tolerable farce, bequeathing the rents of certain lands to provide a money prize once a year, and not only that but a garland also, with which the perspiring forehead of the victor should be decked. Dear maiden humourist! how often must the shades have echoed with imported merriment when the day came round, and all the lads in Askrigg, black with suppressed exertion, red and swollen with heat and loss of breath, went swarming up the fellside! But I grieve to say the Askrigg people have grudged her joke to the fanciful old lady, and no one races up the hillside now; nor are any garlands twined in the summer days at Askrigg. So the world grows sadder day by day, and soon there will be nothing to laugh at any more.

Well, Garland Hill has gone away behind me, and so have the battlements of Nappa Hall—that old house of the Metcalfes, concerning which I might say much were not my head buzzing with the memories of a far nobler family, for the first sight of whose great castle I am continually scanning the slopes of the northern hills. Let others tell the tale of good Sir Christopher Metcalfe and his cavalcade of three hundred of his own name and kin; and all the other legends they can rake together concerning this fine and interesting house. I never promised to leave no gleanings on the ground I travelled; and in point of fact I have scarce lost sight of Nappa when the river, still, as I said, the soul of Wensleydale, begins to break, and here and

Askrigg.

there a patch of foam gleams white upon its even surface, or a
rippling current shot off from the summit of a sunken boulder
swirls aside half across the waterway, while the whole stream,
gathering swiftness, is ruffled by the chafing of some unseen
impediment.   So there floats up once more into the silent air of
the hillside road that fine soft music of a rushing river, which
has beguiled so many a mile of the long journey I have made
in Yorkshire ; and with every turn, as the road rises and the
trees grow thicker, it besets me more ; till, as I come at last to
the cross roads by the inn at Aysgarth and go down through the
churchyard, I pause in wonder whether my own fancy has not
beguiled me, or whether it is indeed the quiet stream I saw at
Hawes, which here occupies the whole valley with so hoarse a
voice. A thick belt of trees hides the watercourse, and I hasten
down through the dewy morning shadows, scarce heeding the
cheerful piping of the thrushes sitting high up in the sunlight,
or the dogroses, white and pink, glowing wet upon some hedge,
till I come out beside a sunny mill at the foot of the descent,
where a wagon and a team of horses stand waiting for despatch
upon some early journey, and the jangling bells sound
pleasantly as now one horse and now another shivers to toss
away the flies.

    Straight before me lies the high arch and parapet of Aysgarth
Bridge, and as I step out upon it, eager to know what has
happened to the river, my slow companion during many a mile,
I stop bewildered.   For the placid stream has gone, and in its
place, surging out from a distant bend of trees, there pours
down a rushing and tumultuous torrent, torn and broken and
driven into eddies by a multitude of rocks, over which it foams
and flashes with wreaths and flecks of white, which in the clear
morning radiance are absolutely splendid.   Far off up the
stream, where the woods lie dark and wet on either bank, there
is only a rare sparkle of the sun, still low behind me in the
eastern sky ; but the scattered water finds the light as it races
down towards the bridge ; and where it drops over a high ledge,

spreading out into a shallow film as it descends, the cascade is all golden, while the deeper pool below is bronze ; and then the whole tortured river slips over another fall and scours away beneath the dark shadow of the bridge.

I do not know whether any acute and learned writer has ever discoursed on the essential and necessary qualities of a bridge. Of course I am not referring to those qualities which affect its stability, which are a matter of calculation and measurement, which appeal particularly to coarse fibred people, and which may, for aught I know, be expounded in a whole shelf of books which I should never dream of opening.   One man's wisdom is not another's.   Let us all be tolerant, and while I concede to modern bridge builders that it may be very right to make the structure strong and stable, fit to carry carts and steam-rollers and other necessary nuisances, I claim to be heard when I point out that it is even more needful that a man should be able to lean over it in comfort.

For who is the real blessing in a country place? Is it the squire, who is absent half the year, or his agent, who will let no poor man crib an inch of land ; or the parson, who deals with the Stores, and preaches on the advantages of thrift? Not so ; the real blessing is the idle man, he who lights his pipe and saunters out in the soft sunshine, and seeks a mossy parapet not quite breast high, on which he can spread his arms, and muse and watch the bubbles drifting, and the foamy water leaping, leaping up the buttresses ; he who finds excitement in the troubles of some fisherman casting his line in a brown eddy higher up, his creel and landing net safe propped upon a jut of rock, or in the flight of the swallows skimming so low that they seem to dip their white bosoms in the fall, while the sun lights up their backs with every shade of royal blue, or yet more indolent, is content to watch the swift water coursing over the golden shallows, happy only to be alive where all nature is so musical, so animated, and so full of colour—till the hour comes for lunch, and he strolls up to the hotel, paying cheerfully for his slice of salmon eight times the price of the London market.

Happy, cheerful idler, easy to please and easy to rob! Who but he brings blessing to a countryside, diffusing a healing dew of good temper and half-crowns! But what is there for him at Aysgarth, where the parapet of the bridge is so high that a man can but just rest his chin on it? I vow I turned away with a bitter heart; I have lost all the pretty musings which must have come to me in that exquisite spot had the bridge only been fit to lean on. Plague on the Aysgarth folk! Did they never see the proper model of a bridge .... a wide, low balustrade, stained with lichen, with trails of ivy and of wandering jew dropping down beneath the arches.? Why, at Tanfield, on this very river, there is one so easy, so sunny, and so full of pleasant murmurs from the rippling river . . . but I really cannot stay to lecture further upon bridges, nor is it necessary, for if County Boards cannot act upon these pregnant hints, they would not heed me though I wrote a volume.

A golden morning is a solvent for ill-temper; and ere I had gone half-a-mile from this unlucky bridge, I had forgotten all about it. For I had left the road, and was threading my way across a piece of common land bordering the river, which was heard, not seen, because a lofty hedge of shrubs and elder trees cut off the view. The ground was dotted over with brambles and dogroses, and presently the path dropped a little, and went down by broken ground to a kind of staircase in the rock, whence I climbed out on a projecting reef round which the water surged noisily, and had before me such a scene as is not to be found elsewhere in England.

For the woods upon the further bank throw out a shoulder, stretching, as it seems from where I stand, half across the river's bed, so that the white torrent, narrowed to but half its width, pours over a ledge between two dark reefs, and as it falls finds instantly a second and a wider ledge, over which it spreads out in a sheet of dazzling whiteness and again it falls over a

third, far broader than the other two, expanding like a fan
wrought by some cunning silversmith of intricate laced filagree,
but leaping and quivering with infinity of wondrous palpitating
lights and flashes all over its moving surface, and so rushes downwards over more stairs than I can count, sometimes curling over
in a full round flood, sometimes broken and torn, and flying like
sea-spray round a black jutting boulder, widening continually
as if it tore out its full course again by sheer power and might
of its descent, while the dark trees shut it in, and here and

Bolton Castle.

there a bare rock face shines warm in the increasing brightness
of the sun.

Ah, exquisite Aysgarth ! Who would not strive and strive
again to reach some true expression of the fair picture which
lies glowing in his memory ! Words are but a palisade, through
whose chinks one can, at most, catch some gleam of all that
beauty, and while I sit and vainly steep my senses in the roar
and turmoil of the flashing water, I know well that I might as
easily describe a swallow's flight as the abounding loveliness
of this great fall at Aysgarth.

R

Well, it is gone ; the rush and glory of the fall have passed into memory ; and I am following a field path scarce trodden out between high swathes of grass waiting for the scythe, while the sun, mounting ever as I loitered by the fall, burns and bronzes all the scorching valley. Full in front of me, scarce two miles distant, lie the dark towers of Bolton Castle, standing strong and grim half way up the green hillside, quivering a little in the shimmer of the heat, which gives them a certain glamour as if the blast of some enchantment might dissolve them suddenly, and send the whole gaunt stronghold flying piecemeal into that limbo of romance whither the Scropes who held it have retreated out of this workaday world, carrying with them their memories of border raids and outlaws of the Marches, of fugitive and murdered kings, and of captive queens, with all the rout of chivalry which followed them. Ah, how silent all the land is where pageants were so common once ! where the Friars Minors came barefoot across the hills from Richmond, with their stinging impulses to uphold the memory of poor King Richard, whom the Scropes loved, and their hints that in truth he did not die at Pontefract, but was alive, and would come again into the loyal north country,—where Mary Stuart rode a hunting with sidelong looks towards the kingdom which she would never see again—where the cannon of the Parliament roared for many a day, while Colonel Scrope ate horse flesh and defied his enemies ! How still it is now all the old hot life has gone ! The land is drowsing beneath the summer heat ; and in some tall tree of a little wood bordering on the farm below the castle, there sits a wood pigeon wiling the heart out of the body of any man who will stop to hear her.

There is one who will, having indeed much to think about in the shadow of the four great towers, still so strong and tall, which Richard, first Lord Scrope of Bolton, built in those days when the poor prisoner of Pontefract was still a powerful monarch. Scrope was his chancellor, an old man who had fought at Cressy six and thirty years before, a stout and faithful

counsellor, too sturdy and too true for the poor foolish king.
For when certain greedy courtiers persuaded the king to grant
them the rents of certain lands of deceased persons during the
time for which, according to the custom of the realm, the king
should hold them, Scrope refused to issue grants under the
great seal, and sent the courtiers away empty-handed.   So they
went back to the king—the story is in Walsingham—and bade
him mark how the chancellor had set his heart to make light
the king's order, and that it became him to suppress such heady
disobedience, else his kingly honour would be stained, and his
orders would not weigh with any one.   Now the king had no
more than the wisdom of a peevish boy ; and, giving way to
passion, he sent a messenger to Scrope with orders to take the
great seal away, and bring it back to him.   But the messenger
returned empty-handed to the king ; and at last, when others
with the same orders were despatched, the chancellor replied :
" I am ready to resign the seal, not to you, but to him who gave
it me to keep, and between him and me there shall be no inter
mediary, but I will give it back into his own hands."   And
so seeking out the king, he gave up the seal ; "and the king,"
adds Walsingham, "having got the seal in his own hands,
did just what he liked for a long time."

It was in 1382, seventeen years before that fatal Irish
expedition, during which Bolingbroke landed and seized the
power of the country, that Richard used his faithful servant
thus ; yet there was surely something which people loved in
the peevish, tyrannous lad who came to regal power so
young, and brought it to an end so wretched, else how could
it have happened that the House of Scrope would cling so
warmly to his cause, when it had no other guerdon than the
block to offer ?   It is true that wise old Richard, the builder of
this castle, carried over his prudent head and his great influence
to the camp of Henry and the cause of good government ;
but his eldest son, the Earl of Wiltshire, lost his life at Bristol
by loyalty to the fallen king ; and the whole Scrope family

appear to have trusted the assurances that no harm should happen to the person of the rightful monarch. Satisfied with this, Archbishop Scrope consented to the deposition, and assisted at Henry's coronation, and might have been a loyal subject to the House of Lancaster, had Henry acted with any kind of faith towards his prisoner.

To this hour it is a mystery what became of Richard. Though the balance of evidence is with the theory that he was starved at Pontefract, yet this is not certain. No man can declare positively in these days what the truth was of the wild stories which the Franciscans, as I have said already, carried up and down the dales and over all the moors and mountains of the north, whipping up men's passions, calling on their pity and their loyalty to the son of the glorious Black Prince, appealing to their hatred of new things, their turbulence, and dwelling hard doubtless on the shame of serving before a throne which was planted on a corpse. Six years these hints and rumours ran to and fro about the country ; and it would be strange indeed if one so acute as Henry had not seen the danger of letting all this gossip last. Yet he produced no evidence as to the mode of Richard's death ; he took no steps to clear himself of the foul charge of having slain him, and year by year drifted by with a growing confidence in men's hearts that the Friars had spoken truth, till one day, in 1405, Archbishop Scrope preached a fiery sermon in York Minster, and set up his banner against the cause of a king whose honour was stained with perjury and murder.

That must have been a great and memorable scene when the Archbishop dared to stand up in the holy stool, and appeal to the excited populace that such deeds should not be wrought by them who governed in this realm of England. The Friars had won their point, though heaven knows what the object was with which they followed it. But the words once said no retreat was possible. Twenty thousand men in arms crowded to the Archbishop's banner, and had there been a prudent head among them they might have struck some blow which would have shaken Henry's throne, and even won it back for the wandering outcast who called himself King Richard. Henry Percy brought his tenantry from Topcliffe and from Beverley —when did a Percy hold his hand from rebellion?—and there, too, was Thomas Mowbray, the Earl Marshal, and many another brave knight ; and the whole host lay in the forest of Galtres, not far out of York. But they consented to treat with the king's army, and the end was that Scrope was persuaded to disband his men, and being then defenceless, was arrested and brought to Bishopsthorpe, where the king then was with Gascoigne, that noble Yorkshireman who has left for an inspiration to all ages the memory of a chief justice who had no fear of man, not even of the frown of kings.

For being ordered to sentence the captive Archbishop Gascoigne answered nobly : "Neither you, my lord, nor any of your subjects can legally, according to the law of the realm, sentence any Bishop to death." But Henry was not to be baulked of blood by legal scruples ; and a king who had sat contentedly these six years under a well-grounded suspicion of murder was not likely to concern himself with forms. What followed I give in the words of the chronicle itself.

"The King immediately ordered Sir William Fulthorpe, a knight and not a judge, to pronounce sentence on the Archbishop in the hall of the said Manor House. Fulthorpe accordingly sat in the judge's seat, and commanded Scrope to be brought before him ; the Archbishop, standing bare-headed, heard the following sentence pronounced : 'We do adjudge thee, Richard, to death as a traitor to the King ; and do, by the King's command, order thee to be beheaded.' To which the Archbishop replied, 'The just and true God knoweth that I never intended evil against the person of Henry IV., now King.' . . . And afterwards he said to those standing around him, 'Pray ye that the Almighty God may not avenge my death on the King or his,' which words he

often repeated, like St. Stephen, who prayed for them that
stoned him. The same day he was placed on a horse worth
forty shillings, without a saddle, for which he returned
thanks, saying, 'No horse ever pleased me better than this.'
He then sang the psalm, 'Exaudi,' riding with a halter, and
habited in a blood coloured garment, with sleeves of the same ;
for they would not allow him to wear the lined vestment worn
by bishops ; and so, with a purple coloured hood hanging down
his shoulders, he was led like a sheep to the slaughter, and
opened not his mouth in anger, or to pronounce sentence of
excommunication.

"Having arrived at the place of execution, he said, 'Almighty God, I offer to thee myself and the cause for which I
suffer, and beg pardon and indulgence of thee for all sins by
me committed or omitted.' He then laid his hood and gown
on the ground, and observed to his executioner, Thomas
Almar, 'Son, may God forgive thee my death, as I forgive thee ;
but I pray thee that thou wilt give me with thy sword five
wounds in the neck, which I desire to bear for the love of my
Lord Jesus Christ, who, being for us obedient unto his Father
till death, bore five principal wounds,' and three times kissed him,
then, kneeling, he prayed, saying, 'Into thy hands, most sweet
Jesu, I commend my spirit,' with his hands joined and his eyes
raised towards heaven. Then stretching out his neck, and
folding his hands over his breast, the executioner at five strokes
severed his head from his body."

Such was the death of the great Archbishop Scrope, a man
as dangerous to Henry after his death as when he lived. For
the love the Yorkshire people bore both to his house and him
was too strong to perish quickly, and, indeed, those were days
in which faith stretched easily across the grave. So Scrope's
spirit lived and wrought among the people ; and as they knew
him to be holy during life, so he continued his protection after
death, and miracles were whispered of him, much to the anger
of the government. When he had been dead eight years, the

new King, Henry V., endeared as he was to all the nation by
his gallantry and fortune, found it necessary to prohibit offer-
ings at the shrine of Scrope, who had then just wrought a
notable miracle by arresting the fire in a belfry in York.   The
King stopped the outward show ; but not even he who won at
Agincourt could destroy the inward reverence, or check the
sprouting of the seed which was ere long to bear such bitter
fruit for his own son.   It was not given to him by fate to win the
whole nation back to entire love and trust in the house of
Lancaster.   Had his short and splendid reign lasted but ten
years more . . . But all this is childish speculation.   In the
book of fate it was written that England should be torn by the
bloodiest of civil wars, and there was no part for any man to
play but that of onlooker, while the passions deepened and
the hatred of one house against another widened day by
day.

I did not mean to say so much when I stopped and rested
in this little wood.   The wood-pigeon has done cooing.   What
has she to do with battles and with executions?   Yet just such
a cooing may have sounded in this wood on that June day
when the messengers spurred up with the news of the Archbishop's death.   Come, let us go up and see the castle.   It
lies facing the wide dale very gaunt and strong.   On the south
front there is no entrance ; and that upon the west, which
passes for the main gateway, is scarcely more imposing than a
postern.   It gives access to a deep, vaulted chamber like a
guard-room, and a series of winding staircases and dark apartments, which have to this hour a certain aspect suggestive of
a prison.   Even the light spirit of Mary Stuart, used as she
was to live in grim old fortresses, must surely have been
troubled when Scrope, the Warden of the Western Marches,
to whom she had surrendered at Carlisle, brought her hither by
the Queen's directions in the early autumn of 1568, listening
courteously to her professions of eagerness to clear herself of
the charge of complicity in that black tragedy of the Kirk o'

Field, by which her husband, sleeping securely, was blown up by gunpowder on a February night.

God forbid that I should touch the problem of Mary's guilt or attempt to reach the heart of that great drama of the casket letters which the Lords, her enemies, produced at York during the period of her stay at Bolton. What have I to do with questions of innocence or judgment? Let historians don the ermine and give their opinion from the judgment seat. Mary Stuart is not arraigned before my bar ; and I thank heaven that it is so. For, in truth, when I look down even from my own exalted moral pinnacle, on that poor, friendless, sinful woman, lost in the abysses, I have no inclination to measure the very depth of her descent, or to know how far in any crisis she only stumbled, and how far she actually fell. How many storms of passion a man must have conquered before he dares to judge her ! How far he must have risen over his own humanity before he can do aught but pity her, and that with-out contempt, but with a warm feeling of common nature which, but for the grace of God—as some one said—might have made his name, too, a byword and a hissing unto half the world, without at the same time winning, as Mary did, the perpetual love and trust of the other half.

The room which was the Queen's chief abode while she remained at Bolton is still shown, a large, gloomy chamber, looking to the west by a window so small as gives some colour to the story that she may have escaped by it. Here she sat and waited during all the autumn days when the authenticity of the casket letters was being discussed, and while the northern Lords were slowly moving forward to that insurrection of which I spoke at Barnard Castle, and concerning which I shall have more to say at Ripon. There is a scene told by poor Christopher Norton in his confession written not long before he suffered the penalties of high treason, which is worth quoting here ; for Christopher was in attendance upon Mary, and may have been the channel of frequent messages passing between

her and those Lords of the old religion who saw in her the
hope of the faith which they supported.   "One day," said
Norton, " when the Queen of Scots in winter had been sitting
at the window side knitting of a work ; and after the board
was covered, she rose and went to the fireside ; and, making
haste to have the work finished, would not lay it away, but
worked of it the time she was warming herself.   She looked
for one of her servants, which, indeed, were all gone to fetch
up her meat, and seeing none of her own folk there, called me

Bolton Castle.

to hold her work, who was looking at my Lord Scrope and Sir
Francis Knollys playing of chess.   I went, thinking I had
deserved no blame, and that it should not have become me to
have refused to do it, my Lady Scrope standing there, and
many gentlemen in the chamber that saw she spoke not to me.
I think Sir Francis saw not nor heard when she called of me.
But when he had played his mate, he, seeing me standing by
the Queen holding of her work, called my captain to him, and
asked him if I watched.   He answered 'Sometimes.'   Then he

gave the commandment that I should watch no more, and said the Queen would make me a fool."

Ah, Christopher! Unlucky, faithful Christopher! It sounds an innocent story told so to the Council in full view of the scaffold. What could a poor lad do when the Queen called him? She spoke not to him. But did ever any man stand before Mary Stuart in the silence and the warm gloom and feel no thrill of love for her? Was it not the flight of some warm human message which Sir Francis Knollys detected, some soft appeal from the liquid eyes, some glance beseeching his devotion. . . . Pooh, what is it that occurs when a raw lad is called to stand beside a captive Queen, and she the loveliest and most unfortunate woman on the earth?'

Christopher Norton was to watch no more. But history records that through his agency there was indeed an effort to escape—a subtle plot in which Lady Livingston was to play the moonstruck damsel consumed with passion to meet Christopher by night outside the moat. What more natural than for the lovebird to pass out with her face close veiled? And who would then know whether it were she or one who had far greater reasons for desiring to pass the guard? It was a pretty plot, but some link in the chain dropped out, and the drama ran to its appointed end. There is a tradition told up and down the dale that the Queen did once actually escape by the window of her chamber, and finding horses and attendants waiting on the hill rode off as far as the ridge by Leyburn, which is called "The Shawl," where she was overtaken by Scrope's horsemen and brought back. The spot is shown where she was stopped. The story may be true. Yet what folly to have skirted along the hillside, within sight and hearing of farms and manors, when she might have struck at once over the wild moors! How small a thing might have changed the history of England and of Scotland at that time! Had the Queen escaped, and ridden at the head of the rising of the north, the whole inquiry into her guilt, all the discussions at

York about the casket letters, must have been dropped hastily.
Or had Lord Westmorland, who waited on the moors to inter-
cept the Scotch lords carrying the casket, managed to seize and
to destroy it ! But it was fated otherwise. True or false, the
casket letters ruined Mary ; her supporters perished on the
scaffold ; and when she left Bolton it was but to plunge further
into that Protestant England in which, after twenty years of
hopes and disappointments, the whole drama ended by the axe
in the courtyard of Fotheringay.

This old tragedy comes very close as I roam about the
corridors where Ross and Herries and the faithful Maitland
used to wait for audience of Mary. But as I climb on up
the winding stair, past halls and state apartments dropping to
decay, and so come out upon the battlements, whence I can
look down on the whole waste and ruined shell of grandeur
—towers, which by the dropping of their floors, are mere tall
shafts ; doorways, which for ages have given passage only to the
birds,—when I reach this point, and all the vast extent of the
ancient castle lies before me, with the green hills rising rough
and broken on the one hand, and on the other the river winding sweetly up the long dale, there come back upon my memory
all those border exploits which are credited to the lords who
were so often wardens of the western marches. " Keen Lord
Scrope's to the hunting gone," and noble hunting he must have
had among the border reivers, the most lusty and audacious
thieves of which English history has knowledge.

> " Of Liddisdail the commoun thiefis,
> Sa pertlie steilis now and reifis,
> That nane may keep hors, nolt, nor scheip,
> Nor yet dare sleip for their mischiefs."

Such were the bad men whom it was the duty of many Lords
Scrope to watch up to the limit of the English border ;
and though the whole delightful subject lies outside my

domain, yet as the Scropes fall within it, I may be forgiven
for telling one story of their stewardship.

> " O have ye na hearde o' the fause Sakelde,
>   O have ye na hearde o' the keen Lord Scrope ?
>   How they have ta'en bauld Kinmont Willie,
>   On Haribee to hang him up ? "

I fear there are many of us poor Southrons who have heard of
neither one nor the other.   Kinmont Willie was one of the
worst of thieves, and by consequence one of the most loved and
respected of mankind in the acquisitive society where Providence
had placed him.   Salkeld was, I fear, a man of no delicacy of
feeling.   For there really was a truce, and he did actually break
it by securing this bad thief when he met him on the mountain
side, and what is more he refused to give him up, truce or no
truce, without the orders of Lord Scrope, who was not then at
Carlisle, but probably at Bolton, and who on his part felt that
such a rascal as Kinmont Willie must at any rate be kept until
the Queen and Council decided whether to hang him or to let
him go.

It was all very natural and human—but how imprudent !
For if you catch a thief, and are not inclined to do the gracious
thing at once, how much better to hang him instantly, and tell
the Queen and Council afterwards !   Scrope ought not to have
needed prompting on this score.   The duties of a Warden of
the Marches might well have taught him greater readiness, while
the constant proximity of the Scots should have convinced him
that when they fail in their ends it is not for want of trying
lustily.   However, that is what he did ; and Kinmont Willie
lay in Carlisle Castle, where it might have been thought he was
safe enough.

But thirty Scotsmen resolved to have him out.   Buccleuch
himself was at the bottom of it.   Dear heavens, does one never
pine among the modern comforts of Dalkeith for the days in
which half the spearmen of the Border were in saddle at the.

signal of Buccleuch! "And for such purpose the Lord of
Buccleuch, upon intelligence that the Castle of Carleill, where
the prisoner was keept, was surpriseable, and of the meanes, by
sending some persons of trust to view a postern gate, and to
measure the height of the wall very closely, he did immediately
draw togither 200 horse, assured the place of meeting ane hour
before sunset at the Toure of Mortoune, the which is ten
miles from Carleill, and upon the water of Sark in the debate-
able land, quhair he had preparation of ledders for scaleing the
castle wall. . . " Pooh, the story needs the lilt of verse, and
the ballad has ten times the spirit of the history :—

> " He has call'd him forty marchmen bauld,
>   Were kinsmen to the bauld Buccleuch ;
> With spur on heel and splent on spauld
>   And gleuves of green and feathers blue.
>
> There were five and five before them a'
>   Wi' hunting horns and bugles bright ;
> And five and five came wi' Buccleuch,
>   Like Warden's men, arrayed for fight.
>
> And five and five, like a mason gang,
>   That carried the ladders alang and hie ;
> And five and five, like broken men ;
>   And so they reached the woodhouselee.
>
> And when we reached the Staneshaw bank,
>   The wind was rising loud and hie ;
> And there the laird garr'd leave our steeds,
>   For fear that they should stamp and nic.
>
> And when we left the Staneshaw bank,
>   The wind began full loud to blaw ;
> But 'twas wind and weet, and fire and sleet,
>   When we came beneath the castle wa'.
>
> We crept on knees and held our breath,
>   Till we placed the ladders against the wa',
> And sae ready was Buccleuch himsell
>   To mount the first before us a'.

He has ta'en the watchman by the throat,
　　He flung him down upon the lead—
" Had there not been peace between our lands,
　　Upon the other side thou hadst gaed ;

" Now sound out trumpets !" quo' Buccleuch ;
　　Let's waken Lord Scrope right merrilie !"
Then loud the warden's trumpet blew—
　　" Oh, wha dare meddle wi' me !"

Then speedilie to wark we gaed
　　And raised the Slogan ane and a' ;
And cut a hole through a sheet of lead,
　　And so we wan to the castle ha'.

They thought King James wi' a' his men
　　Had won the house wi' bow and spear ;
It was but twenty Scots and ten,
　　That put a thousand in sic a stear !

And when we cam to the lower prison,
　　Where Willie of Kinmont he did lie—
" Oh, sleep ye, wake ye, Kinmont Willie,
　　Upon the morn that thou's to die ?"

Then Red Rowan has heute him up,
　　The starkest man in Tiviotdale—
" Abide, abide now, Red Rowan,
　　Till of my Lord Scrope I take farewell."

" Farewell, farewell, my gude Lord Scrope !
　　My gude Lord Scrope, farewell !" he cried—
" I'll pay you for my lodging maill,
　　When first we meet on the border side."

We scarce had won the Staneshaw bank,
　　When a' the Carlisle bells were rung,
And a thousand men on horse and foot,
　　Cam wi' the keen Lord Scrope along.

Buccleuch has turned to Eden water,
　　Even where it flowed frae bank to brim,
And he has plunged in wi' a' his band,
　　And safely swam them through the stream.

> He turned him on the other side,
>   And at Lord Scrope his glove flung he—
> "If ye like na my visit in merrie England,
>   In fair Scotland come visit me!"

Oho, keen Lord Scrope! I wonder how long it was before the
pages at Bolton and Carlisle ceased to go about laughing
secretly when they heard the name of Kinmont Willie! and
what a tale to tell the Council, who at that moment were
deciding whether Willie should be hung or not! But what a
noble, lusty, fullblooded life it was! and who that knows the
tale will ever pass Carlisle Castle without hearing the stir and
the hubbub and Buccleuch's bugle ringing out defiantly the old
slogan, "Oh, Wha Dare Meddle wi' Me!":—

> Yet or I dee
> Sum sall thame see,
> Hing on a tree
> Quhill thay be deid!
> Quo' Sir R. M. of Lethington, Knight."

And if Scrope was acquainted with these spiteful and ill-
tempered verses, he doubtless found much comfort in them.
But this really will not do. Here I am right out of Yorkshire,
and not for the first time! Yet this excursion into Westmorland has refreshed me, as a schoolboy is revived by a détour
into his neighbour's orchard; and I am full of energy as I descend
again into the heat, and run on past the little church, as old as
the days of Richard the Second, and through the village, and
so past pretty Wensley, which has such a charming bridge and
such a lofty notion of its own importance. For it claims to
have given England one Queen, one Prince of Wales, one
cardinal-archbishop, three other archbishops, five bishops,
three chancellors, two chief justices of England, and more earls,
barons, knights, and abbots than it cares to count. So Wensley
goes peacocking about among the other Yorkshire villages on
the strength of all these ancient glories, and every urchin holds
his head the higher and dreams of cardinals.

It is time to get me gone from Wensleydale, though I have

not said one-half of the things I meant to say when I came
down the hill on Hardraw, and first saw the long, still stretches
of the Ure.   The afternoon is waxing late, and my wheels have
brought me into Leyburn, that wide, dull, formless town which
stands so notably just where the high ridges that wall the dale
begin to drop and die away in the vast central plain of Yorkshire, while it any reason were needed for dispatch upon the
journey thither, it is furnished me by certain heavy drops of rain
that splash at quick intervals out of an overclouding sky, and the
rise of a little sobbing wind, which presages a thunderstorm.

Wensleydale.

Indeed, I had scarce reached the shelter of the " Bolton Arms "
when the whole wide dale was filled with driving showers, while
the thunder rattled heavily around the hills, and sharp, stabbing
snaps of lightning flashed suddenly out of the towering clouds
which built themselves up in huge, black battlements above the
moors.   So all the afternoon I watched the storm sweeping in
a great procession through the dale ; but towards evening the
rain abated, and I set out on foot to see the moors which lie
above the Scropes' great castle.   Even when the heavens ceased
to weep, the clouds lay low and heavy on the hill crests, and

the wide mouth of Wensleydale was filled with grey mists, through which even Middleham, which lies but two miles off across the valley, could be discerned with difficulty. The sky was torn and angry, and presently great thunderclouds blew up again from the south-west, and stood in lurid ranks above the sulphurous hills. Then the lashing rain came down once more in torrents ; the grassy track across the moor swam with water ; there was neither man nor animal to be seen upon the lonely waste which lay strewn with scattered ling and gorse, and here and there a standing pool of bog water, extending further than the eye could range across the undulations of the hills. So the storm lasted until dusk. But then a small red spot came and sat upon the summit of one of the inky hills, sole in the waste of angry sky, and by and bye it spread its wings like a crimson bird, and then it was a bar of flame, and then a river of orange and copper flowing all along the ridge, and next a wide gap of gold and crimson in the torn sky, piercing the mists with shafts of radiant light. And then the sun sank, and the crimson paled, and the hilltops swam in a sea of watery green and opal.

Wensleydale.

CHAPTER XIII

LONG and long ago one Christopher Brown fled from this town of Leyburn to the sanctuary of St. Cuthbert at Durham. It was on Saturday, 26th July of the year 1477, that Brown came begging with anguish—" Peciit cum instancia "—the safety and the freedom of the saint; and in the nave of the great cathedral, in presence of a notary and witnesses, he loosed his heart from the load it bore, and told the reason of his terror. In the brief Latin jotting which the monks made, it is but half a story, and it went back no less than eighteen years to a certain day in 1459. It was the Feast of St. Wilfrid, October 12th, and Brown, upon a certain road near Laburn—"apud Laburn juxta Midilham in Coverdale,"—note which were the well-known places in those days—met one Thomas Carter riding with his little son held before him on the horse. There was some cause of quarrel between the men, and as Carter went by, Brown let fly a biting jibe at him, which stung him so that he leapt down from his horse, forgetting the child, and ran to revenge himself on his insulter. But the little lad, left without support, slipped off the horse, and the beast, startled by the suddenness of the movements, reared and plunged, and his hoofs crashed down upon the child, and gave him hurts of which he died.

I do not know with what eyes the two men saw each other, when Carter snatched his little son out from the cruel hoofs of

the frightened horse and both stood looking down on the deed
they had done.   It is a pitiful tragedy, yet, doubtless, not
unexampled.   But what makes the matter more worth notice is
the singular fact that eighteen years passed before Brown's fears,
or his awakening conscience, drove him to flee across the moors
to sanctuary.   I do not know that the one man was more to
blame than was the other.   But did remorse slumber eighteen
years before affecting either of them ?   Less than such an injury
has often in the history of Yorkshire started a blood feud, and
a bitter passion for slaying which has lasted out two generations.
Was there such a feud between the Carters and the Browns ;
or was it merely that the furies, the avengers of blood, were in
pursuit of Brown from the very moment of his deed, till at last
after eighteen years they drove him a shattered, miserable man
into the home of peace upon the Wear ?

Something there was, beyond a doubt, which dogged Brown
all that time ; and if it was impalpable, his terror may have
been the greater.   Four hundred years have not swept
Wensleydale of superstition.   "Some years back," says a
writer in *Folklore of the Northern Counties*, "a man told me
he had met Mr. —— walking on the road ; ' but,' he added, ' it
was nobbut but his shadow, and I don't think he'll live long."
A dozen tales of this sort go chasing each other through my
brain as I go down the long, steep hill which passes out of
Leyburn towards the river   It is a ghostly country, and those
who know best the life and beliefs of the people see in them a
kind of magic clue which, if it be set going, will unroll itself into
far distant days, and guide him who elects to follow it past all
history of Tudor, Plantagenet, or Norman, past Saxon and past
Dane, to an age where there are no landmarks in the mist of
time, nor any certain voices perceptible to modern ears.
Straight and unbroken out of the homes of long-forgotten races
come those creeds and fancies which are cherished in the
cottages of the labouring folk to-day, paganism out of distant
lands growing still in our midst, as it was cherished by those

S 2

who roamed the ocean in their dragon keels, and traced these fancies from ancestors so remote that they themselves had neither memory nor record of their origin. Dear heaven! How infinite is the long procession of the ages; and how blind are we who march in it, seeing neither the ranks which march in front, nor those which follow, but have eyes only for ourselves, stalking proudly across the fields and uplands as if they were our own, and we denied the title of the dead.

The long hill has brought me down at last to a bridge of iron cast across the river. On either side there are wide water

Middleham Castle.

meadows, through which the children will tell you with hushed voices, that Water Kelpie romps, on the watch perpetually for stray children, many of whom she has carried off to the slimy depths of Ure. It may be so, though I have passed this way by noon and nightfall and yet have not seen her, nor do I wish it, for in my heart . . . but that is my own affair. Besides I really have not time to stay beside this stream dilating upon demons. Up above me on the hill, half hidden by the houses over which it used to tower, stands the great castle of Fitzranulph, whose banner hung, among others, in the Hall of Scolland

within Richmond Castle. This was one of the greatest of the
tributary strongholds which gave support to the semi-royal state
of Richmond. But Fitzranulph is gone and long forgotten ; the
children will tell you that this was the castle of the Nevilles, for
in Yorkshire the fame of that great family has by no means
passed away from whose loins there sprang the Earls of Westmorland, Salisbury and Warwick, the Marquisate of Montacute,
a Duke of Bedford, the Barons Furnival, Latimer, Fauconbridge,
and Abergavenny ; and whose main line died away at last in
poverty and sorrow at Sheriff Hutton Castle, whither, after the
fall of the great kingmaker at Barnet, his heir retired stripped
of both property and titles, and died scarce better off than any
shepherd on the wolds.

But the Nevilles were in the centre of their power when they
dwelt at Middleham, and of all their castles there was none save
Raby where they dwelt with more magnificence than here. I
do not know what truth there may be in the suggestion thrown
out long since by wiser heads than mine, that the exasperating
" he " who in the old ballad of " The Nutbrown Mayd " so
tortured and tormented the loving heart which was far too
faithful for a husband so suspicious, and who avowed himself at
last to be " an earlys son " entitled to the heritage of Westmorland, might not be a member of this great family. If so, I hope
his conduct was not typical of the family demeanour to the
trusty woman hearts which followed them. I climb up through
the little town, past the market place, and through a narrow side
street on the left, where the houses stand so close beneath the
old main gateway as to preclude the possibility of seeing the
grim structure at any distance. It is grand and gloomy rather
than picturesque. The old Norman keep of the Fitzranulphs
is still more conspicuous than the later buildings grouped
around it. Strong and dark, its projecting towers and turrets
at the angles stand to this day in firm clear outline, while the
more splendid chambers where the luxury of the Nevilles and
the splendour of a Royal Court displayed themselves, stand

ruined and deserted, a waste of blackened crumbling walls and roofless chambers, of masonry dropping on the greensward, and wallflowers blooming sweetly round the mouldings of the gateways.

I suppose it is mere fancy which sees in any mighty ruin an aspect according with the spirit of the deeds which have been done there. Stone is stone, and mortar mortar, all the world over ; yet where is there a man who can so detach his mind from the impression of past events as to look upon the stone and mortar of Pontefract or Middleham without some thrill of passion which he never felt before a mountain precipice, however lofty ? For my part I cannot pass by Middleham without a shudder ; for over all the knightly and the noble recollections of the Nevilles there broods the most terrible of all figures in our English history, the shade of Richard, Duke of Gloucester, a man in many ways so wise and strong, so clear-sighted and so brave in action that in him villainy was seen surely at its best, and it may be counted most exactly what harvest can be reaped by a man whose heart has rejected pity, what riches can be garnered by one who compasses his ends with secret murder.

I came hither intending to write about the Nevilles ; but I cannot see past this terrible figure of King Richard the Third, who gained this heritage by a marriage with Anne Neville, second daughter and co-heiress of the great earl who fell at Barnet. If on that unhappy day the kingmaker had been able to anticipate the turn of fate, he might have used the bitter words which poor King James uttered of the Crown of Scotland, when they brought him news that a daughter had been born to him. "It came with a lass and it'll go with a lass." It was from the heiress of the Fitzranulphs that the Nevilles got this lordly castle. But it should not have gone with a lass so soon by many a year ; for Warwick's Countess was alive, and partly by life interest, and partly through her own right the estates were hers. Yet the Duke of Clarence, who in Warwick's lifetime, married the elder daughter, held the lands; while as for Lady Anne, who was entitled to the half of them after her mother, he hid her secretly from the pursuit of Richard.

He might as well had hid her from a sleuthhound which had smelt her glove. Richard found her in the habit of a kitchen maid. He was a strangely chosen wooer. He had stabbed her lover in cold blood upon the field of Tewkesbury; he had murdered that lover's father, poor King Henry, at midnight in the Tower with his own hands—so, at least, men still believed—and if it was not his hand that struck both blows, he was at least present when both murders were committed. It is folly to read of old events in the light of contemporary judgments. In those days blood was in the air; men who had shed much were yet not loathed by noble ladies, and it may be that Richard, who was young in crime, did not displease the poor girl who saw no escape from him. So they were wed; and ere long Clarence was slain secretly in prison, men said again by Richard's hand; and an added portion of inheritance of the Nevilles passed to the Lord of Middleham. So did the stewardry of the Duchy of Lancaster, which gave him Pontefract, and the wardenship of the Western Marshes, which put him in command of Carlisle; and while using this vast power in Yorkshire, which he loved, Richard was always at his best reducing the Border to discipline, winning back Berwick from the Scots, so that the Yorkshiremen whom he led to triumph over their hated enemies, gave him their hearts, and for a space of years the power even of this man rested on attachment enough to make him happy.

This is why, of all places in the country, his name should be recalled at Middleham, where some good odour clings to him, where his son was born, where he suffered the agony of losing him, and where, beyond a doubt, he plotted the appalling treachery by which he grasped the throne. He was in York-shire when King Edward died; and what thoughts rose in his heart when he saw two weakly boys stand between him and the

Crown may be guessed by any one who counts his murders
There is nothing told in English history more tragic than the
tale of the crafty toils which Richard used to snare the two
poor lads. When he had them safe within the Tower, and he
himself sat on the throne, he paused a while—so great a
murder as he dreamt of then needed time to collect his courage.
The hour struck. The messenger sent to the Governor of the
Tower found that foolish fellow troubled with stupid scruples ;
whereupon Richard sent back his familiar, Sir James Tyrrel,
with written orders to take over all the keys of the Tower for
one night. It was enough. The two lads were never seen
again.

Poor, friendless children ! They were fearfully avenged. " I
have heard by credible report," said Sir Thomas More," of such
as were secret with his chamberers, that after this abominable
deed done he never had quiet in his mind, he never thought
himself sure. Where he went abroad, his eyes whirled about,
his bodily privily fenced, his hand ever on his dagger, his
countenance and manner like one always ready to strike again.
He took ill rest at night, lay long waking and musing ; sore
wearied with care and watch, he rather slumbered than slept.
Troubled with fearful dreams, suddenly sometimes started he
up, leapt out of his bed and ran about the chamber. So was
his restless heart continually tossed and tumbled with the
tedious impression and stormy remembrance of his most
abominable deed."

Well, these are old tales now, and I daresay some may be
impatient of them. As I came down the hill from Leyburn, I
let fall an observation on the singularity of the indications
given by the monks of Durham of the locality of that now
flourishing tourist centre. Leyburn was " Juxta Midilham in
Coverdale "—an odd description to our ears—for a traveller of
to-day would be more likely to describe Middleham as near
Leyburn, and would not know Coverdale at all, unless he were
a Yorkshireman. I have given reasons for the fame of

Middleham; and now it will be well to walk across the moor
behind the Castle and find out how it happened that Coverdale was so well known at Durham in past ages and so little in
our own.

I venture to hope that nobody will interrupt me at this point
by talking of racehorses. I think no man alive can pause to
rest in Middleham or try to gather any information about that
once famous town without wondering whether, indeed, he was
born to write a sporting calendar or a guide to the turf. You
will ask the fellow who shows the Castle some question
about "The Peacock of the North," and the odds are he will
answer by inquiring what year he ran in, and volunteering the
information that " Flying Dutchman," who won both the Derby
and the St. Leger, was trained upon the top moor, under
the shadow of Penhill ; while if you demand to be shown
the Nevilles' Hall, he will offer to point out the training estab-
lishments of Mr. Fred Bates or the brothers Osborne, and,
perhaps, even to put you in the way, for a trifling consideration,
of some certain knowledge which will make you rich for life.
You may listen to him if you like. But then you must put
knights and monks out of your head. You cannot be both
baronial and a modern sportsman. Some day I will go to
Middleham with "Ruff's Guide " in my pocket and the
Pink'Un in my hand. I will sit down upon the moor and write
my own and other people's sporting reminiscences. But till
that time of leisure comes, I beg that I may not be troubled by
further allusions to the subject.

Yet I know that, human nature being in all ages just what it
is to-day, the monks were sportsmen too, and used these noble
moors much in the same way as the brothers Osborne do.
They were also notable sweet singers, as they well might be
in a spot so pretty, where to this day the thrushes and the
linnets pipe with such soft and liquid trillings as might teach any
man to warble who would but listen to them. The road, after
running for a little distance over the moor, breaks away from

the short turf and the outcropping rock, and falls between
sweet hedges into a wooded valley, a sheltered cleft among the
crowding of great hills, whose gaunt flanks and shoulders tower
over the dale so high that one feels some wonder to see it all so
bright and sunny.   For there is not a tree nor bush which is not
trembling in the gold light and the wandering wind which
carries it.   All the hollow is aglow, and from some depth of the
valley bottom there rises up the sound of a river rushing freshly,
just heard above the murmurs of the leaves and branches.   I
pause a moment on the hillside, half doubting whether I may
not break some spell by stepping down among these sights and
noises ; and, indeed, I wish with all my heart that I had turned
away from the brow of the hill, and searched no further in the
valley.   There was once a monk—everybody knows the story—
who walked out into the forest, a stone's throw from his
monastery, and heard a blue bird singing as if his whole heart
hung on every note.   No thrush or blackbird ever piped with
half such sweetness.   The soul of the monk went out to the
beautiful blue bird, and he followed it fluttering from tree to
tree, singing the while as if all the love and bitterness in the
world lay in his throat—followed in a trance of ecstasy, till he
forgot his cell and his holy duties and his brother monks, and
had ears only for the fluting of the bird.   So at last he lost it ;
but when he sought his monastery again he found it half in
ruins and all its glory gone, and of himself no memory left save
an old tradition that once upon a time—who knew how many
years before ?—a monk had strayed away into the forest and
had been lost for ever in its glades.   And it was for this
that the poor monk came back to the reality of things !   Had he
but been able to follow the blue bird !

Surely it was the piping of the blue bird which sounded in
my ears as I paused upon the hillside, luring me away from the
things I had come to see.   I did not heed it, but went down
through silent, dewy hedges till at last I reached a gateway,
inside which a prosperous and comely farm reared its houseplace

and its byres for cattle.   That is innocent, though unromantic ;
but in the next moment I saw the broken arches of Coverham
Abbey towering over the barns ; I traced out the line of the
once noble church ; I saw what occupied its aisles ; I located the
position of its high altar. . . And I turned away ashamed that
men should not only dwell themselves and keep animals in the
sacred precincts of a church, but even proclaim the fact to all
the world by leaving the remnant of the arches standing still !
It is not a sight to increase one's respect for modern life.   Ah,

Coverham Abbey.

had I but followed the blue bird, and not gone down into the
valley !

If that ground, which is not only consecrated but is also rich
in the dust of saints and nobles, appears to any man a fitting
place to stable cows and rattle milk pails in, one can but shrug
one's shoulders and go one's way.   So I went mine across the
bridge which spans the stream, and on the further side I found
a steep narrow lane, which led me up among trails of bramble
and wild roses and along the slope of the hill till I came out at

last upon the village green of East Witton, a pretty village lying under the great fells that wall in Wensleydale on the south-eastern side. There is nothing much to see in Witton ; and I went on by a pleasant road for something like two miles till the road turned up the hill, and almost at the corner a gateway standing open admitted me to the grounds in which lie the ancient ruins of Jervaux.

Had not my head been full of Bolton Castle as I came down Wensleydale, I should certainly have stopped near Bainbridge to see the site on which the monks who afterwards built Jervaux found their first home. In that bleak country they met with sore privations ; and it is told of them that travelling on a certain time from Byland, to which more ancient monastery they were at first affiliated, they found themselves entangled and lost among the convolutions of the hills. Now the night before, the abbot had dreamt that he was visited in sleep by a Virgin and her child, and that the babe plucked a branch from some flowering tree which stood in the centre of the cloister court. And therefore believing himself under the protection of these sacred beings, he exclaimed, "Since we are thus impeded, let us repeat our hours and the Gospel." Immediately the same virgin and her child appeared, and the abbot cried out loudly, "Fair and tender woman, what doest thou with thy son in this rugged and desert place ? " And the woman answered, "I am a frequent inmate of desert places, but now I have come from Rievaulx and Byland and am going to the new monastery." Then said the abbot, "Good lady, I implore thee to conduct me and my brethren out of this desert place, and lead us to the new monastery, for we are of Byland." She replied, "Ye were late of Byland, but now of Jorvaulx ; " then she said, "Sweet son, be their leader ; I am called elsewhere," and disappeared. The boy holding in his hand the branch plucked from the cloister at Byland cried aloud, " Follow me." At length they arrived at a barren and uncultivated place, where the boy planted the bough, which was instantly filled with white

birds, and having exclaimed, " Here shall God be adored for a
short space," he disappeared also.

There is a certain lack of practical sagacity about this pretty
story, which is characteristic of monkish chronicles ; for it does
not seem that the poor monks were much benefited
by the services of a guide, who did but lead them from one
wilderness to another. However, we are told that they did
reach home not much after the child had left them ; and, at any
rate, it is quite natural that this incident should leave upon their

Jervaulx Abbey

minds the impression that they were in some special degree
under heavenly protection. Perhaps it was so ; for whereas
their rugged pastures in the high dale would grow but little
corn, they obtained no great while later the rich meadows
under Witton Fell, among which I am now standing ; and there
they built one of the very noblest of all English churches, as
may be seen still from the fragments which are left us after the
ravages of past generations.

Not much is known of all the deeds and actions of the monks

at Jervaux; nor even if the story were recoverable would this
be the place to tell it.   But one vivid scene which happened is
well worth transcribing, if only because it brings us to the earlier
days of that great insurrection which is called the Pilgrimage of
Grace, shows us the gathering of the host which we saw
dispersed at Doncaster, and places before us the life of the
monasteries in the very last hours of their long and splendid
life.

In those years which came immediately before the Dissolution, Adam Sedbergh was abbot of Jervaux.   I do not
know whether he was in truth a man of peace, or whether it
was merely policy which made him desire to keep aloof from
the bands of angry peasants who began to rove the country in
protest against the interference with monastic houses.   He may
have hoped that Jervaux might escape, if only it were not
touched by any share in the disorders.   However this may have
been, the poor man had but little choice, for " on a Wednesday
about Michaelmas Day, 1536, there came to the garth or
court of the abbey of Jervaux, two or three hundred of the
inhabitants of Mashamshire and Kirbyshire, and among them
the Captains Middleton and Staveley.   When he heard that
they were there, he conveyed himself by a back door to Witton
Fell, having with him another person or more, and a boy named
Martin Gibson, bidding his other servants get them every man
to his house and save his goods and cattle.   He remained on
the fell for the space of four days, returning to the monastery
every night.   During this time the commons wandered about
the surrounding country and went to Coverham Abbey, then to
Wensleydale and thence to Richmond.   At length, having
heard that he, the abbot, had said, 'That no servant of his
should ever do him service, nor tenant dwell of no land of his,
that should go with them,' they turned back to Jervaux and
enquired for him.   They were answered that he was absent.
Then said they, 'We charge you, the brethren, to choose a new
abbot.'" Upon this the brethren rang the chapter bell and went

towards making a new election, though certain among them said they would in no wise aid to make a new abbot. Half an hour's respite was then given to the monks, with the threat that if they continued to refuse, the house would be burnt over their heads.

If ever any men had cause to pray that they might be delivered from their friends, it was surely these unfortunate monks of Jervaux, and their still more luckless abbot. Terrified by the threats of the mob, which surged through the church and all the abbey buildings, offering each moment to carry out their threat, the monks sent messengers in all directions over the hill to seek the abbot; and at last one William Nelson found him by a great crag upon the summit, and told him of the strait in which the abbey stood, and how nothing would pacify the mob except his presence.

I doubt that Abbot Sedbergh, as he listened to the breathless tale, and looked down from his safe hiding on the fell to where the tower of his abbey stood in the lovely valley, saw any ending of this matter but the gibbet for himself, and destruction for that fair and goodly building. He held back and hesitated; till the man who found him pointed to a column of black smoke which rose up heavily among the trees, and showed him that the threats had been fulfilled, that the abbey was indeed on fire, and that if he would save any part of the structure, for which it was his duty to lay down his life, he must go down into that angry throng and do the best he could. So urged, the abbot hurried down the hillside; but when he came to the outer gate, he was seized by the people, torn about and almost killed, among deafening shouts of "Down with that traitor." At last his friends and followers managed to rescue him, and the whole throng crowded into the great hall, amid a scene of such turmoil as those quiet cloisters had probably never witnessed to that hour. The passions of the people were mightily inflamed; and as the abbot set foot within the hall, Leonard Burgh, one of the leaders of the people, drew his

dagger and made a sudden slash, which had gone near to end
the abbot's troubles and dismiss him from this weary world by
a road more straight and easy than the one designed for him.
But others caught the ruffian's arm ; and as the abbot came on
further into the howling mob, one William Asleby, a chief
captain in those parts, cried out, "Traitor, where hast thou
been?" while others cried, "Geate a block and strike off his
head."

Such was the conduct of those godly men towards an abbot
who displeased them. And, indeed, I know not whether the
sacredness of his person would have gone far to save him on
this occasion, had there not been some among the party cool
enough to reflect that an abbot living might profit them better
than an abbot dead. So they gave him the alternative of join-
ing their insurrection or of losing his head ; and he very wisely
took the course which offered him at least a chance of saving
it—a chance which might well appear a certainty when not long
afterwards all the scattered bands of insurgents were combined
into a mighty army under the banners of almost every lord of
note and power in the north: Nevilles and Lumleys, Scropes,
Conyers, Nortons and Constables, Fairfaxes, Ellerkars—how
could any heart which loved its cause and thought it just not
beat high and fast when it saw such a noble gathering of all
the pith and marrow of the north gathered under the holy
banner of the five wounds of Christ?

I think that most men who have written of the doings of that
mighty host have credited it with just and upright purposes ;
and have seen in its leaders men capable of any noble work to
which their monarch might have put them, had he cared to
conciliate and treat them leniently. But he chose rather to
hang them in many parts of England for the crows to feast
upon ; while his ruthless minister, Thomas Cromwell, found in
the rash ardour of men whose faith roused no echo in his heart,
and whose honour did but make his treachery the easier, pre-
cisely the opportunity he sought of extirpating the great lords.

Where Nortons and Constables suffered, it was not likely that abbots would escape; and so Adam Sedbergh, who had come down from Witton Fell with such reluctance, found the end he had foreseen, and was hanged at Tyburn, a tragic witness of the fate awaiting those who are not strong enough to swim against the stream.

I stand beside the gateway where he met the seething crowd, looking up at the high fell. Its flanks may have been bare moorland in those days, but now the skyline is crowded with dark fir trees, marked out by lighter green of larches, and beyond the trees a line of crumpled hill-tops. Around the old grey ruins two or three gardeners are working. One of them has set down his water-buckets on the gravestone of some abbot, and draws off the water as he needs it, without a thought of who lies under that great stone marked with the crozier. Another mows the grass, sweeping with steady strokes up the nave and into the choir of the church, pausing now and then to jest with his companions. They make it very nice and neat. One would not have it otherwise. And yet there is something incongruous . . . pooh! I am growing captious, and had better go my way up the hill. The ruins of Jervaux are beautifully kept. I can expect that the work will be done at night by fairy hands. It is a pleasant road which runs over the roots of the ridges towards Masham, a road bordering green meadows and pretty woods, but having no conspicuous interest until it debouches on the hillside above the town of Masham, and the valley of the Ure lies spread out below, wide and green, and set between low hills. Masham was a place of note in ancient days, being, indeed, the seat of the younger branch of the great family of Scrope. But they, like their cousins of the house of Bolton, perished off the earth long since; and even the church, a modern building of no striking beauty, contains no memorials of them.

I shall not loiter in this old hill-village, but push on by a somewhat scurvy road until I come to a wayside house which

T

marks the entrance to Hackfall Woods, which are beyond doubt
the loveliest spot upon the Ure, with the possible exception of
the falls at Aysgarth.   There is no luxuriance of beauty at the
outset, for the path by which one is admitted strays on beside
a little rivulet which is pretty enough, but by no means striking.
The ground drops quickly and the beck plunges down deep
dells of fern and bramble, making little falls and splashings
which are very pleasant to the ear ; while the woods tower up
on either hand, and through the green shadows of the trees, on
the very summit of the hill, there gleams a grey stone building,
catching the full power of the sun.   At last the path drops no
longer, and suddenly it leads out upon a little plateau overhanging the river, where a hut or summer-house has been built
for the accommodation of those who desire to loiter in these
woods, which must be among the most beautiful in Yorkshire.
For the river, which since it boiled over Aysgarth Falls has
rippled on for the most part quietly enough, now chattering,
now deep and silent, but rarely broken into foam, has found
once more a broken and a stony channel, and the black water
races through the gorge flecked with white, gleaming spray, and
walled in by fine scars of rock, over which the trees rise on both
sides the river in a sea of gold and green.   Far down the stream,
where it shoots away around another bend, a lofty rock stands
out boldly from the forest in the full glow of sunlight, its riven
precipices and brown weathered flanks adding to the outlook
over rushing river and exquisite gold woodland a sense of age
and immobility.

Fountains Abbey.

CHAPTER XIV

FOUNTAINS ABBEY

I SUPPOSE there is no doubt at all that every wise man, and especially every wise cyclist, would go from Hackfall by the road to Tanfield, in which wide and ancient village he might tickle his antiquarian tastes by examining the very splendid Marmion tombs in the church, might sketch the gatehouse of their castle, and best of all might idle away a happy hour on a bridge possessing all the qualities whose absence I deplored at Aysgarth. Moreover, he would go on from Tanfield by a good and pleasant road, skirting a park of ancient hawthorn trees so wide and beautiful as one may not often see in England, and thus come at last to comfortable Ripon, where he would find good entertainment worthy of the wise.

It is late for hawthorns now. They are turning brown in all the hedges : and the road by Tanfield has lost its most conspicuous beauty. Yet I doubt whether it is wise to go plunging

into such a mesh of bad and hilly cross-roads as I engage myself in for no better reason than to get a distant view of Ripon.
Let no one imitate me who has less than my placidity of temper ;
yet if he follow on my tracks, striking ultimately the good highway from Ripon to Pately Bridge, about three miles out from the

West Tanfield.

old cathedral city, he will see a view such as will linger in his
memory for many a day,—a rich country falling rapidly to a
deep hollow, a high ridge rising on the further side, and near
its top, backed up by dark woods and picturesque town build-

ings, the two square Minster towers standing grandly in the shadow.

There are many Ripons to be seen from many points in the surrounding country, but this is the only one which is really fine and striking ; for even the Ripon which confronts the wayfarer from Boroughbridge is not seen at such a distance, nor backed by such a noble hill. I turn away from the broad high road with a longing look at its smooth surface, and following the lane which turns off to Aldfield, pass quickly through a little group of hillside farms and cottages, until my attention is arrested by the shattered summit of a vast square tower rising out of the brown woods into the clear sunlight of the summer morning. So strong, so solid is the dark outline of this massive tower that only the swallows which dart through it out into the light again betray it to be a ruin. The broken pinnacles, the absolute stillness of the air, impress my fancy ; and the interest deepens when, following with my eye the contours of the ground, I see that what lies before me is no hillside tower, but one which rises from the very bottom of the valley.

A little further down the hill the road falls into woods again, and one is almost at the foot before seeing more than a pretty, narrow valley, with a steep ascent upon the further side. But at the bottom the road winds off upon an old stone bridge, which the monks may have flung across the noisy little river for better access to their mill ; and one has no sooner stepped out on this bridge than there comes in sight, built close under the steep escarpment of the rock, a house with shallow wings, so grey and old, and having a front so finely broken with tracery of window and intricacy of rich carving, so subdued in colouring, so worn into a harmony as perfect as that of a mossy bank, that I know not how to analyse or convey to others the delight with which I saw it. The river slips along beneath its front, bordered by an exquisite garden of old-fashioned and sweet-smelling flowers. There are high-clipped yew trees such as the world loved two centuries ago, and a round arched gateway of

the Jacobean days, up whose worn and slightly broken steps
yellow poppies bloom and seed themselves and flower year by
year.   This is Fountains Hall, a place which time has touched
very gently and with loving fingers since old Sir Stephen Proctor,
quarrying in the ruins of the abbey close at hand, wrought out
in stone this fancy so beautiful as to deserve forgiveness even
for the loss of that which he destroyed.

It is but a little way past the front of Fountains Hall,

Fountains Hall.

beneath high scars of rock upon the left, until one passes
under a mouldering archway which opens on a broad and
level sward occupying nearly all the valley bottom ; for here
the Skell sweeps suddenly aside and washes the high wooded
slopes upon the right.   On the other hand there are red walls
of cliff ; and set in the very centre of the meadow, stretching
well-nigh across the whole expanse, stands what I have dreamed
of and desired in vain to see throughout the whole route I have
travelled—a great abbey of the Cistercians, roofless it is true,

and sorely shattered, but neither shapeless nor desecrated, broken yet not ashamed, tended lovingly, and standing grand and solid to this hour with an aspect little changed since those old days when pilgrims and travellers knocked at the gate which now lies open, knowing well they would be fed and sheltered and sped upon their way again.

I say the place is but little changed ; and it is true, for here, alone among all the Yorkshire abbeys, is a ruin which is no puzzle even to the ignorant. There is still the empty window of the church, through which one sees the whole vast length of nave and choir, standing perfect save that the blue sky roofs it and that an even stretch of close-cropped turf gives it a floor more lovely than it ever had in its days of pride And there stretching far across the valley to the right is the long, low, round arcade of the domus conversorum, the workroom of the lay brethren, and above it the walls of the great dormitory, almost perfect in their height, so that I see an outline not very much unlike that which the Cistercians planned when, as the years of poverty passed by and riches showered down upon them, the little band of starving fugitives grew by their own energy into one of the greatest brotherhoods of England.

In this June weather a wonderful beauty has descended on the valley. For the first touch of summer has made the grass spring and the leaves bud fresh and vivid ; while underneath the shadow, far as one can see, along every slope right up to the wall of the abbey and far beyond, there flows a sea of luminous and tender blue, myriads of forget-me-nots flowering in the green grass. Far away under the shadow of the yews which top the red cliffs on the north one can see the soft azure glow ; down by the water's edge it gleams as brightly ; and up the hill, as far as where an old broken wall marks the limit of the monastery, the exquisite blue flush spreads over hillock and over hollow, round copse and tree trunk, while from the still sky, unbroken by a cloud, there descends a flood of early morning light so soft and lucent, casting so warm a radiance on the

magical expanse of flowers, that the heaven itself is not more
blue or lovely than the earth. A few weeks ago the whole
valley was adorned in the purity of snowdrops; but as the days
lengthen, and the sap rises in the trees, and the blood beats
higher in the heart of man, the old earth of Fountains, which
holds so many baffled schemes, where so many noble dreamers
have laid down their aspirations, puts forth this warmer and
more human plea, " Forget-me-not."

I cannot cast aside this plea. For what else did I come
but to remember those who wrought so greatly in this valley
in past days? I turn aside a little to my right, where there is
a thicket of yew and beech trees, amid which is one so ancient
that its vast girth and boughs are propped by strong supports,
so as to maintain as long as may be the ebbing life in its old
limbs. The Skell chatters down beneath the shadow of these
trees, a narrow, noisy rivulet, passing under an old mossy
bridge; and on the hillside just above there stand the wasted
remnants of two other yew trees, last of those seven which
beheld the first comers to the valley. Twelve hundred years
and more the sap has risen in those gnarled old trunks. They
were old already at Christmastide of 1132 when Archbishop
Turstan, on his way from keeping Noël at his house in Ripon,
dropped on this spot the thirteen monks whom he had rescued
from St. Mary's Abbey, as told in the third chapter of this
work. Those old yew trees saw them coming on that bleak
winter's day, saw the rich cavalcade which accompanied the
great archbishop, saw the thirteen brethren left in the wilderness in the gathering dusk, with little shelter or protection.

Skelldale was a place of evil reputation in those days, and
even four centuries afterwards men remembered that it had
been called Thefesdale. " It was a spot," says the old
chronicler of Fountains, "left uninhabited in all ages of
the past, a mere jungle of brambles, and so placed in the
hollow of hills and overhanging rocks that it seemed more fit
for the den of animals than for human use." In this solitary

waste these thirteen monks set themselves to realise their
dream of holiness. " It was sure a noble sight," the chronicler
. breaks out, "to see men girded with such faith and fervour
that they were not turned aside by the bitterness of winter, nor
the terror of their loneliness, nor yet by the lack of every kind
of goods. . . . In their purses was no money, in their barns no
corn, and for their daily food they had nothing save what the
occasional kindness of the archbishop sent them."

" In the centre of the valley," the chronicler goes on, "there
stood an elm tree, leafy after the manner of its kind, which
used to shelter beasts in winter and in summer, and to it these
holy men came for refuge, making beds upon the ground with
straw and stubble. . . . All slept or took their meals together
underneath this tree, a brotherhood poor indeed, yet mighty in
the Lord. . . . By night they rose for vigils, by day they set
themselves to labour, some weaving mats, some cutting wood
to build an oratory, some tilling garden plots. There was none
who ate the bread of idleness, or took his ease till wearied out
by toil. They came to meals when hungry, they lay down to
sleep when tired ; but of sadness or of murmuring there was not
one sound, but every man blessed God with gladness."

Now some time afterwards there descended a famine on that
land, and the holy men were vehemently stirred, for they had
neither bread to eat nor money to obtain it, yet a crowd of
poor flocked to them for succour. The abbot sought in all the
country round for bread and found none who could give it
him. There was want on every side, and at length they were
driven to take the leaves of the trees and the herbs that grew
upon the ground and make them into pottage. . . . And while
this famine lasted there knocked one day at the monastery gate
a certain wayfarer clamouring for aid in the name of Christ.
The porter answered that he had no bread, but the poor man cried
out the more that he was starving, and would not go until he
had an alms, begging that for Christ's sake the brethren would

ease his hunger. Now the porter being thus appealed to sought the abbot, and told him of the poor man's importunity ; and the abbot, struck with pity, sent for the brother who had charge of the loaves, and bade him give to the suppliant. But the brother said that there remained for the use of all the monastery only two loaves and a half, which were wanted for certain workmen whose time for meals was at hand. " Give one loaf to the poor man," said the abbot, "and keep the rest for the workmen. Let God provide as He will for us." So the poor man took his loaf and went. And lo ! there stood before the gate two men from Knaresborough, driving a cart laden up with loaves, sent by Eustace Fitzjohn, to relieve the brethren.

Such was the struggle of this little band of pioneers against poverty and every adverse circumstance that could daunt the heart of man ; and there came a time when, wearied out with labour and anxiety, they lost their courage, and had no longer any hope of maintaining themselves in the lonely vale of Fountains, so that they resolved to send their abbot to St. Bernard at Clairvaulx, to set before him, as their father, how great had been their sufferings, and how fruitless. So the abbot went and told his tale ; and St. Bernard was moved to compassion, and bade him bring the monks across the sea, and place them in a grange which he would give them, where they might follow out their vows in peace and safety. But while the abbot was still in France, there died at York one Hugh, dean of the cathedral, a man of great wealth ; and God put it in his heart that for the welfare of his soul he should betake himself with all his goods to the monastery of Fountains. And shortly after, a canon of York, one Serlo, who was also wealthy, did the same ; so that when the abbot returned to the north country the afflictions of the brethren were already at an end ; and from that time the abbey grew and flourished with abundant strength, sending out colonies who carried the rule of the Cistercians into distant lands, and adding year by year to the grandeur of their abbey buildings till they reared the vast pile which makes this lovely valley famous over all the world.

It is true all this was very long ago, and as I glance out through the trees, across the sparkling stream, and down the flower-strewn slopes to the old broken walls of church and cloister, I realise, with a little shudder, how many generations of mankind have been born and died since the first wattled huts were set up in this valley. But the tale of man's suffering and labours is never old and never fails to touch our hearts, whether it be of to-day or of a thousand years ago, and the noblest memory of this valley is still that of the poor enthusiasts who sought to hew a path to heaven over thorns, and who, we need not doubt, did actually find it.

There is a path which leads out of the thicket up on the side of the hill above the abbey, whence one may look down at the whole pile of buildings, and marvel at the skill with which the monks, when cramped for space by the narrowness of the valley, threw out tunnels over the stream and built across it up to the very margin of the valley. And here in the rock wall which the pathway skirts is a well set back under a pretty arch-way, bearing the name of the great outlaw with whose exploit I should perhaps have begun the story of Fountains, for, indeed, it was not likely that a sequestered dale called Thefesdale would have no tale to tell us about Robin Hood. The monks are said to have preserved bold Robin's bow ; and though this may be a fable, yet we need not doubt that they held in vast respect the vagrant earl who robbed so piously, and gave so freely to the poor, and was actually worsted and tossed into the Skell by one of their own cloth.

It was, I suppose, before the days when Turstan brought hither the truant monks of St. Mary's, that the curtal friar kept the dale against all comers. I grow tired when I attempt to reconcile the dales, so it is better not to try. However, there

the curtal friar was, and his fame was an annoyance to Robin
Hood.

> So Robin he took a solemn oath,—
>   It was by Mary free ;
> That he would neither eat nor drink
>   Till that friar he did see.

The vow was perhaps more valorous than prudent ; for if it
is ill jesting between a fu' man and a fasting, it is even worse
fighting ; and that Robin might have known. Yet it is for
these follies that we love the man, and our hearts go with
him—mine does at any rate—as he travelled off to find the friar.

> And coming into Fountains dale
>   No further would he ride,
> There was he ware of the curtal friar
>   Walking by the water's side.
>
> The friar had on a harnesse good,
>   And on his head a cap of steel.
> Broad sword and buckler by his side,
>   And they became him weel.

What a freshness and lusty insolence there is about this fiction
what an atmosphere as of the morning of the world.

> Robin Hood lighted off his horse,
>   And tied him to a thorn :
> "Carry me over, thou curtal friar,
>   Or else thy life's forlorne."

Now the friar instead of resenting this insolence by felling Robin
to the earth, took him meekly on his back and carried him across
the Skell

> Lightly leapt Robin off the friar's back.
>   The friar said to him againe,
> "Carry me over the water, thou fine fellow,
>   Or it shall breed thee paine."

And Robin, not having yet made up his mind about the friar,
or settled with himself how far a bout with him would be enjoy-
able, took the corseletted man of peace upon his back, and
carried him again to the bank from which they came. But on

[To face page 284

"*Robin Hood and Littlejohn.*'

the way he made up his mind, and had no sooner set the friar
down than he repeated :

> "Carry me over the water, my fine fellow,
>   Or it shall breed thee paine."
>
> The friar took Robin on's back again,
>   And stept in to the knee ;
> Till he came at the middle stream,
>   Neither good nor bad spoke he.
>
> And coming to the middle stream
>   There he threw Robin in
> And "Chuse thee, chuse thee, fine fellow,
>   Whether thou wilt sink or swim."
>
> Robin Hood swam to a bush of broome,
>   The friar to a wigger wand,
> Bold Robin Hood is gone to shore,
>   And took his bow in his hand.
>
> One of the best arrowes under his belt,
>   To the friar he did let fly,
> The curtal friar with his steel buckler,
>   He put that arrow by.
>
> Robin Hood shot passing well
>   Till his arrowes all were gone.
> They took their swords and steel bucklers
>   They fought with might and maine.

I really cannot spare the time to recount this battle in all its
incidents ; and it is the less necessary to do so since I suppose
most of us remember how the two men fought valiantly up and
down the meadow without result, till bold Robin sought a boon,
to wit, that he might blow a blast upon his horn ; and how the
friar, breathless but undismayed, replied rudely, that he hoped
his foe would blow so well that both his eyes would drop out.
And what followed ? Why,

> Robin Hood set his horn to his mouth
>   He blew out blastes three ;
> Half a hundred yemen with bowe bent
>   Came raking o'er the lea.

I fancy this must have been the only occasion on which Robin showed a disposition to hit below the belt ; but it profited him little, for the friar at once capped his stroke by asking leave to "set my fist unto my mouth, and whute whutes three," and at the whutes half a hundred bandogs came running o'er the lea. And then . . . but why go on ? do not we all know how the yeoman shot at the bandogs, and how the bandogs caught the arrows in their mouths, and how at last both parties called a truce and joined their forces, and the curtal friar became as famous in all Sherwood as Little John himself, or as Maid Marian, or any other of that group of immortal deities of the great forest, who have come down to us through the night of time, fresh and dewy, and carrying the odour of the woodlands and all the wondrous beauties of the age of pure romance. Who cares in what century of this dull world they lived ? Where is the man who will try to bring them down from the lovely land of fancy where they dwell into the thick air of history, and the gross realm of fact ? Why, they have soared above it all, as much as a butterfly with gold and azure on its wings is above its chrysalis ! In God's name let them stay there, and delight us still, though all the professors in the kingdom seek to prove them shadows !

Well, I have done with Robin for the time, and, indeed, his horn has but little right to ring among these hollows, where for so many longer years it was the chanting of the monks which broke the silence of the winter's night and the early summer dawn, when the grey light came stealing down the crags, and the first whistles of the thrushes responded to the echoes from the lighted church. From this spot where I stand beside the well I look down on the great range of ruined offices— no shapeless mass of humped and neglected mounds, as at Rievaulx—but a clear and ordered sequence of apartments, leading to the great hall of the Abbot's house, where the bases of the pillars still remain in a grand double colonnade, and one set up erect proclaims how noble was the beauty which has been reft from us. I go down by a steep path and stand in

the warm sunshine in the very centre of the hall. Ruined as
it is, all is yet so beautiful that there is nothing to regret. The
broken pillars are exquisitely stained with lichen, and little
flowering plants with delicate tendrils and white blossoms have
rooted themselves in the clefts and wrinkles of the crumbling
stone. Before me there lies spread out the long narrow valley,
of which the Abbey occupies the gate—a vast expanse of lush
green meadow land, dappled thickly with buttercups, closed in
on either hand by high, dark woods, ringing with the melodious
whistle of the blackbirds and with the chatter of the noisy
river.

Here, or in some chamber giving on this hall, it was doubtless that the Abbot Thirsk, last but one to occupy a dignity
which would have been better bestowed on a better man, had
those queer interviews with a goldsmith from Cheapside which
were commented upon so sharply by the commissioners sent
out by Secretary Thomas Cromwell when he was preparing the
Dissolution. " Please it your mastershippe to understand,"
so ran the dutiful address of the scandalised commissioners,
" please it your mastershippe to understand that th' Abbot
of Fontance hath so gretly dilapidate his howse, wastede the
woods . . . diffamede here a toto populo. Six days before
our accesse to this monastere, he committede theft and
sacrilege, confessyng the same. At mydnyghte he causede his
chapelaine to stele the sexten's keis and towke out a jewel, a
crosse of gold with stones. One Warren, a goldsmith of the
Chepe, was with him in his chambre at that howre, and then
they stole out a gret emerode with a rubie. The said Warren
made the Abbot believe the rubie to be but a garnet, and so for
that he payede nothing. For the emerode but xx *li.* He
sowlde hym also plate without weight or ounces. Howe much
th' Abbot therfore therin was deceived he cannot tell, for the
trewith ys he is a varra fole and a miserable ideote."

Thus angerly wrote the worthy commissioners ; and a more
delightful instance of Satan reproving sin is, I should think,

scarce to be found in the annals of mankind. The Abbot committed theft and sacrilege when he sold the plate? Perhaps he did ; and what was the nature of the act committed by the King when he gave the whole of Fountains to Sir Thomas Gresham not four years afterwards? Had I been Abbot, and seen that blow coming, as those surely did on whom it fell, I should have stripped the treasury of all its jewels, and had up, not a single goldsmith from the Chepe but every one who would make the journey, rather than leave the contents of the shrines and treasuries as a prize for greedy courtiers, Unscrupulous the Abbot may have been, but his conduct was no proof of folly ; and, indeed, the affectation of simplicity is so naturally assumed by the weak seeking to justify themselves before the strong, that I am disposed to guess that Thirsk was in truth no more a "miserable ideote" than the two commissioners themselves.

But what a light this throws on the scramble for the treasures of the monasteries which was going on in those last years before the old foundations were broken up ! Was Warren the only goldsmith from the Chepe who scented from afar the wondrous bargains which might be wrenched from the sore necessities of the monks? Surely there must have been a regular stampede of honest traders out of Goldsmiths' Row into all the solitary valleys of the realm, where the munificence of past ages had stored up such priceless jewels, such wonders of rich work in gold and silver, that scarce has there arisen any such chance for plunder or keen bargaining since England was a kingdom.

Sinner as he may have been, old Abbot Thirsk saw some nobility of action before he closed his eyes on a world which had grown troublesome to monks ; for he joined the Pilgrimage of Grace, and whether it was with his own good will or not, it can scarce be that he rode to Doncaster with Robert Aske and picked up no crumbs of gallantry and courage on the way. At any rate he swung at Tyburn side by side with the Abbot of

Jervaulx, and so takes his place for ever in that long roll of
gentlemen who gave their lives for a cause which none can call
unworthy, whether he esteem it wrong or right. He was succeeded in his office by one Marmaduke Bradley, a very wise
monk in the opinion of the commissioners, with which doubtful
praise I should be content to pass him by, were it not that old
Jenkins used to come and see him. Jenkins, at the time when
Bradley ruled at Fountains, was butler to Lord Conyers at
Hornby in the gate of Swaledale : and used to be sent frequently to Fountains to inquire how the Abbot did. Jenkins's
word is, of course, the sole authority for the passage of these
courtesies ; but the interesting thing is his account of how the
monks regaled him. The Abbot always ordered him, he said,
a quarter of a yard of roast beef for refreshment,—nine inches of
good solid beef. I wish he had told us the thickness of it ; but
so far as one can judge, it must have been a portentous meal.
He had besides wassel, served in a horned cup ; and while thus
banqueting, old Jenkins saw very nearly the last of Fountains and
its monks, for Abbot Bradley ruled for no more than three
years, and then the crash came. The monks were driven out
of the Eden they had made, stripped of the revenues they had
perhaps abused, and Fountains Abbey, that great and lordly
House of God, entered on the path of ruin which has given us
the wondrous beauty of to-day.

Clear and sparkling, flashing under trails of ivy and a hundred
creeping plants which trail their tendrils in the water, the Skell
goes murmuring through the old arched tunnels out into the
dappled sunlight, filling all the valley with a pleasant sound.   I
walk on through what was once the Abbot's garden, to the east
end of the church, where an archway leads me to the Chapel of
the Nine Altars, whose lofty pillars are a miracle of grace,
and so I stroll all through the building, stopping now to
wonder at the grandeur of the arches, now at the tender
grace of the trailing ivy which drops down, all vivid with the
sunlight, between each of the barrel arches of the aisles ; now

U

pausing in the great Refectory, now in the Chapter House, till
there is borne in upon my mind a great pity for the loss of the
ideals which led men to conceive this exceeding splendour.   Do
we not know how a man loves anything which he has wrought
and fashioned with his own intelligence ; how his aim expands,
how it gains nobility, and his heart shows him uses for his work
of which he never dreamed when he began to labour?   Such,
and a thousand times greater, was the love of the better class
of monks for this great Abbey, and such the measure of. their

Fountains Abbey.

sorrow when those who had no care for the ends they cherished
wrested the tool out of their hands, and would not even use it
for a noble purpose, but broke and blunted it in mere
debauchery.

And so I come at last to the *domus conversorum*, opening out
of the first bay of the nave upon the southern side, cool, dark,
and grandly vaulted.   Through the empty windows the sun
casts flickering lights across the floor, and from the river flowing
just without, wavering reflections dance among the black arches
of the roof.   In this long, solemn cloister is no sign of ruin ;

and as I pace along its vast length, letting my sight stray here
and there among the clustered shadows at the foot of the great
pillars, past and present melt insensibly together, the music of
the running stream puts on all the modulations of a low and
distant chanting, swelling and falling ; and it is only by an effort
of imagination that I am able to realise there is no solemn
function in the Church behind me ; no busy concourse in the
Chapter House; no white-robed Cistercians stepping gravely with
their downcast looks up the hillside or treading down among
the flowers ; that the hive is empty, both of bees and drones,
and that I, who pace under this superb arcade, half-timid at
the sound of my own footfall—a layman, a stranger, and an
alien in creed, may wander where I will into the most
sacred of those chambers which were once seen by the brethren
alone.

I turn out again into the place of flowers, and before I go,
stand once more in wonder at the strange, soft beauty of the blue
flush which covers all the ground,

> " Those dressed in blue
> Have lovers true."

So says an old north country rhyme ; and, indeed, if Fountains,
which does but pass from one form of beauty to another all the
year, ever lacked true lovers, it would not be in the few days
when the forget-me-nots are flowering on the slopes.   It is so
that Fountains comes back always on my memory, and I see
again wide fields of luminous soft blue, out of which the Abbey
rises grey and stern, while the ancient tower soars up into the
clear air and sunlight, and the swallows skim through the openings of the shattered windows.

My way leads out of Fountains by the Hall again ; but
before I go I ought to say a word of the great beauty of
the gardens of Studley Royal, which one reaches by following
the valley ; of the grandeur of the trees which flourish in that

U 2

sheltered spot, and even more of the generosity with which Lord
Ripon throws all, or almost all, of his beautiful domain open
to visitors, to wander where they will.   But, indeed, my gratitude to him for the care he spends on Fountains absorbs all
other feelings ; and I can but wish and wish again, though
with little hope, that certain other gentlemen in Yorkshire, who
have become the guardians of ruins scarce less precious, would
but remember how gracious an act it is to render public services
which no man can demand of them.

I pass out again by Fountains Hall, and climb up the hill
upon my left, whence I have a fine backward view of Fountains,
from which, however, my attention is called off by the singular
outline of a pointed hill which rises a little way before me,
carrying a small building surmounted by a cross, which I should
set down as a hermitage or chapel, did I not see garments
indescribable flapping on a clothes-line underneath the sacred
emblem.   Hermits, as all men know, never washed.   Did not
St. Cuthbert banish soap and water from his island save when,
once a year, he received a visit from the monks of Lindisfarne?
It cannot, therefore, be a holy man who dwells there ; yet I am
not on that account less anxious to go up it, and as I trudge up
its steep sides, I discover that it must be Howe Hill, and that
in truth there was once long ago a chapel standing where now
a labouring man rears pigs and poultry, and hopes the devil
will not come again within his time as once he did to view the
country all round from this high eminence.   I suppose I may
as well say what the devil wanted.   There can be no danger in
my speaking of him, when I have just rendered so long homage
to the monks.   It was Aldborough which excited the ire of the
irritable fiend—an ancient Roman city on the hither side of
those Hambledon Hills which are just coming into sight, blue
and sulphurous in the haze of the afternoon.   I shall not see
Roman Aldborough even from this high ground, for it was
all destroyed and buried, history says by the Danes, and legend

by the devil. At any rate, the devil got on the very top of this peaked hill, and setting one foot before and the other behind, he sang out in a voice of thunder :—

> " Borobrigg, keep out of the way !
> For Aulboro town
> I will ding down. "

Which he accordingly did with huge bolts of stone, of which the incredulous, if there be any, may see no less than three sticking bolt upright in the ground near the doomed and miserable town at which the devil hurled them.

But if the vestiges of Aldborough are not in sight, there is, at any rate, a noble and inspiring view spread out before me. For Ripon lies, as I have said, on the last undulations of the broken hill country which occupies the whole of Western Yorkshire, and the height of Howe Hill is enough to top the ridge on which the old town lies, and give a clear, wide view over the great plain, lying green and rich and broken with red farmsteads up to the very foot of the great Hambledons upon the east ; while southwards it expands so far that all the·outlines melt in haze, and the sight loses itself in an infinitely soft misty blur, just where people say that in clear weather York Minster raises her twin towers on the very sky line. I would that the Cathedral were in sight, for the distant view of that great Minster, which has in all ages summed up the grandeur of the life 'twixt Tees and Don, and made itself a central point in all the stormy vicissitudes of Yorkshire, would be a fitting background to a prospect which ranges almost from the Field of Marston to that on which was fought the Battle of the Standard.

Looking down upon this noble country, studded with famous houses, sown with tragedies, a man might muse daylong on tales which find their niche in history or legend. But the afternoon is waning fast, and I am due at a certain farm I know of. I must tell my tales to-morrow ; and so I saunter down

the hill again, and strike across the summer lanes till I reach a
pleasant meadow, where a little stream runs down through its
own well-wooded valley to the Skell.   Just at the head of this
tributary valley, where the pasture breaks off and the woods
begin, there stands a goodly farm, a long, low house facing to
the south, so that the roses climbing round its windows catch
the sunlight.   In the porch stand the farmer and his wife with
a north-country welcome, than which none other is more cordial
and frank.   The house is full of the sweet odour of fresh-baked
bread.   In the house place, large enough to seat fifty people, a
Yorkshire supper is set out, such as those who have sat down
to it may well dream of all their days, and the hospitality is graced
with kindness so downright and so frank that the time goes by
without my marking it.   When I go to the door again, the moon
has risen high and silvery over the dale.   The apple trees are
still in flower, and a sloping gravel path runs down beneath
them till it is lost among tall woods, out of which the plashing
of the little stream rings out plainly over the still fields.   The
birds have done singing, and the night is falling fast.   There is
a keenness in this northern air, after sundown, which makes it
comfortable to shut the door, and see the lamplight gleaming
on the old polished pans and pewter hanging from the wall, and
listen to the farmer's stories of old life which he remembers,
until my hostess shows me to a room all sweet with lavender,
and telling me some story of a ghost which haunts it, to
which vain legend I pay no more heed than any tired man
would give it, leaves me to my slumber.

CHAPTER XV

RYE pudding makes, as I am told, an excellent dish to set before hungry men. It is not that they like it, as a rule ; indeed, I have not yet heard of any one who chose it for a birthday feast, or who begged his cook to make him one because he loved it. But it is clogging to the appetite, and is thus high in favour with those housewives who have many mouths to feed. There was one such worthy dame at Markenfield, not far from Fountainsdale. Her rye puddings were daily set before her twelve farm labourers, and they were as hard as brickbats, and the twelve men loathed them. Now, one day a noble pudding of this kind had just been taken from the copper, and was being borne in state into the Great Hall at Markenfield by four strong men, when suddenly it bounced off the dish and began to roll. The four men grabbed at it, but it rolled too fast and went by them easily, bounding nimbly through the hall, banging open the door, which stood ajar, and so out into the quadrangle, across which it skimmed and twisted as if shot out of a catapult, till, underneath the outer gateway, it encountered the twelve labourers coming into dinner. Right into the midst of them it charged, while the men, who had never seen a rye pudding acting so before, scattered right and left in terror. But one, more plucky than the rest, threw his reaping-hook at it as it went by, and hit it,

and split it open. Otherwise, so I am told, there is but little
doubt that the pudding would have been rolling to this hour.

Now this is a notable event; and I know some other reasons
for seeking out Markenfield; so that it will be time well spent
to diverge from the direct road to Ripon, crossing one or two
pretty fields—all fields are pretty in this angle of the earth—
and penetrating a small wood, till we reach the old grey hall
lost in the middle of the meadows. Doubtless there was once
a fit approach to Markenfield; but I have never found it.
One wanders up and down among a maze of gates and sheep-
folds; and, after floundering to and fro sufficiently, one emerges
on the corner of a moat, one scarce knows how. A small
bridge thrown across the moat leads into a fine courtyard, on
the further side of which the great windows of the Hall and
Chapel break the irregular outline of the centre building. The
house is of many periods; some part, perhaps, as ancient as
the Edwards; some betraying by its handsome windows that it
was built in an age when there was but little fear of Scots' in-
cursions. In this wide courtyard the tenantry must have been
mustered for the march to Flodden, where Sir Ninian Markenfield held a command; and here, too, three generations later,
there were gatherings in a cause perhaps as gallant, but by far
less glorious. For Thomas Markenfield, grandson of the old
warrior just named, was one of those north-country gentlemen
who, in the days when English Catholics had hopes of setting
Mary Stuart on the throne, and were busy seeking aid from
Alva and his Spanish pikes, met at the Percies' house of Maiden
Bower in Topcliffe, not ten miles away to the east of Ripon,
and there sat waiting for news that the men of the East Country
were up, with the Duke of Norfolk at their head. But the
Duke was taken, and the eastern counties did not rise; and
the gallant company of gentlemen at Topcliffe would have
done well to ride back to their homes again. But rarely did a
Percy or a Neville hold his hand from a rebellion; and many
another gentleman who sat beside them on that October night

at Topcliffe was sick at heart with disappointed hope that he
might live to hear mass sung again in Ripon Minster, and to
see the monks march back again to empty Fountains in a long
procession.   Markenfield himself had lived many years abroad
because England Protestant was distasteful to him ; and
coming home for one purpose only, had found a fiery
coadjutor in Richard Norton, whose name is still remembered here at Ripon, where he dwelt at Norton Conyers, as
clearly as at Bolton, where the verse of Wordsworth has linked
it with associations among the loveliest in literature.

"The residue of your doltish captaines," broke out another
Norton in an "Addresse to the Quene's Majestie's poor
deceived Subjects of the North," "the residue of your doltish
captaines, what be they ? Thinke you they be men able to
beare you out against the power of a prince, all his nobilitie,
cities, realme, subjectes, frendes, and allies ? One with little
witte far sette (Swynborne), another in his old age weary of his
wealth (Norton), another a runneaway with a young wilde
braine tickled to see fashions." This last was Markenfield, as
an unfriendly and contemptuous opponent saw him ; and since
every man may belabour the fugitive adherent of a lost cause,
it has been scarce worth the while of any wanderer in these
bypaths of history to correct or test the judgment. What does
it matter now whether Markenfield was light of wit or not ?   It
is not always those whose brains are firm and steady who figure
best in the judgment of posterity. Perhaps poor Markenfield,
when he thought of Mary Stuart languishing at Tutbury, was
blinded by a glamour which turned many an older head than
his. But does any one think it was self-interest which made
him mount his horse here for the last time on that October
day, and ride off to tilt against the Government of Elizabeth
Tudor, who neither pardoned nor forgot ? Idealist he may
have been, but there was no mean motive in his heart when he
staked the home and possessions of an ancient family, and set
out upon that quest whence in a few short weeks he sped back

a broken fugitive, a landless exile, who saved his life with difficulty oversea. Even his young brother John, a lad not twenty at the time, was attainted, so that there might be no male heir entitled to the lands ; and so perished the old family of Markenfield, lost like many another in this great kingdom by adherence to a cause which, having ceased to touch men's reason, did but appeal the more passionately and poignantly to their hearts.

I do not doubt that in all parts of England there have been many found who staked their lives as nobly as the Yorkshire-men upon a falling cause. Nor do I fail to see that in the great revolts which have seared the life and beauty of that vast county, there were many motives : much love of turbulence and fighting, not a little frothy passion, doubtless many mean and selfish ends to serve. But in looking down the centuries, and marking how the Yorkshiremen clung with the whole power of their strong and simple wills to first one and then another of the lost causes in this kingdom ; how they were Cavaliers among the noblest ; how they rose in two armed revolts on behalf of the old religion which they loved ; how the Red Rose of King Henry and the White Hart of the Second Richard were enshrined in the hearts of rich and poor alike, long after the last lance had been splintered and the last blood shed which was poured out so freely for those fugitive and unhappy monarchs ; when I remember all these acts of pure devotion, I am inclined to credit the men of York with carrying, under a somewhat rough exterior, all the faith and courage of idealists. One respects good judgment, but one very often loves the bad.

As I turn away and regain the rough lane which leads me towards Ripon, I can see beyond the ridge where the Minster lies in morning shadow a mass of woods which catch the sun-light. There, or thereabouts, lies the house of Norton Conyers, home of that old Richard Norton, who was so fierce a fellow-rebel with Markenfield and Swynborne. It is a noble house, and I would fain ride out there where the memories of the

Rebellion lie so thick, and thence to Topcliffe, that ancient village of the Percies, where so many plots were hatched. But " Maiden Bowere," that great mansion of the noblest and most

Ripon.

tragic Yorkshire house, is nothing but a grassy mound, and Topcliffe is only a wide, silent village, sleeping on the memory of its stormy days. There are men yet in the village who will point out with a certain awe the lineal descendant of him who led a mob against the house of Maiden Bower four centuries ago, and slew with his own hand Henry, Fourth Earl Percy—so long does the memory of tragedies linger in country places in the North. But for the most part the villagers of Topcliffe value as their chief celebrity a certain villager who is old enough to remember that in the days when half the coaches for the North stopped to change horses at the inn, he and other urchins used to listen for the first distant tootling of the horn, and scurry down and scramble for the penny which was the guerdon of the boy who first caught the leader's head.

There is nothing else to be found at Topcliffe; but there clings a tale to Norton Conyers which is well worth telling. Long after the Nortons had been lost and scattered, the estate was the property of Sir Richard Graham, who, following the losing side as resolutely as any Norton, was sore wounded on the field of Marston Moor; and when the day was lost, and he himself, spent and bleeding, had no longer power to strike one blow for the King, he turned his horse's head towards his home at Ripon, with the sole desire to die among his own people and under his own roof. But Cromwell—so the story runs—had watched Sir Richard riding off the field, and resolved that he should not so escape, and came riding in his traces at the full speed of his great warhorse. But Sir Richard had the lead, and was well mounted, and his horse smelt home. So the two men galloped through the summer dusk, through Hammerton and Boroughbridge, and by a score of farms where the lights were out and labouring men and women were sleeping without thought of war, till Sir Richard gained his home far in advance of Cromwell, and lay down in his chamber hoping to die in peace. But the breath was still in his body when Cromwell thundered up, and without dismounting rode straight into the hall and up the staircase and into the chamber where Sir Richard lay—you may see the impression of his horse's hoof on the top of the oak staircase to this day; and there, in

a very ecstasy of fury took the dying man in his gauntleted
arms and shook him till he died.

Such is the wild tale which legend, seeking always to localise
itself on well-known people, has fathered upon Cromwell.   It is
a striking piece of folklore, and I hardly care to point out that

Ripon Cathedral.

it does not square with the known facts about Sir Richard
Graham, since it belongs obviously to an age far more remote.
But here is Ripon, an unimpressive spot when one approaches
it from this side, though, as I have said, a rare, picturesque old

town when seen from the proper quarter. A steep street leads
up to a wide, square market-place, rather picturesque, though
once, surely, it must have boasted a fine cross, where an ugly
obelisk now stands. Out of this square a narrow lane runs
down to the Cathedral, small, but pure in style, and having a
west front of austere simplicity, which is probably as fine an
example of Early English as could be found. In a county
where noble churches were less common, Ripon would hold an
honourable place. But in Yorkshire it suffers from the force of
contrast. I remember Beverley, and Ripon leaves me cold.
Silent and empty stand the aisles which were once so thronged
with pilgrims, and many a day has gone by since St. Wilfrid,
who breathed courage into the hearts of the warriors beneath
his banner on the plain beyond Northallerton, has cared to
show that he remembers his ancient city on the Ure. There
were wondrous stories told about this city once—or, rather,
about the Monastery round which it grew. For here St.
Cuthbert sojourned when a young man ; and being guest-
master for the monks, was blessed so far as to receive an angel
of the Lord. For going out early to the Hospice on a winter
morning while it was still not day, he found a young man sitting
there whom he conceived to have travelled through the night
and snow, and to have turned aside at dawn in search of rest.
So he gave him water to wash his hands, and himself bathed and
wiped the stranger's feet, chafing them with his hands and
warming them in his own bosom ; and he begged the guest to
stay till the third hour of the day, that he might take food and
start refreshed upon his road again. The stranger answered
that he was travelling to an abode very far away, and that he
could not linger ; but Cuthbert was the more urgent, and
implored him in the name of God that he would not depart without refreshment. So the guest stayed ; and after the prayers of
the hour of tierce were over, and meal time was at hand,
Cuthbert laid the table and brought food, and hurried away in
search of some new bread, which he thought must then be

ready. But when he returned he found no guest, and going to the door, and looking out over the new-fallen snow, he saw no print of feet upon the threshold, nor any sign to show which way the traveller had gone. So wondering greatly, he turned back into the guest-room, and found it full of a marvellous sweet savour, and looking round to see whence that odour came he saw three loaves of extraordinary whiteness lying warm beside him. And he said, trembling, "I see that he whom I received was an angel of God, coming to feed, not to be fed. Lo ! this earth cannot produce such loaves as he has brought,

Ripon Cathedral.

for they excel lilies in whiteness, roses in scent, and honey in savour. Clearly they have not sprung from this heavy earth of ours, but from the Paradise of Eden. And no marvel that he who enjoys the Eternal Bread of Life in Heaven should refuse to partake of earthly food."

It is a thousand years and more since the angel visitor fled away from the monastery gate over the untrodden snow ; and Cuthbert, who chafed the stranger's feet and warmed them in his own bosom, has slept almost as long in Durham, himself a saint, and the best loved memory in the Church history of

northern England. In all Ripon I doubt if five people know
this tale; though in a city set so plainly on the bedrock of a
vast antiquity, men's thoughts must often be turned backwards
to the lives of those who dwelt before them on the hillock by
the Ure. Even the horn which is blown nightly by the market
cross might serve to carry back imagination almost as far as the
horn of Bainbridge ; for indeed that blast has rung through the
market place of Ripon night by night for more centuries than
any one remembers, a summons out of old past times, a
challenge to our careless minds and hurrying feet to pause when
the rush of work is over and silence is dropping on the city,
and remember that we who count these cities ours did not
make them, but are only travellers through, bound to pass on
like all the others, giving place like them to new generations,
who will set aside our claim to ownership with just the same
haughty insolence towards the dead.

As I turn down the hill and pass through the lower quarter
of the town, where the river slips by quietly beneath an old
stone bridge, I have some trouble in remembering that this is,
indeed, the water which came over Aysgarth Falls, so tamed and
broken is the wild mountain freshness which streamed down
the limestone shelves in Wensleydale. Some anticipation of its
outfall into the sluggish Ouse has sobered the wilful river,
which slips along between the meadows towards Newby as if it
had no thought but to reflect the hawthorn and wild roses. But
in the winter, Ure is often turned into a deep and swirling
torrent ; and I do not know how I can go on by the road to
Boroughbridge without mentioning the tragedy which happened
thirty years ago a little way below this spot, and which has left
on the minds of most men living in the district a trace of terror
and of pity which will last their lives.

There was a large flat-bottomed ferry-boat which plied across
the river by a chain just opposite to Newby Hall ; and on
February 4th, 1869, the York and Ainsty Hunt, after a fine run
from Monkton Whin, came down this way. The fox took the

water; and the hunt crowded into the ferry boat, men and horses, some dismounted and some riding still. The river was high and flowing rapidly. The chain ran on one side of the boat, which had thus a natural tendency to tilt downwards on that side. The boat was overcrowded, men and horses were alike excited, and when near the bank, Sir Charles Slingsby's horse began to kick. Other horses became restive, and pressed down towards the chain. The next moment Sir Charles Slingsby's horse leapt overboard, and in an instant the boat turned over like the leaf of a book. No one who saw that awful scene cares to speak much of it. Sir Charles, last heir of a race as noble as any in the north, was lost with two other members of the hunt, as well as the huntsman and both ferry-men.

There is no lack of tragedies both old and modern on this country side; and here already are the wide dull streets of Boroughbridge, where some may spare a thought of pity for the great Earl Thomas of Lancaster, who was beheaded at Ponte-fract, as I have said already. For it was here that after waiting vainly for the Scots, on whose aid he reckoned, he flung himself on his knees before a crucifix in a chapel of the town, crying out, "Good Lord, I render myself to Thee, and put myself in Thy mercy." But he erred, for it was into the mercy of that weak and violent monarch the second Edward, that he put himself; and the king's mercy ended in the edge of the sword on a hillock outside Pontefract. Let him go by out of memory; for, worshipped as he was by the common people, I doubt if he was in truth heroic. It is a greater and an older tragedy which makes this region famous; but to find its scene we must go on from Boroughbridge for a mile or so, till we come to a small sloping village, set pleasantly on the side of a low hill, in the midst of a rich and fertile country, studded with orchards and gardens, where masses of pinks and stocks and every other fresh sweet-scented flower fill the air with fragrance. So bright and sweet is all the country round that it is easy to believe that this

may indeed have been the summer city of the Romans, the
pleasant quarters among fields to which those rulers fled
when the low streets of York grew thick and sultry, or
when in autumn the vapours from the marshy shore of Ouse
set them longing for the sweet air that blows down from the
moors.

Few people who pass through this long irregular village could
dream that any relics of a splendid past lay hidden in the earth.
For above ground there is no sign of ruin, no indication of
importance in the past, no hint that the pretty village had
caught up a tale which it could not finish, or thrust itself upon
a site which still possessed the prestige of former greatness.
You will go into the garden of the inn, and follow your guide
down all its length till you come to a rough shed, just such a
one as any gardener might use for tools. The guide unlocks
it, discloses a floor thickly strewn with sawdust on which he
begs you not to step ; and while you stand aside, wondering
a little whether anything of value can indeed be stored up in so
poor a place, he seizes a broom, and brushing off the sawdust
reveals a mass of glowing colours, out of which but little of the
beauty has yet faded, though fifteen centuries or more have
passed since the cubes of the mosaic were set by the cunning
workman in the wet cement. A star of eight points issues from
a circle, the whole a miracle of dainty workmanship, a gem of
colour, surely the masterpiece of some great craftsman who
came from over seas at the summons of a lord of wealth and
power.

The sun gleams through the open doorway on the vivid
colours. The guide stands leaning on his mop. Just outside
there is a bed of onions, and a pile of baskets waiting for the
crop of ripening strawberries. But this fine pavement was not
set in any garden. It must have been the ornament of some
great noble's house. Day by day the shadows of a pillared
colonnade slanted over it, and all this ground now given up to
raspberries was doubtless set with statues and with fountains,

triumphs of craft as precious as the pavement. "Surely," one
thinks, "it was the country villa of some great official, count
of the Saxon shore, or master of a legion." A few yards away
there is another pavement, and in a cottage higher up the
street there is a third, and in all Aldborough there are no less
than nine entire, with relics of some others ; while you cannot
scratch the soil in any spot within the circuit of the old city
walls without the prospect of disclosing pottery, or tools, or
coins, such as were long known as "Aldborough pennies," and
seem actually to have formed a currency in the district by their
very plenty—bronze of Constantine and Hadrian passed at the
village shop, or paid to wipe off the score for beer chalked up
behind the tavern door !

Thus it is clear that in old days when the Roman wall held
back the Picts in their own wild country, Isurium—such was
the name of the lost city—was a group of palaces. One asks
what was the end of all that splendour ; and the question is
one that is very quickly answered. For here and there where
excavations have been made, there is found strewn over all the
ruins of the buildings a layer of dense fine ashes. Not in one
spot or two, where it might have been heaped up by chance,
has this tell-tale dust been found. It pervades the town ; it
has fallen black and heavy over house and temple, speaking
clearly of the terror of those days when the fierce barbarians
broke in upon the pleasure-loving city, stripped long before of
the legions which gave it safety while they taught it luxury.
I do not know how long Isurium survived after the Romans
went, before the wolves swooped down on it. Perhaps, before
the final slaughter, many of the citizens may have fled up into
the hills, trusting themselves and their children rather to the wet
caves of Settle than to the hands of barbarians who knew no
mercy. But for every one who fled to that slow death in
misery and darkness I do not doubt that five remained here
in Isurium ; and when the last day came, and the axes went on
hacking through the streets, and the temples were profaned,

X 2

and the palaces stripped of all their wealth, there was beyond doubt a piteous scene of slaughter acted on this hillside, children and women hunted through the streets where their husbands and fathers had been slain—and in the end, when the conquerors were tired of killing, and of plundering things whose beauty they did not understand, they set fire to the whole, and from their distant refuge on the hills the frightened exiles must have looked down day by day on the site of their noble city veiled in a black cloud of smoke, till at last the embers ceased to smoulder and the exiles were all dead, and the country scourged by the Danes was left desolate and uninhabited, so that grass grew upon the ruins and the city was not rebuilt, but only a vague memory lingered of an "old burgh" that had stood there.

Such was the end of old Isurium. The tale has made me melancholy; and, indeed, if I may venture on a gentle criticism of a country which I love, it does appear to me that tragedies lie rather thick about this district. Yorkshire-men in all ages have shown a genius for getting into trouble ; and here before me, in the charming old town of Knaresborough, whither I am going between the wild rose hedges and the honeysuckles as fast as my two wheels will carry me, is another tale of woe, of which I was so heartily tired before I ever came to Yorkshire that I vowed I would not mention it,--nor should I have done so were it not that I find the folk of Knaresborough a trifle apt to expect all strangers to drop a tear in memory of that atrocious scoundrel, Eugene Aram. I say at once, there-fore, that I have no sympathy at all with this poor drivelling creature, who could not even keep his counsel about the sordid crime he had committed. To be a criminal may, or may not, be a proper object of ambition. To be an unsuccessful one is plainly base ; and when the failure comes by reason of the weakness of a sloppy, sentimental mind, which must needs confide its guilt to the unsympathetic bosom of a small school-boy, I can only say that Aram had quite mistaken his own

Knaresborough.

talents, and should have chosen some much easier path, where a weak and silly head would be in less danger of the gallows.

But here upon the hillside are the first houses of the ancient town, as old, perhaps, in its origin as Isurium itself, for the Romans were prompt to find out mineral springs, and doubtless knew the properties both of "Sweet Spaw," which bubbles up some three miles out, within the bounds of the old famous forest, and of that which has been both elegantly and justly called "Stinking Spaw." On approaching Knaresborough from Boroughbridge one has no more idea of the beauty of the town than one has on approaching Richmond; and it is only on following the steep descent till it runs out upon a handsome bridge that one sees the many coloured houses climbing in a dense mass of roofs and gardens up a lofty cliff, while the river, swift and smooth, sweeps round sharply through the woods which close the prospect, and over all the blackened ruins of the castle recall the day when feudal lords of vast power dwelt in this stronghold on the borders of what was then a wild and solitary forest, well stored with game and traversed only by few paths which travellers could follow.

These lords of Knaresborough possessed the true north-country aptitude for taking a hand in any mischief which was going on. The murder of Becket was one of the most striking pranks of mediæval times, and, accordingly, no one will be surprised to find that the Lord of Knaresborough, Hugh de Morville, was one of the four knights who broke into Canterbury Cathedral in the dusk of the winter afternoon and slew the great archbishop. It is said that the four murderers took refuge in this castle, where they dwelt for a full year cut off from all society—I should have thought there was not much to lose in Knaresborough so very long ago. However, in the end all was made well by the customary expiation of a journey to the holy land; so I suppose there is no truth in those veracious tales still current in Devon which avow that Tracy, another of the four, spends his time still in howling upon stormy nights

up and down the coast near Ilfracombe, unable to win pardon
or repose.

Knaresborough would have been of little account in Yorkshire
had it been ignored by holy men ; but with rare wisdom it
concentrated its holiness upon a single hermit, in preference to
spreading it over a whole monastery, and so succeeded in pro-
ducing a saint, which Fountains, with all its superior grandeur,
was never able to do.   St. Robert, while still young, tried
several monasteries.   He coquetted with Whitby and with

Knaresborough.

Fountains, but found no scope in either of them ; and at
length, wandering up and down in the neighbourhood of
Knaresborough, he met a hermit, whose way of living pleased
his fancy so enormously that he persuaded the good man to let
him share his cell. Had the hermit known how difficult Robert
had found it to live in the society of many at Whitby and at
Fountains he might have doubted the prudence of admitting
one so restless to a share of the parched peas and crystal well
which had been his solitary joy. The event was what might

have been foreseen. Two hermits in a cell agreed no better than two boys in one bed. Robert was soon left in sole possession, which suited him exactly. He said the original hermit had gone back to the world again. Perhaps he had. Nothing to the contrary is known ; and Robert, succeeding to the sanctity of both, very soon became a saint indeed.

William Estoteville, who was Lord of Knaresborough in those days, was incredulous about the piety of the hermit. " He is rather," said the surly baron, "a receiver of thieves." I wish Estoteville had given the evidence for this opinion ; because I myself . . . but that is of no interest now. At any rate, it is admitted that whereas Robert began in a dreary cave all by himself, it was not long before a rich matron gave him the chapel of St. Hilda, with some land "and its appurtenances." I do not know what the appurtenances comprised ; but they enabled this poor hermit to keep four servants, two of whom were employed in tillage, one on "various occasions"—a pretty and suggestive phrase—and a fourth, whose sole business was to collect alms from the pious. I sometimes wonder whether Robert found it better to confer this honourable duty on a small and weakly man, whose emaciation might rouse pity in the traveller, or on some sturdy ruffian, who might collect alms with a cudgel. Perhaps he kept both kinds among his servants ; and that is why Estoteville spoke so harshly of him, and ordered his cell to be torn down.

It was of very little use in mediæval days to tear down the cells of hermits who were backed by the powers of heaven— not to mention four servants ; and so Estoteville, riding in the forest not long after, saw smoke curling up among the trees, and asked his attendants whence it came. They said it came from the cell of Robert the Hermit ; and Estoteville, who had fancied the holy man was disposed of, swore by—somebody has blotted out the oath with so thick a pen that I could not read it, though I held the page up to the light—swore in this awful manner that St. Robert should no longer play the hermit in his forest. But of what use is it to swear at hermits ? In a few weeks Estoteville was St. Robert's chief supporter ; and having thus won over all his enemies, the saint went on growing holier and holier, as well as richer, till, when he died, the monks of Fountains, who were always worrying round Yorkshire for a saint, being, as I have said, quite unable to breed one for themselves, came over in force, and did their very utmost to secure his bones. However, they went back again without him ; and I really do not know where the dust of the hermit reposes at this hour. Nor is it now of more than antiquarian interest, for the dry bones have long ceased to work miracles ; and as that is so, we may as well go on from saints to witches, who may possibly possess more power.

Happy, yea, thrice happy, is the town which the powers of heaven and of hell have combined to render famous ! It is a rare case, and I doubt if there are five towns in this illustrious kingdom which can show two natives so justly famous as St. Robert and Mother Shipton.

Ursula Shipton's mother was a witch. She entered on that high vocation at the early age of fifteen. The parentage of one who has left so strong a mark on the intelligence of servant girls must be a matter of decided interest ; and, therefore, I think it well to say that Agatha Shipton was much annoyed at the excessive interest manifested in her proceedings when, in or about the year 1486, she made the usual compact with the devil. Prying people seemed to her to sin against good manners, so she resolved to read them a lesson, and a suitable occasion presented itself not long afterwards at a breakfast party where most of her ill-bred neighbours had presented themselves. The first thing that happened was that one worthy gentleman found the ruff torn off his neck, and certain faggots hung there in its place. This seemed very comic to the friend who sat by him, and he chuckled vastly over the joke, until he found his own hat whisked away and replaced by a pewter vessel. A young lady sat opposite to these two sufferers, and seeing them adorned so quaintly she was quite unable to refrain from laughing; and having once begun to laugh, she could not stop, but sat laughing for full a quarter of an hour, while all the rest of the company were so inordinately merry at her mirth that they too laughed, and not one of them could stop, but all guffawed so loudly that the master of the house came running upstairs hastily to know what had happened. But when about to enter the room he found he could not, and no wonder—for the oldest man living, says the chronicler, never saw a larger pair of horns than he had on his head. Suddenly all these witcheries vanished into air ; the guests sat silent, resting their tired sides, and in the same moment there resounded from the ceiling a sound as if a hundred persons were laughing boisterously at their discomfiture, yet no one could be seen.

This was a thought disquieting, and the guests resolved that they had better go home at once. They had no sooner descended to the courtyard than they found themselves pelted with rotten apples, thrown by unseen hands ; and when, terrified and breathless, they mounted and spurred away from the enchanted place, behind every man there rode a little deformed old woman, whipping up the horse, till the poor beasts flew rather than galloped back into the town. Of course there was an inquiry before the magistrates. Agatha Shipton quite admitted that the whole disturbance was her work. She scoffed at threats of punishment ; declared that if they worried her she would do as much again ; and, finally, bored by the solemnity of the proceedings, called out loudly "Updraxi, call Stygician Helluei," whereupon there appeared in court a horrid winged dragon, and carried her away triumphant on his back.

From a parentage so potent great things were naturally looked for ; and Mother Shipton disappointed no one's hopes, being, indeed, from the moment of her birth a portent more remarkable than any other which had tumbled from the skies since Yorkshire was a county. Exact descriptions of her

[To face page 314

"Sat laughing for full a quarter of an hour."

appearance are on record ; but she was so very ugly that they make me shiver, and I will not print them. She led her nurse an awful life. The poor woman did not know sometimes for days together what had become of her small charge, who used to come tumbling through the ceiling just when she had abandoned hope of ever seeing her again. Even this was not the worst that she had to undergo, for demons of all kinds were always about the dear child's cradle. Beelzebub taught her fairy tales, and Belphegor dandled her upon his knee.

Of her performances in riper years need I say much ? Is there a child among us who does not know the things she prophecied—the motor cars, the ironclads, the Crystal Palace, the Crimean war, yes, even Klondyke was not hid from her far-seeing vision. Does any one doubt it ? Let him listen.

> Carriages without horses shall go
> And accidents fill the world with woe.
> Iron in the water shall float
> As easily as does a wooden boat.
> A house of glass shall come to pass
> In England, but, alas !
> War will follow with the work
> In the land of the Pagan and the Turk.
> Gold shall be found, and found
> In a land that's not now known.

There is a great deal more of the same sort, with many cryptic sayings which make my head ache when I try to interpet them. Go thy ways, good Mother Shipton, born of demons, and taught by the enemies of all mankind. Of all thy prophecies and wisdom there remains nothing but the giggling of silly servant girls and a shrug of the shoulder from the wise man passing on to other things. But Knaresborough is still itself, undecayed and beautiful as in all ages of its history. The castle may have crumbled. Great families may have come and passed. Storms, and revolutions, and sieges have broken on the town and swept off like the changes of a dream. The forest is disparked. No horn ever rings within the glades, nor has any living man heard the baying of the gazehounds re-echo over moor or hollow where once the merry music used to float down the wind so often.   The very art of archery is lost.   The boys who used to learn so painfully the forest bounds were long since grandfathers, and not one urchin nowadays could say where the forest ended.   Customs, habits, yes, the very language have all changed.   Nothing is the same except the hill and the many coloured houses with their sloping gardens, and the brown moorland water sweeping round its base so swift and steady.   It is evening, and a small feathery moon has risen over the treetops, casting a faint shimmer on the water.   One or two lights are gleaming on the hillside, and a boat comes up against the stream with a brilliant Chinese lantern in its stern.   There is a sound of voices on the water, boys playing in the empty boats as others must have played before them any time these ten centuries and more.   Silence is dropping down on Knaresborough; and as I walk back through the empty streets to my hotel, the summer night is filled with infinite sweet odours and with little rustling sounds, as if some presence out of the old past were labouring to tell me something high and solemn, and yet was inarticulate.

Ripley.

The Wharfe at Bolton Abbey.

CHAPTER XVI

WHARFEDALE, BOLTON PRIORY, AND SKIPTON.

I WISH I had not heeded old Sir Thomas Brown when he told me many chapters back that deliberating delay would be a wise cunctation. I was all too much inclined to loiter when the worthy knight pulled me by the sleeve ; and encouraged by his sententious suggestions, I have let time slip and slouched along the hedgerows picking flowers as if I were no more bound to hasten than any vagrant gypsy, who may unyoke his pony by the roadside when he pleases, and cares not if he reach his journey's end that night or not.

Dear old philosopher, that attitude of mind may do for Norfolk, where the acreage is less, and the interest—if I may say it—so far inferior. But here in Yorkshire he who loiters will pay the penalty by leaving many a place unseen which he

would fain have visited ; and as I ride swiftly on from Knaresborough, past the unlovely outskirts of Harrogate, towards the
opening of the long Wharfe Valley, I remember with a pang
that I had meant to visit Adel, and Harewood, where that
sturdy old Chief Justice Gascoigne, who feared neither king
nor prince, lies sleeping in the church ; and Farnley, with many
another place which I have dreamt of seeing since my childhood, but now must go by, lest I leave out greater things.
Perhaps it is as well ; for who can carry in his mind every
noble thing there is in Yorkshire, or store his memory with all
its excellences without reducing the whole to one mixed blur?

Harrogate.

Otley lies in the opening of Wharfedale, a wide and spacious
gateway to the moors. Low hills, well wooded, flank it on the
south, and on the north a few ridges of high ground far away
across the fertile valley mark the entrance of that wide dale
which narrows quickly to a beauty so exceeding. The town
has little distinction, save in the noble wooded slopes which
drop down from the Chevin and from " Jenny's Hill " to the
very borders of the town,—a foretaste of the heights to which
the valley bounds will rise when the gorge narrows and woods
and pastures give place to the brown moor. There is no waste

land as yet upon the slopes ; and through the wide green valley the river runs on placidly with an unbroken surface, yet swirling here and there in eddies which betray the power of the current. "In summer, too," says Camden, "it is very dangerous; as I experienced to my cost in my first tour in these parts." I wish the good man had not given only half his confidence ; yet even as they stand, without the details, these few feeling words may serve to restrain the eagerness of any who might think it safe to dabble in the Wharfe.

> "Wharfe is clear and the Aire lithe,
> Where Aire kills one, Wharfe kills five."

Pass. Bolton to Harrogate.

So says an ancient saw. Indeed, I am very glad that Camden was not one of the number, and that he paid no heavy price for the lesson to mistrust the pretty swirling stream which washes up so pleasantly among the forget-me-nots and meadow-sweet upon its banks.

As I follow up the valley, threading the fields over an atrocious road, the river begins now and then to show its teeth, the brown water flashes into white over a jagged rock, and an occasional waste of moorland on the left shows that I

am drawing near the region of those downs where the monks of
Bolton used to graze their herds of sheep and cattle. Presently
a fine crag rises on the hilltop, a dark splintered cairn of storm-
worn rock.   It is Ben Rhyddyng, and the turrets of the great
Hydropathic are just below, almost at the beginning of the
moor, which sweeps on brown and sombre from that point,
roughened here and there by woodlands, till it is lost in thin
blue haze.

The heart of every riverside town is undoubtedly its bridge ;
and it is to the old grey arches which span the river at this
point that I turn my steps before all else in Ilkley.   On this
fine summer morning the river flows on brown and cool.   It
has gained already the aspect of a mountain stream, broad and
shallow, singing over a bed of many coloured gravel which
flashes in the sunlight, and among which one sees from time to
time the slow moving body of a blunt-nosed trout.   A little wind
stealing off the moors shakes the shadows on the bank, just
where the scyamores dip their lower branches in the stream ; and
a little higher up a few boulders make a freshet, and send down
a scum of bubbles discolouring the clear water.   On the further
bank there lie wide meadows of lush grass all bronzed with
buttercups and sorrell, and shaded by high hedges where the
hawthorn is in blossom yet.   Further off again there are well-
wooded hills stretching far into the blue haze which wraps both
moors and valley in a mystery not yet scattered by the sun.

Here upon the bridge, and in all the meadows round, there
is no haze, but exquisite clear morning, with a mountain freshness in the air.   It is early still.   There is no bustle in the
town ; and here by the riverside, where the stone coping of the
bridge is but just warmed by the sun still lingering near the
hilltops, there are no noises but those made by the river and
the birds.   Just such a morning it must have been when
William Butterfield, long ago, surprised a tribe of fairies at the
wells a short way up the hillside.   He remembered noticing
particularly, as he went very early at midsummer to set open

the door of the bath-house, how the birds sang so sweetly and
cheerily and vociferously, making the valley echo with the
music of their voices. He paid but little notice to this as he
went up the hill ; but afterwards it seemed to him that all
nature must have been a-revelling with the sports of the small
people, and that the sweet gaiety of the linnets and the
thrushes had in it a note of joyousness which he never heard
again.

As he drew near the wells he took out of his pocket the
great iron key, and placed it in the lock ; but there was something "canny" about it, and instead of the key lifting the lever,
it only turned round and round. Then he tried to push the
door open, but he had no sooner made it give a little than it
was pushed to again from within. At last he set his shoulder
to it, and forced it open with a bang. " Then, whirr, whirr !
such a noise and sight ! All over the water and dipping into it
were a lot of creatures dressed in green from head to foot, none
of them more than eighteen inches high, and making a chatter
and a jabber thoroughly unintelligible. They seemed to be
taking a bath, only they bathed with all their clothes on. Soon,
however, one or two of them began to make off, bounding over
the wall like squirrels. Finding they were all ready for decamping,
and wanting to have a word with them, he shouted at the top
of his voice, but could find nothing else to say than 'Hallo
there !' Then away the whole tribe went, helter skelter,
toppling and tumbling head over heels, and all the while
making a noise not unlike a disturbed nest of young partridges.
The sight was so unusual that he declared he either couldn't,
or daren't, attempt to rush after them. . . . When the well had
got quite clear of these strange beings, he ran to the door and
looked to see where they had fled, but nothing was to be seen.
He ran back into the bath to see if they had left anything
behind, but there was nothing. The water lay still and clear
just as he had left it the night before, so he gave up looking,
and commenced his usual routine of preparing the baths."

Poor stolid William Butterfield, who saw the sight we have all dreamed of, yet could find nothing better to say than "Hallo there!" What was the cursed trick of fate which threw so rare a chance in the way of a fellow so poor of fancy and resource! Yet, to have looked even once across the barrier into Elfland must, one thinks, have changed a man's whole life; and surely sometimes, on warm summer nights, Butterfield must have heard the fairy laughter tinkling on the hillside when the stars hung large and golden over Rombald's moor!

The Valley of the Wharfe.

But he is dead long since, carried off, perhaps, to Elfland, and in the Ilkley of to-day, prosperous and full of ordinary lodging-houses, I can find no trace of fairies; which is just as well, for I am full of eagerness to move on up this valley, the scenery of which is growing beautiful beyond my expectations, and am content to leave the Roman relics and the ancient crosses, and even the fine moorlands and the crags which over-hang the town, by which one may wander in the most glorious keen air all the way to Skipton.

As one follows on the road from Ilkley the moorland ridges
break and scatter into fine hills, now sloping steep and dark
from a bare summit, now marked by two or three lonely fir
trees on the height. Lower down the woodlands are all
swathed in heat. Even the fresh wind that sways the grass
and sings over the dimpled river, filling all the valley with low
music, cannot scatter the thin grey haze upon the slopes. Only
in the valley bottom there is bright sunlight ; and the air is full
of the scent of wild flowers innumerable. Far in front of me
Barden Fell and Simon's Seat lies like two vast blue clouds,
shutting off this land of Eden from the working world.

At last, passing by the way to Skipton, I emerge upon a
wooded corner by a group of pretty cottages ; and passing
through a gateway in the wall, I find myself descending a steep
slope of grass and fern towards the river, beyond which rises a
bare red cliff, breaking the line of woods, all green and brown
and golden in the fine fresh sunlight. On my left stands Bolton
Hall, and further on, scarce seen as yet, a grey arch peeping
through the trees recalls the days when in this lovely valley
there dwelt only monks. It is not at this hour of the day that
those old ruins put on their chief beauty. I shall return and see
them towards evening when the light has mellowed, and the
glitter has gone out of it. So I go down towards the stepping
stones round which the water sparkles so bright and clear, and,
passing up the broken woodland paths, come at last to a copse
of oak trees, where I pause to wonder at the exceeding beauty
of the scene.

I cannot see the ruins, which are hidden by the thick growth
of oaks and beeches. Below me is a steep green slope among
the tree trunks, with here and there a stray belated bluebell,
while over the fresh green twigs of the lower trees I see the
brown river sparkling, and beyond that again another noble
woodland, which rises from the water till it cuts the slope of
Barden Fell lying in purple shadow and Simon's Seat all green
and brown in the clear sunshine. A rushing wind sings

Y 2

through the treetops from the moor; and following in its
track a dense mass of shadows blows up the valley; the sky
turns grey, the sparkles go out of the water, and the leaves
shiver. Suddenly a little flash shoots out among the greenery,
the oaks turn golden as the sun returns, and the long reach of
brown water is once more so clear that even at this distance on
the hillside I fancy I can see the blunt-nosed trout glancing
here and there among the stones.

There is no turn in all the convolutions of this valley which
does not stamp some beauty on the memory. When I rose

Bolton Abbey.

and wandered on again, I came to a spot where a smaller valley
cuts down into the larger one, and a little stream, half dry,
struggled on to meet the Wharfe beneath banks as high and
steep as would have well become a torrent. But no king's
raiment was ever stained so gorgeously as that high bank. For
over its whole surface, up to the very skyline and far away
beneath the shadow of the trees, there flowed a sea of colour.
Wild campion, which the boys called ragged robin, the large
star of the wild garlic, hyacinths, forget-me-not, speedwell, and
a thousand more, were blooming there in strange profusion, so

that the whole slope positively glowed and burnt with the intensity of its royal colour.

A mile higher up the valley narrows, and the river bed is contracted further still by broad shoulders of jutting rock, grey and mossy. Through the narrow channel the river flows but slowly, the scum of bubbles drifting past the corners sulkily, giving out now and then a sucking noise which seems to come from a great depth. A few yards more and the black water swirls and writhes in a narrower channel still, while a little further up there is no black water at all, but only a white mass of foam, plunging like a living thing as it roars through a deep narrow cleft in the dark rock.

It is not difficult to leap across this roaring chasm to the ledges on the other side, but it is death to fail. This is the Strid, that famous passage of the Wharfe, out of which a white horse rises, vaporous and shadowy, in warning that another life is about to end in the whirlpools, where so many others have gone down since the Boy of Egremont missed his leap and fell there, dragged back by the hound which he was leading by a leash, and which faltered at the noise of the rushing torrent. Men say the story is not true ; or, at least, that it was not sorrow for the poor lad's death which led Cecilia de Romille to grant Bolton to the monks. I care not what the truth may be, for, true or false, the old tale is as much a part of the beauties of this valley as the river or the rocks, and the student is not born who will divorce them. It is at least true that since the days of the Boy of Egremont lives almost countless have been lost in the black swirling water of the Strid ; and there are not wanting people who can tell how they have seen the white steed rising from the depths, mysterious and shadowy, in the first stillness of the dawn, or when all the valley is filled with silver lights from the full moon rising over Barden Fell.

Above the Strid the woods close in around the river, and now and then the whistle of a solitary bird is heard above the rushing of the water, breaking and struggling over rapids, whose abrupt

descent is scarce less striking than the Strid. A little further
on, the woods, which have been so dense and shadowy since I
entered the grounds of Bolton Priory, melt away in fine,
undulating lawns, the river courses under steeper slopes, and
there, set beautifully on the side of the mountain, stands Barden
Tower, an ancient building which is steeped in memories of the
Cliffords.

Far back in the early chapters of this book, when I came in
sight of the country lying round Londesborough beneath the
low ranges of the wolds, I might have spoken of the shepherd

Barden Tower.

lord who, when he came into his own again, was Earl of
Cumberland, and lord of all those territories which made the
family of Clifford as great in the north-west of England as the
Percies in the north-east. He was son of that Lord Clifford
called the Butcher, who fell bravely on the day before the
fight of Towton, in the cause of good King Henry, for whom
the northern nobles risked so much, and whom they loved with
a passion that long survived his capacity to serve them. But
when Clifford fell, and the Yorkists triumphed next day
upon the field of Towton, a hurricane of woe swept over the

north country, and Lady Clifford fearing justly that her two
young sons would be taken and slain, sent them to a seaside
town, whence the younger embarked for the Low Countries. But
the elder son, the heir, was brought back by a feint, and placed
in charge of a woman who had been nursery maid at Skipton
Castle, and whom the child thus knew and loved. The woman
was married to a shepherd at Londesborough, which estate was
the property of Lady Clifford; and there the young lord lived
as the child of those two peasants till the rumour began to
spread that he was yet alive, and his mother, fearing that he
would be discovered, transported him with his poor protectors
to the Scottish border, where in the safe seclusion of that wild
country the lad grew to manhood, with no knowledge of his
parentage, nor any training other than that common among
shepherds.   He was near thirty when a monarch of the House
of Lancaster once more gained the throne; and the House of
Clifford was raised up from the dust to its ancient honours and
possessions.   But from that time the shepherd earl, unused to
State and dignity, loved this small Tower of Barden, set
among the woods and lonely fells, better than all his stately
castles; and here he used to dwell, studying alchemy and
science—if the tales be true—with the canons of Bolton, a
scholar, a recluse, yet having in his veins so much of the noble
blood of Clifford still undulled that he could shake off his
solitary habits and play a man's part on the Field of Flodden,
when the fear of Scotch invasion called out the tenantry of
Craven, and all Wharfedale and Langstrothdale re-echoed
almost for the last time in our history with the pomp of feudal
warfare.

Well, he is gone; but I like to think that his shadow hangs
about these hills as truly as that of the scholar gipsy flits
about the Cherwell and the Cumnor Hills; and as I climb the
steep side of Simon's Seat I find here and there a jutting slab
of rock, where I may be sure he must have sat half buried in
the scrub of cloudberries, whose red flowers star the hillside,

while here and there a stray purple berry anticipates the next
month's harvest, and leaves a red stain on my careless hand.
Far below over the rough slopes lie Bolton Woods, a thin line
of forest in the valley depths, while out of it the green fields
rise sharply, breaking into moor at last, ridge rising over ridge,
shoulder falling behind shoulder, valley intersecting valley, far
as the eye can wander through the foldings of the hills, till the
sight loses itself in the dim haze of heat and can distinguish
nothing certainly.   High up on the opposite western slope lies

The Bridge at Barden.

a little tarn on a tableland among the hills, gleaming steel-grey
like a mirror.   One grey gable of Barden Tower projects out
of the brown woods far below, but far as I can see there is no
other habitation, nor any sign of man or living thing, save only
a great hawk wheeling on steady wing above the moors—a
prospect unchanged at any point since those old days when the
shepherd lord used to dream out the long days upon this
mountain side, drinking in the keen pure air, and watching idly
the changes of the light among the sunny green bushes of the
cloudberry and the darker masses of the heather.

I think it is scarce possible to avoid dreaming when one lies among these hills, so famous and so beautiful; and dreams would be worthless if they were not free to wander where they please; but I do sometimes regret that the great vision which came to Wordsworth in this valley regarding the tragedy of the Nortons had not issued from the gate of Horn. For, indeed, the true tale is piteous enough; and the ruin of a family so noble needed not the addition of miseries more bitter than those which were in truth incurred in the lost cause for which

The Valley of the Wharfe.

Yorkshire paid so heavily. There was rivalry between the Nortons and the Cliffords; and I suspect the fact that the former had joined the Rising of the North would of itself have been enough to incline the Lord of Skipton in the opposite direction. At any rate, though Clifford may have wavered, he stood loyal in the end, and his ancient house suffered no loss when so many others were ground down in the dust. His name must always have counted for more than that of Norton along the banks of Wharfe; for the true power of the latter

was, as I have said already, at Norton Conyers, close to Ripon,
and that is doubtless why but few of the poor hinds in Wharfedale where hanged up when the time came to pay the penalty
of failure, and in Richmondshire and all the villages round
Ripon the poor labouring men dangled from the trees in
groups of twenty and thirty at a time.

Richard Norton had been a man of note and mark, one of
the Council of the North, and Governor of Norham Castle in
Queen Mary's days. He had been out in the Pilgrimage of
Grace, and I suppose that in all the north, where, as was truly
said, "the ancient faith lay like lees in the bottom of men's
hearts, and came to the top if the vessel was but ever so little
stirred," there was none who clung more passionately than he
to the institutions of the perishing society which the land was
shaking off beneath his eyes. The old religion, the power of
the great feudal houses,—they were slipping by like milestones
left behind upon a road which one has travelled. One by one
Norton saw himself borne past them; and he lost both wealth
and home in a vain effort to turn back the march of time.

But he did not die. In those dark winter days when the
rebels saw that everything was lost, and scattered in small
parties up towards the Scottish border, hoping that among the
moors of that wild land they might find safe shelter and in the
end escape to Flanders, there came to Richard Norton one Robert
Constable of Flamborough, his kinsman, and advised him
urgently to take shelter with him. I know not how it happened that Norton distrusted this cousin of his own so far that
even in the misery in which he lay he rejected the hand held
out to him, and chose rather to take his chance in cold and
wretchedness among the mountains. Perhaps he was warned
by some knowledge of Constable's past life; for no man surely
drops from an honourable past to the baseness of deliberately
trapping noble gentlemen who put their trust in him. This was
Constable's sole object. He was both a traitor and a spy;
and earned an infamous success in the vile mission which he

had taken on himself, staining a very noble name with practices besides which the treachery of Murray of Broughton shines almost as the conduct of an upright gentleman.

Guided by some good angel Norton escaped this false adviser and fled to Flanders, whither his eldest son, that Francis of whom the poet tells a tale so dolorous, also fled. In fact, of all the eight sons whom the poet represents as perishing . . . . But surely it is a mean task for history to criticise a dream because it is not fact. In heaven's name let us take the gift without this scrutiny.

Well, the light is changing, and it is time to go. As I come down the steep fell the rich sunlight of late afternoon has turned all the lawns round Barden Tower golden, and the still woods behind are lit up with a rich illumination. The brown gravel in the river's bed glows deeper and ruddier than before ; and every sedge and bramble that is swayed and drowned by the flowing water catches a share of the warm light. This is the hour in which to see the priory ; and so I pass on through the long woodland paths above the river, past the Strid and the little islands and all the wide brown reaches of the river, while the air grows so lucent round the top of Simon's Seat that every stone and boulder on his rough flanks stands out clear cut with its own separate distinctness, till I come out at last upon a height to the north of the old ruin, and see below the river sweeping close in beneath the hill upon the right, so as to leave a wide and sunny meadow in the bow.

Over this broad lush sward of grass there are red cattle grazing up to the very margin of the river, and on the further side, just where a red bank breaks the line of sloping meadow, and a few hawthorn bushes still bear the remnants of their waning blossom, rises the grey shell of the priory, the five lancet windows of its choir framing glimpses of the distant hills which are far lovelier than the decorated tracery which they have lost. For Bolton, never a house of grandeur comparable to Fountains or Rievaulx, has been touched very

Bolton Abbey.

tenderly by time, which has added one of nature's ornaments
in return for each of those fashioned by the hand of man which
has been torn from her, setting a scented gillyflower in the
niche whence some saint used to call the dalesmen to adora-
tion, flinging down a screen of ivy, or a trail of wandering jew,
across the wall which was once made rich by all the blazonry
of Clifford ; and opening through every shattered door and
archway some new view, now of the brown rippling river
stealing by the sunny pastures, now of the high woods steeped
in the magic colours of the sunset, now of the great crags upon
the fells stretching blue and clear far down the vale into a

The Castle, Skipton.

distance which seems infinite and boundless, till one's heart
leaps with the very beauty of the scene, and one thinks that
the loss of all which has perished here at Bolton was not a
price too heavy for this ruin, glowing in the rich light, which
has drunk in the overplus of beauty in the valley, and brought
it out again so nobly that no man having looked on it can fail
to bear it in his mind for ever.

It was a bright evening as I rode on towards Skipton, and the
high downs which lie along the road stood up clear and golden
against the pale sky. It was growing dusk as I came down the
hill beside the castle wall, and paused before the two round

towers of the gateway, hesitating whether I should not wait for day before entering the old stronghold of the Cliffords. But there is something very gracious in the soft onset of the dusk in early summer; and the first golden sparkle of a star in the wan sky tempts me under the old archway full of shadows, and across the courtyard to the ancient quadrangle upon the left, where a tall tree growing in the midst gathers the coming darkness round itself, and makes a little rustling as the night wind steals downwards from the moors. The heavy mullioned windows are unlighted. There is no sound of service from the long hall or the kitchens, once so full of cooks and scullions, the withdrawing rooms are empty, the guardrooms absolutely silent; and neither lord nor lady paces through the courtyard. Yet if ever ghosts revisited the glimpses of the moon, how many a man would give his heart to see those which flit about this house of shadows. For there would come fair Rosamund, —she whom the cruel Queen Elinor tracked out in her labyrinth by a clue of wool—" Rosa Immunda " as the punning epitaph described her all too truly, yet a Queen of Hearts and Sovereign of Love unto this hour, made dear by a thousand stories of our childhood and the romance of seven centuries.

There, too, one would surely see the black-faced Clifford unhelmed and bleeding in the throat, as men saw him fall at Dintingdale, butcher perhaps, but a brave and hardy warrior such as any house might count among its ancestors with pride. Perhaps the shepherd lord would wander with the father whom he hardly knew, unless, indeed, his spirit chose to stray at moonlight over Barden Fell; but there certainly, since he chose to sleep his last sleep within Skipton church, would come George Clifford, Earl of Cumberland, that gallant admiral who wore the Queen's glove in his hat, and sailed his ship, the *Bonaventure*, into the press of the Armada fight, and bore the news to Tilbury that the Spaniards were scattered north up channel like a flock of sheep. " His fleet," says Fuller, " may be said to be bound for no other harbour but the Port of Honour,

though touching at the Port of Profit in passage thereunto." I
know not which of those two ports the old Admiral loved best ; to
Drake and Hawkins the one was as dear as the other, and why
not ? Doubtless both prompted him to the great voyage in the
Malice Scourge, when he took San Juan in the Isle of Porto
Rico, and had other gallant adventures, as we may read in
Pinkerton. So there he goes with the royal favour in his
hat, and a slight rolling gait, carrying still upon his lips the salt

Skipton Church.

of many oceans, and in his ears the humming of the cordage
and the creaking of the spars as the ship swung round upon
another tack, and plunged forwards towards unknown lands.
And, surely, in this house, which she beautified and restored,
one would not sit among the falling shadows in the courtyard
without seeing Lady Anne Clifford, Countess of Dorset,
Pembroke and Montgomery, who gave so haughty a reply to that
Minister of Charles II., who required her to return a certain

candidate for one of her many boroughs. " Sir," she wrote, " I
have been dictated to by a king, I have been bullied by a
usurper, but I will not submit to a subject. Your man shall
not stand." Dear, noble lady ; surely she must return to this
her castle ; and on some such summer night as this, when the
stars hang warm and golden in the sky, pace once more along the
terraces or the battlements which formed her proud inheritance !

But they have all passed on, like travellers who will never
turn back to their last night's inn ; and I stand here in the silence
and the gathering darkness, half timorous, half looking for I
know not what, till I hear the heavy footstep of the guide
returning through the archway, and I follow him out into the
castle yard again. A faint peal of organ music fills the air,
followed by a low sound of chanting. There is practice in the
church where the Cliffords lie ; and as I pass out into the road
again, and stand hesitating in the gateway, I am drawn across
the churchyard by the jewelled lights within the stained glass
windows, gleaming red and purple through the dusk ; and
pushing open the old, heavy door, I stand within the gloom
of the last and final castle of the whole house of Clifford. At
this west end of the great church there is almost utter darkness,
the lights in the choir, where boys and organist are trying over
chants and hymns, do but make an oasis in the desert of the dark.
Gradually the vague outlines of the old recumbent statues near
the altar grow distinct, and I can see the tomb of the shepherd
Lord, and the stately monument of his son, whom a ghoulish
antiquary, breaking open the silence of the vault beneath the
altar, dared to unwrap from the graveclothes in which his body
rested, and to glut his curiosity by gazing on the features of
the dead. Surely, it is a miserable trick of destiny that the
more a man achieves greatness while he lives, the more he is
exposed to have his bones disturbed, and his last sleep broken,
not by the hands of those who loved him, but by the prying
touch of strangers, greedy to boast of having seen the very
shape and outline of the body which was the home of the

great spirit long since fled. Let us thank God for His precious gift
of obscurity, which will defend us from the jackals after death.
And, with that pious thanksgiving lingering on my lips, I grope
my way out into the summer night, and find the new moon
rising over Rombald's moor, and a fresh breeze filling all the
quiet streets with pure mountain air.

Kettlewell.

Valley of the Wharfe.

CHAPTER XVII

GORDALE AND INGLEBOROUGH

In Skipton in Craven
Is never a haven,
But many a day foul weather.

AND as this jingle has been dinned into my ears oy almost
every man whom I have met in Yorkshire, I set it at the head
of this new chapter, partly to disarm any reader who has been
holding it ready to pelt me with, partly because I do not
believe it to be true.

At any rate, it was a cloudless morning when I rode out of
Skipton on the road to Gordale ; and as that highway is a
thought uninteresting, I shall use my leisure to set down, before
dropping wholly the subject of the Wharfe valley, a legendary
tale belonging to the higher regions of the river, which may serve
for an example of the wild and merry ways of the inhabitants in
those old days "when virtue was a country maid," and lusty

monks from Fountains had their cronies among the peasantry
of the fells where the Abbey flocks were grazed in countless
numbers.

There was a shoemaker, one Ralph Calvert, a cheery dog
with a melodious throat, and a store of old gay ballads which
made him popular both in Thorpe, the village where he lived,
and at Fountains, to which his duty called him periodically.
From Thorpe to Fountains is a long journey, and I blame no
man for thinking that it excuses some refreshment. But even

Thursfield.

a merry cobbler, with a bag full of shoes, would have done
better not to slumber by the wayside after lunch; for they who
do so are sure to dream of the devil, which is exactly what Ralph
Calvert did.

He dreamt that the fiend caught him unawares, and holding
him aloft with one hand, untied with the other the neck of the
bag which he carried on his back, and thrust the poor shoemaker
in. He was in the very act of tying the strings again when
Calvert woke up with a shriek, and found himself lying quite

alone upon the dusty grass which bordered the wayside. He got up nervously and looked about for the devil, and then walked on a bit and peeped round the corner of the hedge to see if he was there, but could find not even a hoof mark in the dust ; and so gradually he recovered his spirits and persuaded himself that it was nothing but a dream, and walked on singing for his own encouragement till he came in sight of Fountains Tower rising out of the deep woods, and spent a merry evening with the porter over a yard of beef and a bowl of foaming wassail.

Next day he started homewards by the Pately Road without a care. But as he went the further from the Abbey, he thought the more of the devil : and at last he thought so much of him that when he got to Pately Bridge he stopped and had a glass or two before climbing up that worst of hills which leads up out of Nidderdale again. Thus fortified, he trudged on bravely over the high moors : and when he came at last to a swollen river, took off his boots and went through it gaily. He was sitting down on the other side to put on his shoes and stockings, singing the while,—

> " As he was riding along the highway
> Old Nick came unto him, and thus he did say,
> Sing link-a-down, heigh-down, ho-down, derry."

When a voice at his shoulder trolled out lustily—

> Tol lol derol, derol dol, dol dol derry."

Ralph turned round like a man shot, and there at his elbow stood Nick himself, horns and hoofs in plain evidence, and bag slung over his shoulder, just as Ralph had seen him in his dream, but inclined apparently to do no evil, since he did but inquire how far it was to Grassington.

Now I cannot tell whether Ralph's head was still humming with the Pately ale, or whether he thought there could not be much harm in a fellow who was so ready to bear a hand in a

"Old Nick came unto him."

[*To face page* 340.

chorus. But the fact is that he answered cheerily, "'Too far to
go wi'out a bite," and brought out an eel pie and a bottle of
wine, which his gossip at the Abbey had packed into his wallet.
Old Nick's eyes glistened—may every one of us be as well pro-
vided when we meet him on the moors!—he sat down gladly,
he trolled a catch, and Ralph responded to it, he told a merry
tale of two monks in an orchard, and the cobbler capped it with
the very latest scandal about the Prior: the eel pie vanished,
the wine washed it down,—never were two cronies half so jolly,
and the sheep came to the brow of the hill and gazed down in
wonder, having never heard in all their fleecy lives so vast a
sound of laughter in this lonely place. Ralph found it true that
Nick is a gentleman, for no painful subjects were alluded to,
and his bag lay unheeded on the grass. At last the devil rose
to go, courteous to the last : and Ralph, too, staggered to his
feet, hiccoughing out, "If tha be 't devil or not, tha bees a
merry chap : but if tha be, bigg us a brigg over this river." The
devil did not hesitate. "In three days it shall be there, gossip,"
he said : and catching up his bag, made two strides to the
summit of the hill. The fuddled shoemaker watched him go,
but lost him in a black cloud which whirled suddenly across the
hilltop, and burst somewhere out of sight, sending down a
torrent of foaming water breast high in the already swollen
river.

So Ralph went home, shaking his head wisely. But in three
days the bridge was there, and stands there to this hour, as I
can testify, having stood on it and mused on this veracious
story,— for the main facts of which, having given but little
personal attention to matters diabolical, I am indebted to Mr.
Edmund Bogg, who walked "a thousand miles in Wharfedale,"
and who, therefore, ought to know all about it.

But I have left Wharfedale far behind, and am lost among
the country lanes upon the slopes which drop to Airedale, last
of the great Yorkshire rivers which has claims upon my interest,
and that less by virtue of its own beauty than of the grandeur

of the hills reached by following its valley. Already I am
mounting on the lower ridges of the water parting ; and at last
the road, which has been heading straight towards the hills,
turns off and runs beside them, dropping fast into a circus of
green fells, dotted here and there with little farms. The
Gordale cliffs, hidden by a jutting down, betray themselves by
their craggy summits towering over the high pastures ; and one
follows up the course of a little stream underneath green slopes
and low walls of limestone till a sudden turn lays open the whole
depth of the ravine.

On the right a blackened cliff, strangely furrowed, and so far
scooped out at its base that the crags upon its summit overhang,
sweeps round in a lofty semicircle, while on the left, dropping
straight and sheer as if levelled by a plummet, a whiter cliff
of the same immense height thrusts its shoulder out across the
curve. Out of the cleft between the two, a stream falls in three
heavy leaps ; while if one penetrates the gorge a little further
one sees that at a greater height the brook makes a wilder
plunge into the chasm, striking in its fall against a ledge of rock
which scatters half its volume into drifting spray. Thus the
whole abyss is filled with the sound of rushing waters, beating
against the blackened cliffs. A raven flaps heavily across the
gorge, croaking harshly. The rowans growing on the upper
ledges of the precipice are dry and wasted, and the desolation
of the cliff is in striking contrast with the fresh colours of the
turf, short and verdant and elastic as is usual in limestone
countries.

This precipice, so lofty and so sheer, is but one face of the
great Craven fault,—a dislocation of the strata which has left
huge cliffs at many different points among these high downs,—
there is another not less grand a mile away across the moor at
Malham Cove,—and seems to have possessed a singular faculty
of terrifying poets. Gray indeed, who wandered through this
country a century ago, or more, was so much impressed that
he stayed here no less than a quarter of an hour, and notes,

quaintly enough, that he thought his trouble well repaid ; while Wordsworth plunged boldly into the unknown in search of a

Malham Cove.

comparison, and said it was "terrific as the lair where the young lions couch." For my part the couching of young lions recalls

nothing but the gardens of the Zoo : and I do not find in myself
that ready sense of awe which overwhelmed the poets.

Now, in the long convolutions of these Craven dales there
are many scenes as wild and beautiful as Gordale ; and if a man
will spend the summer day in wandering from there to Malham,
which is scarce a mile away over the short turf, and thence, re-
gaining the main road, pass on to Settle, he will find such
scenery as will delight his memory for many a day after the
dull town life has closed round him once again, and the rattle

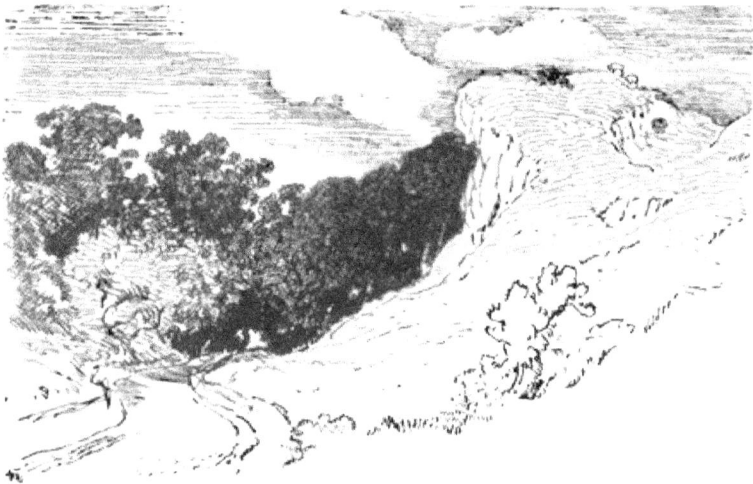

Near Settle.

of the hansoms has driven out of hearing the music of the
streams and the cheep of the moor-tits flitting quickly from
stone to stone. But, as for me, my face is set for Clapham by
the shortest road, for my time in Yorkshire is but short, and
there are sights in that high region which I cannot leave unseen. And so I pass on quickly under the great downs,
threading the country which used to be so sorely harried by
the Scots. I know not why these raiding enemies of England
descended so often upon Craven, which was so many miles

from the Scottish border, unless it was that the flocks browsing
on the great fells formed an easier booty than the crops in
more fertile regions of the north.   But whatever their motive,
the Scots came repeatedly and drove off the Craven villagers
in flocks—if one may trust the brutal details given by Richard
of Hexham ; though why should one set down the tale of a
monkish chronicler as weighed and sifted fact ?   "They first
massacred, says the pious Richard, "in the most barbarous
manner possible children and kindred in the sight of their

Settle.

relatives, masters in sight of their servants, and servants in the
sight of their masters, and husbands before the eyes of their
wives ; and then, horrible to relate, they carried off like so
much booty the noble matrons and chaste virgins, together
with other women.   These naked, fettered, herded together, by
whips and thongs they drove before them, goading them with
their spears and other weapons. . . Afterwards, when they were
distributed along with the other booty, a few from motives of
pity restored some of them to liberty at the church of St. Mary
at Carlisle ; but the Picts and many others carried off those

who fell to their share to their own country. And, finally, these brutal men, when tired of abusing these poor wretches like unto animals, made them their slaves, or sold them for cattle to other barbarians." Such were the tales which ran from mouth to mouth in the monasteries, where idle men, straining their own ears constantly for the tramp of Scottish hoofs, lent easy credence to the tales of frightened peasants, and the yarns told in their cups by the troopers of some baron who had sought the abbot's hospitality. From such tainted

The Market Place, Settle.

sources doubtless came the facts which the good Richard set down ; yet the story serves us, whether true or false, as a proof of that strange horror with which the border fighting was conducted, and which gave it at certain epochs something of the character of a holy war.

But all these woes are forgotten long ago ; and England holds no quieter or more peaceful country than that which lies in the shadow of the mountains which are now gathering round me. This long time I have seen the crest of Ingleborough.

Settle lies behind me some miles back ; and at last I enter the
small village of Clapham, which nestles at the foot of the
"muckle flat-topped hill" which caught some tender spot in
the soft heart of Jeanie Deans as she trudged southwards on
that journey over which races yet unknown will weep when

Catterick Force, Settle.

English is a dead tongue and "The Heart of Midlothian" a
classic and a schoolbook for all who wish to master it.

There is not much to say about the bright clean village
which straggles up the hill on both sides the beck. There is
a bridge half way up the street, from which one can look down
on a thread of water dripping among great mossy boulders, or

over it towards the small low church and the hill rising steep
behind it.   But it is not the village nor the church that brings
strangers to this place.   It is the far-famed cave ; that winding cleft which pierces through the very heart of the great
mountain, and in which there lie miracles of loveliness wrought
in silence and in darkness by the water slowly dropping through
unnumbered centuries.

At the head of the village a gate gives entrance to the
grounds of Ingleborough Hall, through which one is permitted
to climb the first slopes of the mountain up a dell as lovely
and as little spoilt by art as any to be found in Yorkshire.
The 'seasons loiter in the keen air of these highlands, and
there is still a flush of wild hyacinths on one bank, and here
and there a stray primrose nestling by the brown stream ; and
so one passes on through pleasant woods, while the lawns give
place continually to outcropping scars of rock, till at last
one pauses by a crag which gapes a little from the ground, as
if some one had pulled out a mammoth brick from the wall of
limestone, and left a low entrance leading into darkness.   From
a shelf within the iron gateway which bars the ingress of too
curious boys, the guide takes down rough wooden candlesticks,
each holding two vile dips, and serves them out to all the
party, for in traversing the narrow windings of the cavern one
must guard one's steps too carefully to rely on other people's
light.   So armed, he leads us out of the cheerful day round a
corner of the limestone which shuts off all light instantly, save
the flickering of the candles, which, to eyes dazed by the
sudden blackness, do but serve to make the darkness vaster.
The impression of illimitable space is heightened by little
gleams and red reflections from the water which lies in pools
upon the floor of the cavern ; but as I tread cautiously along
the firm and easy path my sight adjusts itself, and one by one,
falling as it seems out of the thick dark, the walls and roof of
the cavern grow distinct before me ; rough wet wrinkled slabs
of brown and blackened stone, worn into strange irregularities

which, in this dim and wandering light, seem to slip and slide together in a wild confusion. But here and there among these knobs and boulders, found more thickly as one plunges deeper into the convolution of the chasm, are shapes of delicate and cunning workmanship chased and fretted like miracles of art, strewn profusely up and down the ledges and the floor of the cave, now like delicately woven lace thrown down by some careless beauty, now dropping in long filaments from shelf to shelf like the tresses of a woman's hair, and again recalling those great spongy corals which the fisher in the Indian ocean sees wavering far down beneath the clear blue water.

These are the incrustations of the limestone water dripping from the roof through more centuries than any one can measure, and as I go on silently and cautiously, crossing now a footbridge thrown over a deep pool, now stumbling among boulders all wet and slimy with the pervading moisture, I begin to see that the same agency has covered the roof with long twisted pendants, glistening at some times almost snowy white, and others having more the colour of a brown moorland water. From time to time the cave expands into a wide and lofty chamber, where our united candles in the centre make a dull glow in strange contrast with the blackness lurking a few feet away, and once or twice the water, whose trickle whispers and echoes through the whole of the abyss, takes a deep choking sound as if struggling out of reservoirs and chasms which lie unsuspected close at hand. Indeed, there is a spot far on into the hill, rarely shown to travellers, where the water ends in a black lake which can only be explored by swimming, and which is fed by one knows not what streams lost upon the mountain side, and swallowed up in unfathomable depths.

It is a strange and rare experience thus to be carried into the bowels of the earth, stumbling and creeping upon hands and knees so vast a distance underneath the sunny slopes where the curlews are calling over the brown moor; but I sighed for the bright day, and the first gleam of sunlight striking on the

rough walls of the entrance pleased me more a hundredfold
than any of the wonders I had seen in the realm of shadows.
Ah, how sweet the soft northern sunlight was as it fell through
the ash trees on the short turf and sparkled on the stream and
old stone walls, mossy and stained with the droppings and
the storms of a hundred autumns. From the cave I turned
up the hill. The woodland grew scant, only larches and a
few scattered hawthorn bushes cast their shadows on the
grass. On my right the steep mossy turf is warm and sunny,
with grey boulders jutting out all down the hill; and a little
further on the path leads through a noble gorge, between two
lofty broken cliffs of limestone, topped by a few gaunt firs.
The morning sun shines straight into the ravine. The shadows
of the bushes lie across the grey face of the rock. The sunlight brings out every kind of tender colour, brown and yellow,
lavender and delicate shades of purple, while further on a
gnarled hawthorn of enormous age throws a black cool shadow
all across the sheer face of the cliff.

It is an absolutely solitary spot. My guide turned back and
left me at the entrance of the cavern ; and here in Trow Ghyll
there is neither sight nor sound of any living creature, while
even the slightly traced path which guides me through the depth
of the ravine is strewn so thickly with old unbroken branches
and the droppings of last autumn leaves, as to make it clear
that neither men nor sheep pass this way save at long intervals
and in the summer weather which is coming. Far up above
me a curlew wheels and cries in the still air ; and led on by the
shrieking of the bird, I climb out quickly on to the brown moor
where the three peaks of the great ridge of Ingleborough seem
close at hand, rocky on the highest summit, where there is an
old entrenchment, set in old days as a watch tower on this lofty
ground whence the slopes and valleys of a hundred hills are
laid open to the sentinel.

Over the long brown grass which clogs the undulating surface
of the moor I trudge on for some half-mile or more, trending

upwards as straight as the nature of the ground permits, till
there strikes suddenly upon my ear the last sound I had
expected on this high grassy hill—the sound of falling water.
There was something curiously startling in the low whispering
splash which stole across the silence of the mountain. I paused
and looked around. As far as I could see the moor lay unbroken, swelling and falling into knolls and valley, but offering
no cliff over which a cataract could fall. I could not even see
a beck ; yet the air was charged with the rustle of water scattered

Ingleborough from near Settle.

in its fall over some great depth, and the light wind which stole
down from the peak blew the murmur round me with such
varying intensity that I could not tell whether it was near or
distant. At last, wandering to and fro in some doubt whether
I was not the victim of a trick of fancy, I struck the hollow
course of a small stream, which flowed deep-set below the moor
over a bed strewn with boulders. I followed down the slope.
The boulders grew larger and more frequent, and at last the
hurrying little thread of water was lost beneath blocks and slabs

of limestone too large for it to pass. The beck seemed to burrow underground ; but the noise of falling water was now loud and clear, and climbing over the great slabs I came suddenly in sight of a vast black chasm gaping dark and unfathomable in the very track of the rivulet, which, drawn by some horrible attraction to the maw of this abyss, gurgles sparkling out from beneath the limestone slabs again, and hurls itself down the pit.

Awe is an emotion which I rarely associate with scenery ; yet there was something which excited it in the aspect of this vast rent in the mountain one had thought so solid, in this immense shaft driven into the very bowels of the hill, and the loss of the pretty beck which bubbled on so confidently only to be gulped in such impenetrable depths where never any beam of sunlight can pursue it, nor moorland wind strew its waters with fresh scents. Across the black jaw of the chasm there drifts perpetually a dim white smoke, the scattered spray of the broken stream, impinging far below upon some shelf of rock, whence it drips down into those subterranean recesses out of which come the waters that whisper so stealthily in the darkness of Ingleborough Cave.

Gaping Ghyll, the country people call this spot ; and there are few who would care to explore its sheer black depths, or discover what are the things which it has gaped for during all the years or centuries since first it opened on the slopes of the mountain. Yet I am told that not many years ago a Frenchman swung himself down with ropes, and, what is more, came up again alive. I turn away with a shudder from the steaming chasm, and breast the hill again with a sense of pleasure in the bright sun and the keen wind blowing from the old deserted camp, which I did not feel before I saw the hidden cavities laid bare before me. There are great wonders in the caverns of the earth, but the surface is all that I ask for myself ; and as I mount higher on the slopes, accompanied by a pair of curlews which wheel round and round me with their hoarse despairing cry, my eye is caught perpetually by some gleaming whiteness on the distant mountains, some flashing patch of snowy whiteness which reflects the sun. At this season there is no snow on any of the hills, and at such a distance no mass of flowers would be perceptible. The mystery is solved when, after ploughing through wet bogs upon the summit of the mountain, I come out in view of the long green dale upon the further side. For there stretched out upon the slope by which I must descend are vast flat tables of gleaming limestone, bleached into vivid whiteness by the storms of untold centuries, under the hot sun which beats upon this slope of Ingleborough. These immense tablelands of barren stone are absolutely dazzling to the eye, great stony deserts unrelieved by any tuft of grass or heather, and ending abruptly upon sweet pasture starred with flowers.

It is a wide grassy dale into which one looks down from the northern slope of the mountain. The noble hill country which lay behind me as I climbed up the other slope is entirely hidden by the flat tableland which I have crossed ; but before me lies the vast bulk of Whernside, a ridge rather than a mountain, having no great beauty in its outline, while at the foot lie a few farms and houses, making up the scattered village of Chapel-le-Dale, dear to the hearts of those who know their Southey as they should. It is a long climb down into the valley, and no scenery comparable to Trow Ghyll beguiles the way. But at last the level ground is reached, and as it is not of any striking beauty, I turn the more readily to the little inn. What occurred there is nobody's business but my own ; but when I emerged again, nearly an hour later, I was more charitable to the attractions of this valley full of high fresh pastures, and strolled across the fields towards Weathercote Cave with all the kindly feeling of indulgence towards mere works of nature which distinguishes the man who has but just done lunching after a long mountain walk. "Obviously," said I, as I slouched over a stile, "there

A A

can be nothing on these even slopes of any remarkable
interest ; but since one may not walk to Ingleton so soon, let
us see this cave of which the people say so much."

In this patronising mood I found my guide, and followed
him into a small plantation, out of which came the sharp
sound of falling water. Passing through the trees, I paused
upon the brink of a torn, ragged chasm of depth sufficient to
conceal the tower of the loftiest parish church in England. A
vast cavernous abyss, with sheer sides of blackened limestone,
out of which, at a point some twenty feet below the surface of
the ground, there bursts a full and copious stream, making
one leap into a dark pool at the bottom. The noise of its
fall, caught and thrown back by the rough walls, reverberates
around the cave, and re-echoes in a steady roar such as one
marvels to hear from a stream so small, and which makes it
easy to believe that when the volume of the water is swollen
by the burst of storm-clouds on the hills, or the melting of the
snows at the first touch of spring, the sound becomes of over-
whelming power. At such times, so my guide assures me, it
has occasionally happened that the rush of waters down the
bed of the small stream is so enormous that the outlet at the
bottom of the cave cannot carry it off as fast as it pours in.
Then the brown foamy water, lashed perpetually by the fury
of the fall, rises steadily in the chasm, creeping up from ledge
to ledge, drowning first one rock and then another, till the
sheer depth is like one vast caldron filled with whirling water,
seething and foaming under the shadow of the black rocks.

Such a sight could be watched by no man without some sense
of terror ; but on this bright summer day there is nothing in
the aspect of the chasm save a rather gloomy grandeur. It is
a place of vast brown shadows, cool and dark, having a certain
beauty even in the shapes of its rock masses ; and the gloomy
archway, under which a staircase is cut in the face of the abyss,
conducts one to the very foot of the lofty fall. But of these
things, of the bushes tipped with sunlight, or the trails of ivy

hanging down the face of the rock, one sees but little and one
remembers less. It is the silvery column of the water which
draws one's eyes and thoughts perpetually. Even in the lowest
depths of the chasm it sparkles into diamonds, bringing its own
light with it—I know not how; and the abiding impression on
my mind is of that stately pillar moving and flashing like a living
thing into the dark depths of the abyss.

Sobered and humbled out of all my patronising mood I took
the road to Ingleton, an uninteresting four miles of the hottest
road conceivable; so that when at length I came out over the
craggy slopes above the little town, and saw the valley opening
below me on my right, with its cool brown shades of coppice,
under which the river brawled along secure from the scorching
sun, I could not help turning aside and climbing over the rough,
slaty shingle of the paths till I found a bank of turf at the foot
of a grey rock, very deep and sheer, where I could lie in shade
among the cloudberries, and look up at Ingleborough turning
purple in the evening light, or down upon the river splashing
over pretty falls and rapids far below; and there I lay until the
hills grew clear and the mountain lost its colour, and a cool
breeze began to blow out of the west, and here and there a star
climbed up from behind the ridges and glittered among the
crags. The town was growing quiet as I rode through. The
excursionists were gathered on the station platform, and as I
rode on down the valley towards Clapham I heard them singing
in the distance as they waited for the train at a junction on the
moor,—very clear and pure the voices sounded as they floated
down the wind across the heather and the gorse.

There is something in the aspect of this still evening which
turns my thoughts far back into the past, and I remember that
southward across the hills lies a country not so very far away to
which I had intended to make a pious pilgrimage in memory
of that saint, that poor, persecuted king to whom the Yorkshire
people gave their hearts many years after he had laid down his
troubles and left his throne in peace to his chief enemy.   I

speak of Henry of Windsor, the only king whom Yorkshire
people deemed a saint, though he was not duly canonised.
But the common people who had fought and suffered in his
cause cared little about that,—yea, and their children and their
children's children loved him equally, of whom the chronicler
said that "His face was beautiful, in the which continually was
resident the bountie of minde wherwith he was inwardly
endowed. He did abhorre of his awne nature all the vices as
well of the body as the soule, and from his verie infancie he
was of honest conversation and pure integrity, no knower of evil,
and a keper of all goodness." It is in the wills and testaments
of poor men that one must seek now for the traces of love
which these qualities excited. King Henry had been dead
well-nigh fifty years when John Watton wrote down in his last
testament that his body was to be buried "in the chapel of
Terrington before King Herry." And ten years after that there
died at York a butcher named John Cowper, whose desire it
was "that Margaret my wyff, or another, ride or goo pilgramege
for me, that is to say, to our Lady of Burgh, to our Lady of
Kerlell, to Kyng Harry of Wyndesour . . ." and to other spots
hallowed by the memory of those whom he trusted might yet
aid his soul. Poor, honest, faithful people! And for every
one who cherished King Henry in their hearts so many years
after his death, how many score were there who would have
died for him when he was yet alive? It was over there among
the hills at Bolton by Bolland that he lay in hiding for many
months after the battle of Hexham, waiting secretly in hope
that his queen would yet knit up his cause again among the
northern barons, who did in truth pour out their blood like
water for his house, so that at length upon the field of Towton
half the chivalry of northern England fell under the banner of
Lancaster.

It was one of the great family of Pudsay who sheltered his
king at Bolton Hall. The story is not doubtful. The loyalty
of the Pudsays was conspicuous even in those days of passionate

devotion and of enmity as fierce. Full sixty years after the king's death Ambrose Pudsay wrote : " In witness whereof this my last will and testament, I dide write it with my owne hande at Bolton Haull, in a chamer that goode Kyng Henry the Sexte lay in, and therfor it is called his chamer to this present daye." Doubtless he conceived that this the last and most solemn action of his life, gained a special sanctity from the fact that he performed it in the chamber hallowed by

Bridge by Bolton in Bolland.

the prayers and sufferings of the fugitive king ; and it may even be that having written out the document he made use of some one among the prayers addressed to the king which were current in his family. The book containing them is still extant, and was described by Canon Raine. It is a small octavo, bound in strong oaken boards, and covered with tarnished purple velvet. The contents are in manuscript of the fifteenth century, and consist of some of the services of the Roman Catholic Church, with genealogical notices of the family of Pudsay. But on the fly-leaf is the following prayer, thus headed : "Oratio beati Henrici sexti, regis Angliae et Franciae, &c., hic vir dissipiens (*sic*) mundum et terras, triumphans, divitias celo condidit corde, ore et manu. Ora pro nobis, beate Henrice, ut digni efficiamur." Then follows the prayer itself, in these terms : "Deus qui unigenitum Filium tuum, Dominum nostrum Jhesum Christum famulo tuo regi nostro Henrico corpore et anima glorificatum demonstrare voluisti, praesta, quaesumus, ut ejus meritis et precibus ad eternam ejusdem Domini nostri Jhesu Christi visionem pertingere mereamur ; per dominum nostrum Jhesum Christum, Filium tuum, qui tecum vivit, &c., per omnia saecula saeculorum. Amen."

Sawley Abbey.

Chapeltown.

CHAPTER XVIII

KIRKSTALL, WAKEFIELD, AND THE APPROACH TO SHEFFIELD

I DO not know how far a traveller in Yorkshire may be expected to rise superior to the traditions of the people ; but the point is of little consequence, for I can lay no claim to what Boswell would have called "fortitude of character" and Dr. Johnson "stark insensibility." I make no difficulty about admitting that I am afraid of the padfoot, and that is why I did not ride on through the dark last night towards Leeds. It may not be well known to all who read this book what the padfoot is. He is different altogether from a footpad, and much more terrifying to encounter. Nobody sees him clearly, because they meet him only on dark nights. But sometimes on a lonely road the solitary wayfarer hears a light footfall padding by his side, now running on a few steps in advance and now retreating to his rear ; while suddenly out of the dense gloom there comes a

shriek so loud and curdling, so wild and lost in the abandon-
ment of its despair, that those who have heard it ringing at
their shoulders can compare it to no other sound they ever
heard, unless indeed they have been followed by the barking of
the Gabriel hounds borne through the air on the storms of some
winter night.

There appears to be a loose notion in the minds of many
worthy people at the present day that superstitions such as that
which I have just mentioned are apt to be eradicated by the
elevating and intellectual influence of mines and collieries, those

Kildwick.

well-known modes of diffusing purity of thought and manners
among a benighted peasantry, clinging still to the half-forgotten
creeds of their pagan ancestry.   Dr. Whitaker, that excellent
though peevish antiquary, was contemptuous of this doctrine,
going indeed so far as to declare that the discovery of a
lead mine or the introduction of machinery was the greatest
curse that could befall a village or a country side.   This view
he held lustily against all comers ; and indeed those people who
hold that piles of slag and ashes lead on the people to new
heights of intellect, and volumes of black smoke purify their

A Black Country Road.

minds of folly, might do well to stroll round the mining districts of the West Riding, and find out for themselves how rigidly the faith in witches is held still.

For my part, shrinking as I do from taking either side in so dangerous a dispute, I cannot but think that dwelling in a country such as this would be more apt to breed superstition in the choicest product of a Sunday school than to root it out of any one. For even in summer, when the dusk gathers and the hills grow shadowy, there is something rarely striking to the dullest mind in the aspect of the furnace fires gleaming out one by one from the recesses of the valley. You will see a vast dark hillside thrusting its great ridge across a quarter of the heaven. Suddenly a little tongue of flame quivers up amid the blackness, and another follows as if responding to a signal, and a third succeeds, till a long, long line of rosy flames gleams along the hill like torches borne by men in some great midnight ceremony. And while one wonders at the beauty of these leaping flames, there comes a sudden rush of smoke and light high up from some tall chimney, streaming half across the sky with volumes of pale green and rose colour, scintillating and eddying with a thousand glowing changes and suffusions ; and sinks again as suddenly as it rose up, leaving the night sky dark and the stars large and golden.

I say it is no wonder that those who live constantly among such sights as this dream in their hearts of witches' Sabbaths. And as the more nearly one approaches Leeds the less there is of beauty in the land, I will set down here the tale of a witch of Halifax, as it is recorded for the confusion of the doubting in the learned pages of the Folklore Society. The witch was called Betty, and she elected not infrequently to assume the form of a cat, notwithstanding which disguise her identity was no secret to some of those who dwelt in the locality, and one old man undertook to catch her and draw blood from her, that being, as is well known, the best way to render any witch innocuous. He armed himself accordingly with a large fork ;

Bradford from the Leeds Road.

and, following the prescribed procedure for those who desire to commune with a witch, he set a cake to bake before the fire of the house which Auld Betty frequented, and sat for some time watching it without result. Suddenly, looking up from the fire, he saw a large black cat sitting quietly beside him, engaged in washing its face. The hour had come ; and the old man grasped his fork firmly. "Cake burns," cried the cat. "Turn it, then," he answered firmly, but the cat, instead of doing as he bade it, said again, "Cake burns." The old man made the same rejoinder, and the cat again proffered the same remark. This went on for some several rounds, till the witch-finder, maddened by the monotony of the conversation, forgot the caution he had received to name no holy name in presence of the witch, and cursed her soundly in the name of the Almighty. Instantly the cat flew up the chimney with a squall, and the old man, seeing his prey escape him, plunged after her, jabbing at her retreating body with his fork. There was a dreadful scuffle in the chimney, and the witchfinder got woefully scratched ; but he drew blood at last ; and the next day the witch was ill in bed, suffering from incised wounds upon her unholy person, while the innocent victim of her malice was left unmolested from that hour.

"For my own part," said Tristram Shandy on a notable occasion, "for my own part, as heaven is my judge, and to which I shall ever make my last appeal, I know no more of Calais than I do this moment of Grand Cairo." Notwithstanding which misfortune of ignorance he went straightway and described it,—and that, although he had but the moment before protested that he thought it "very much amiss that a man could not go quietly through a town and let it alone, when it does not meddle with him, but that he must be turning about and drawing his pen at every kennel he crosses over, merely, o' my conscience, for the sake of drawing it!" Now, with one small reservation, I am as ignorant of Leeds as Tristram was of Calais, and I shall show the better judgment

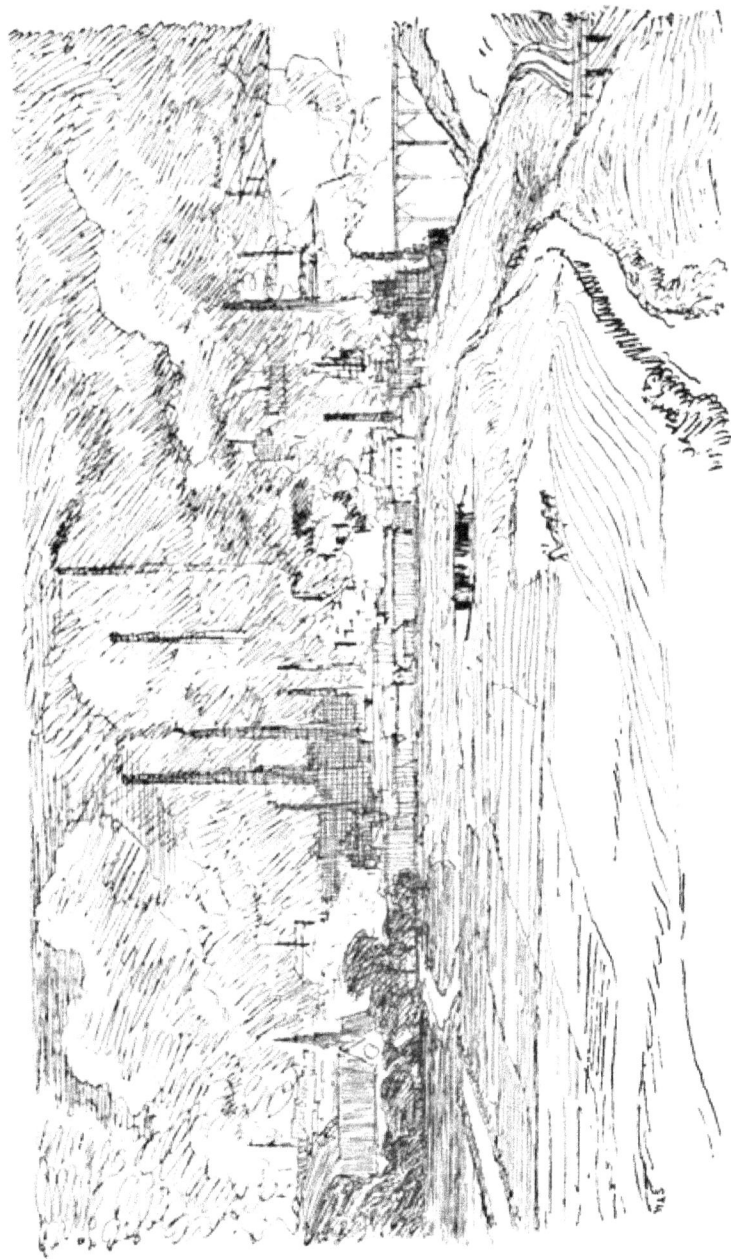

In the Black Country, Leeds.

by adhering to his principle rather than his practice, and
making no effort to describe it. Indeed, of all that wilderness
of bricks and mortar I have no more than two clear memories,
those, namely, of its ruined abbey and its most atrocious cobbles.
On the subject of the cobbles I desire to say only that any cyclist
who can ride out of Leeds upon the Wakefield road without
forfeiting his title to salvation, has my hearty admiration for his
patience.

But the abbey is another matter. Some three miles out of
smoky Leeds one finds it in the shallow valley of the Aire,
a shattered ruin, full of dignity and rigid beauty, speaking
oddly of long past days of solitude and meditation here, where
the clank of engines and the thud of anvils creep daily nearer
to the roofless ruin. It is easy to see how pretty this wide
and open valley must have been, and how sweetly the Aire
once wandered through the buttercup meadows which lie on
every side of Kirkstall ; poor, pretty river, how changed and
soiled ! Just below the abbey it still sparkles, because it falls
over a weir, and the sun will dance even on the inkiest stream
when it is broken into foam. Elsewhere I do not care to look
at it, but turn away to the fine Norman arches of the abbey,
to its church with shallow choir, and transepts fairly perfect
yet ; to the cloister where doubtless upon summer mornings
long ago the old monk Serlo sat, who had seen the first monks
of Fountains, and known their sufferings and their endurance,
and told the tale years afterwards to Hugh of Kirkstall, that
chronicler from whom I have already quoted it. What would
not one give to see the wealth and grandeur of the abbey as it
stood when the old slow voice of Serlo, prosing through the
quiet hours, was the only sound that broke the silence. The
sacred uses of the building are all gone ; but the wealth, if one
may trust the popular tradition, lies hidden still in some
chamber of the earth, guarded by those who will defend it till
the rightful owner comes again, though he linger for many a
century yet. "'Th' man was threshing in th' abba lair," so

Kirkstall Abbey.

runs the tale, "and at nooning a' thocht he'd strecken his back, an when he gat out he saw a hoile under th' abba, and he crept in and he fun' an entry and he went doon it and at bottom there was a great houseplace. There were a gert fire blazing on t' hartstone, an in ae corner were tied up a fine black horse. And when it seed him it whinnied. An behind the horse was a gert black oak kist, and at top o't kist a gert black cock, an cock crawed. Th' man said to hissel, ' Brass in t' kist, I'll hae sum on't.' An as he went up to't t' horse whinnied higher an higher, an cock crawed louder an louder ; an when he laid his hand on t' kist t' horse made such a din, an t' cock crawed and flapped his wings an summat fetched him such a flap on t' side of his head as felled him flat, and he knawed nowt more till he came ti hissel, an he was lying on t' common in t' lair, an never could he find the hoile under the abba again."

So there the monks' treasure remains to this hour. For I do not doubt it was they who tethered this whinnying horse beneath the earth, and set the crowing cock to give warning of the ravisher's approach. Doubtless the chest is full of jewelled croziers and golden crucifixes, such as would make the most moral man among us call loudly for the melting pot, could he only find them. Who doubts that the keen wit of the monks must have scored some points against the commissioners of dissolution? If only one could get a cart . . . and go by night . . . for the laws of treasure trove are the unjustest laws in all the world ! . . . There, let me get away from Kirkstall before all my morals ooze out into some hole in the ground, and I have none left to carry me to Wakefield, where, heaven knows, a man needs all his piety to carry him over the cobbles.

Wakefield is but seven miles of road from Leeds, a sorry road, a scandalous and bumpy road, a road of pitfalls and deep ruts ; and when at last the town is reached, which was made illustrious by its association with the Pinder who fought

Wakefield.

B B

with Robin Hood—dear Pinder of our childhood, I salute
thee !—I have neither patience nor leisure to search through
the hilly streets for characteristics of the citizens, but with one
half-hour spent in the noble church—surely not far inferior to
Rotherham in beauty !—I pass on down the hill until I come to
an inky river flowing sluggishly beneath an ancient bridge,
whose builders never thought to see it so defiled with dust
and soil of collieries.   On it stands the little rebuilt chantry,
perishing and worn, which still recalls the memory of that
great Duke of York, who fell fighting rashly in this very
neighbourhood.   It may or may not be a true tradition which
links the memory of the great duke with this lovely little
wayside chantry, and indeed chapels upon bridges had other
objects than to commemorate the dead.   But events so tragic
as those which happened here sweep men's minds clear of
other recollections ; and since it is the great defeat and
slaughter of the followers of the White Rose which remains the
dominating interest in Wakefield, I make no effort to inquire
further, but cross the bridge and go on up the hill for some
half-mile or more, till, diverging to the right, I find the mound
of Sandal Castle still surrounded by its old dry moat, but
never a sign of the great buildings which almost equalled it
with the rival Lancastrian stronghold at Pontefract.

Hither travelling " by small jorneis " came from London the
great protector of the realm, Richard, Duke of York, bound
northwards in opposition to the fiery queen, Margaret of
Anjou, who was seeking to burst the bonds in which the lords
who followed York held her poor weak husband, and set him
upon an untrammelled throne again.   It was on December 2nd
that the Duke left London for the north, where the flames
and ashes of English turbulence and insurrection were most
lightly stirred, and where the chief power of Lancaster always
lay.   The Earl of March was to follow him with a larger host ;
two younger sons, the Earls of Salisbury and Rutland, were
riding with their father.   So all the company rode into Sandal

Castle upon Christmas Eve; and day by day through all
the festive holiday the friends and tenantry of York were
marshalled and assembled within and without the walls, till a
sturdy host of some five thousand men was gathered under
the Protector's banner; and the duke waited only for the
coming of his son with the main body to attempt some forward
movement.

Now, if York had not been audacious to the verge of rash-
ness, he would not have selected Sandal Castle, though it was

The Chapel on the Bridge, Wakefield.

his own, in which to marshal his adherents and to wait for
reinforcements, for by entering the north at all he was driving
a wedge into a hostile territory. North of Trent the Red
Rose flourished everywhere, and if the White strayed into
any garden it stood a good chance of being torn up by the
roots. Queen Margaret lay at York, not thirty miles away,
" Havyng in her companye," says Hall, " the Prince, her
sonne, the Dukes of Excestre and Somerset, the Erle of
Devonshire, the Lorde Clifford, the Lord Rosse, and in effect

all the lordes of the northe parte with eightene thousande
men, or, as some write, twentie and two thousande." What
kind of policy was it that made York lie waiting for his
strength within thirty miles of such a mighty enemy? Did
he dream that his son's host was so near that he could afford
to scout the queen when she took the step which it was
certain she would take, and marched with her army to Wakefield,
and out upon the level ground before the castle bade him
defiance, offering battle in his very sight? Yet all might
still have gone well with York had he been content to endure
a siege, and wait the coming of his son. That was the advice
of his proved and trusty friend, Sir Davy Hall ; but when he
heard it, York cried in a great fury, "A Davy, Davy, hast thou
loved me so long, and now wouldest have me dishonoured?
Thou never sawest me kepe fortres when I was Regent in
Normandie, when the Dolphin himself with his puissance came
to besiege me, but like a man and not like a bird included in
a cage I issued and fought with mine enemies, to their losse
ever—I thanke God—and to my honour. . . . And sureley my
mind is rather to die with honour than to live with shame,
for of honour cometh fame, and of dishonour riseth infamy.
. . . Therefore avance my banner, in the name of God and
Sainct George, for surely I will fight with them, though I should
fight alone."

So the castle gates were thrown open, and with the words of
this noble speech, instinct and glowing with all the pride of
ancient chivalry, still ringing in their ears, York and all his
company closed their visors, set in rest their lances, and rode
down the hill into another world, carrying with them their
unsoiled escutcheons, and, I think, the love of posterity.
For men's hearts go out to bravery, not judgment, and the
wisest of us may go down the hill to the spot where Richard
struck his last stout blow on the casques of a crowd of
enemies, and stand before the recent monument with all the
will in the world to call the battle folly, and yet find the

kindly tender feelings rising from the bottom of his heart, and his lips shaping no other words than "of honour cometh fame, and of dishonour riseth infamy. . . . Therefore avance my banner." Good headlong knight, rest there in peace! for England, which has such need of wise heads, is served nobly also by those who can only teach their fellows how to die.

"While this battaill was in fighting," says Hall—for I may not omit to tell how Clifford gained his surname of the Butcher. —"a preste called Sir Robert Aspall, chapelain and school-master to the yong Erle of Rutland, ii. sonne to the Duke of Yorke, scarce of the age of xii. yeres, a faire gentleman and a maydenlike person, percevying that flight was more saveguard than tarrying both for him and his master, secretly conveyed the Erle out of that field by the Lord Clifforde's band towards the town ; but or he could enter into a house he was by the sayde Lord Clifforde espied, followed and taken, and by reson of his apparell demaunded what he was. The yong gentleman dismaied had not a word to speake, but kneled on his knees imploring mercy and desyring grace, both with holding up his hands and making dolorous countenance, for his speache was gone for feare. Save him, sayd his chappelain, for he is a Prince's sonne, and, peradventure, may do you good hereafter. With that word the Lord Clifforde marked him, and sayde, by God's blode, thy father slew mine and so wil I do the and all thy kyn ; and with that worde stacke the Erle to the heart with his dagger, and bade his chappelain bere the Erle's mother and brother word what he had done."

That story, which for full three centuries no man has read without a shudder, is not wholly credited by the best opinion of to-day. I know not what the truth may be ; but to me it seems that the mere fact that such a tale could be believed, lifts the curtain on a ferocity of party passions such as no other strife in all our stormy history has called out. Did we but know the bloody details of those wars, we should have a tale of such mingled terror and nobility as would outmatch any record now lasting in the world. But, thank God, there was no diarist ; and the grass grew no quicker on the graves of butchered citizens and knights than oblivion about the cruel details of their fate spread through the kingdom. In one short generation all the widows had gone to join their husbands, the servants had found other masters, the children had forgotten the tales told them at their nurses' knee. The world was changing, and the chivalry was gone And so the old passion died out very quickly, and York and Lancaster worked side by side in the creation of the greater England which rose upon their fathers' graves.

It is not here as with the field of Towton, where a man can look down still upon a country little changed since the hosts were marshalled under the Dun Bull upon the slopes by pretty Saxton. From the mound of Sandal Castle I look out over a country of wide valleys and low swelling hills, obscured upon the north where the prospect is black and dim, for Wakefield belches smoke enough to hide the sunlight. So the lusty strength of modern Yorkshire crops out upon the scene where the vigour of old days spent itself in blood ; and the clank of spindles rings as loud as that of harness along the river's bank. Peace and industry are born together in the land, and the wildest brain does not dream of other civil wars in England.

Do but see how I linger as I draw near my exit from this great county, how I catch at this feature and at that of the noble scenes which go drifting past me as I dally with my route ! I go into the Castle Inn, and see the landlord's picture of the old perfect castle in its grandeur, and listen to his gossip, rambling on from it to the famous naturalist, old Waterton, who used to live at Walton Hall, a bare mile away ; and all the rest of the grand country life which is being slowly driven out of the pleasant valleys of South Yorkshire by the advancing collieries and heaps of slag. The day grew old and I still loitered on the hill above Wakefield ; till at last as I went on by the pretty road to Barnsley, rising and falling among well-wooded hills, the moon was rising in a golden mist, blackbirds were piping in the woods, and a great cloud of rooks were rising up into the cool grey sky.   There are still so many parks within this region, and the trees are even now so fine, that it is easy to believe in the reality of that great Sherwood forest which must have run out in this direction, though with uncertain borders and some intermissions, as far as Kirkless Priory, where, as all men know, Robin Hood met his death and lies buried to this hour, one of the few heroes of the people to whom there is

Kirkless Hall.

attributed no uneasy slumber, no hearkening for the sound of any signal which shall call him up to roam the forest again as he did when the world was young.   It may be that the simple fancy of the ballad writers saw that the restless slumbers they assigned to Arthur, a king broken by the storms of policy, betrayed by the treachery of wife and friend, were inappropriate to Robin, whose heart was in the deep forest glades and who endured no troubles but the weather and the pursuit of enemies, to which all the forest life was also subject.   So that when his joyous life had ended, he slept as sweetly as any deer in all wide

Sherwood, or as the woodwele which woke him by its singing, until it fell at last among the dead leaves in some lonely corner of the forest.

As I lounge up these pretty hills under the grey evening, the rooks stream in increasing numbers on their way homewards through the sky, and a great sound of cawing floats downwards from the untrodden country where they sail so steadily ; while I go on as reluctantly as a child called to come out of its pleasure ground because the dark is near, and the time for playing is all over.   It is with the heart of a child that I have gone round Yorkshire, catching at whatever pleased my idle fancy : and now it is with the lips of a child that I find myself repeating, without any consciousness of what it is, the old burden, " Down, a down, a down," and then the words " Went o'er yon bank of broom," until at last the whole stanza leaps into my memory :—

> When Robin Hood and Little John,
>   Down, a down, a down,
> Went o'er yon bank of broom,
> Said Robin Hood to Little John
> " We have shot for many a pound,
>   Hey, down, a down, a down."

And then it goes on, sadly enough,

> " But I am not able to shoot any more,
> My arrows will not flee."

It was westward from this spot, not many miles away, beneath the reddening sky, that Robin sought for succour in his mortal weakness, and found only treachery : for in a room which one may see still, the Prioress of Kirkless blooded him while one drop of blood would run.

> There he did bleed all the livelong day
> Until the next day at noon.
>
> He then bethought him of a casement door
> Thinking for to be gone.
> He was so weak, he could not leap,
> Nor could he gat him down.

He then bethought him of his bugle horn
Which hung low down to his knee.
He set his horn unto his mouth
And blew out weak blasts three.

Then Little John when hearing him,
As he sat under the tree,
" I fear my master is near dead
He blows so wearily."

How that weary blast ringing faintly over the woodland out
of Kirkless Tower calls down all the empty centuries and
knocks at our hearts for sympathy! That is true romance,
pure gold coined by the sweetest fancy of some forgotten
singer,—as any child will testify by the eager eyes and the
parted lips with which it hears the story, listening for the
hundredth time to the tramp of Little John's hasty feet as he
ran to Kirkless, and burst the locks to reach his master who
was sick and needed him, and to his rage when he heard the
treachery of the Prioress, and asked only leave to burn the
priory in revenge.

" Now nay, now nay," quoth Robin Hood,
" That boon I'll not grant thee.
I never hurt woman in all my life
Nor man in woman's companye.

" I never hurt fair maid in all my time
Nor at my end shall it be.
But give me my bent bow in my hand
And a broad arrow I'll let flee.
And where this arrow is taken up
There shall my grave digged be.

" Lay me a green sod under my head
And another at my feet,
And lay my bent bow by my side
Which was my music sweet,
And make my grave of gravel and grene
Which is most right and mete.

" Let me have length and breadth enough
  With a green sod under my head,
  That they may say when I am dead
  Here lies bold Robin Hood."

So the arrow sang through the warm air of the summer afternoon, and dropped upon the sweet turf a short bowshot from
the grey stone casement where the gentlest of all outlaws sat
watching it with God knows what yearning for the wild-rose
thickets, and the open glades and the bank of broom, round
which the bees went humming in the sunlight : and not long
afterwards Little John laid his tired master down upon the bed,
and went out into the forest by himself, and digged the grave
at the spot where the arrow fell, and lined it with green sods ;
and there lies Robin to this hour, having length and breadth
as much as even he could wish, for the measure of both is as
wide as the hearts of all the people in the land, and as boundless as the love of all the children born in merry England.
God a' mercy of his sins ; and lay no greater ones to the charge
of any soul among us !

I have no appetite for further sights in Yorkshire, though
there is more than one noble park within this region that I
had desired to see.   But the night is falling, slowly, as it does
in summer, yet marching steadily among the woods ; and now
and then I see a furnace fire flare out among the hills, warning me that the land I am approaching is no longer full of
shadows, that it has forgotten old times, and is prosperous and
new, and for the most part grimy.   I have passed by Barnsley,
its steep streets mercifully shrouded by the dusk.   I have run
on past the turn which, had it been bright day, might have led
me off upon the right through Wortley, that fine park and
pretty model village, out to Wharncliffe Chase, and the deep
woodland gorges of the Don.   My road is piled up on both
sides with dusky heaps of ash and slag, and strange glowing
galleries and chimneys belching fire break out upon the skyline on every side.   Already a lurid glow in front of me marks

Sheffield.

the proximity of Sheffield. It is the last of Yorkshire. Moors and valleys swept by storm winds, rivers casting over the whole land a network of low, rushing music, becks splashing softly from a height into cool beds of moss and fern, castles, monasteries, tales of knighthood and of tragedy, all are done, all lie far behind me ; and now the night wind, which sighs at this moment over Beverley, or brings down sweet odours from the hills into Fountains Vale, blows towards me charged with fumes of sulphur and the acrid odours of the forges.

It is, I say again, for me the last of Yorkshire, that very noble county which has contributed so large a portion of the strength and sorrows of the North ; and as I run on slowly through the dark towards the town of glowing furnaces, I find myself wondering how many out of all that motley host of visitors who come to Yorkshire year by year have given their hearts to her, or, indeed, to England, with any sort of understanding love. I know all that can be told me of the soldiers and the sailors who will die for England, of the administrators toiling day and night in some lonely outpost of the Empire, sustained and fortified by the desire that the joints of the imperial structure may be some whit the stronger, the justice done some whit the purer and more true, for all the tragedy of their unrecognised lives and soon forgotten deaths. That is no doubt the greater part of love for mother country,—but is it all ? A woman may be proud that her lover will work and die for her ; but will she be content if he never comes and sits beside her, and takes her hand in his ? If he stay away from her because other women whom he meets in Rome or Naples are lovelier, will not she feel that her very pride is turned to bitterness, and that the love which is not personal is, indeed, no love at all ?

As the world shrinks, and other countries are brought nearer to us, I suppose it is inevitable that love of country should cease in some degree to be a passion, and subside into a principle. But if any man will spend a month in wandering round Yorkshire, with ears awake to all the great voices of the past, and eyes open to the beauty which is so peculiarly English he will find the passion roused again, real and living; and thenceforth the rivers and the glaciers of other lands will be to him no more than the parks and palaces of other men, compared with the white gateway and the low verandah which speaks to him of home.

Bradford.

INDEX

THE END

RICHARD CLAY AND SONS, LIMITED, LONDON AND BUNGAY

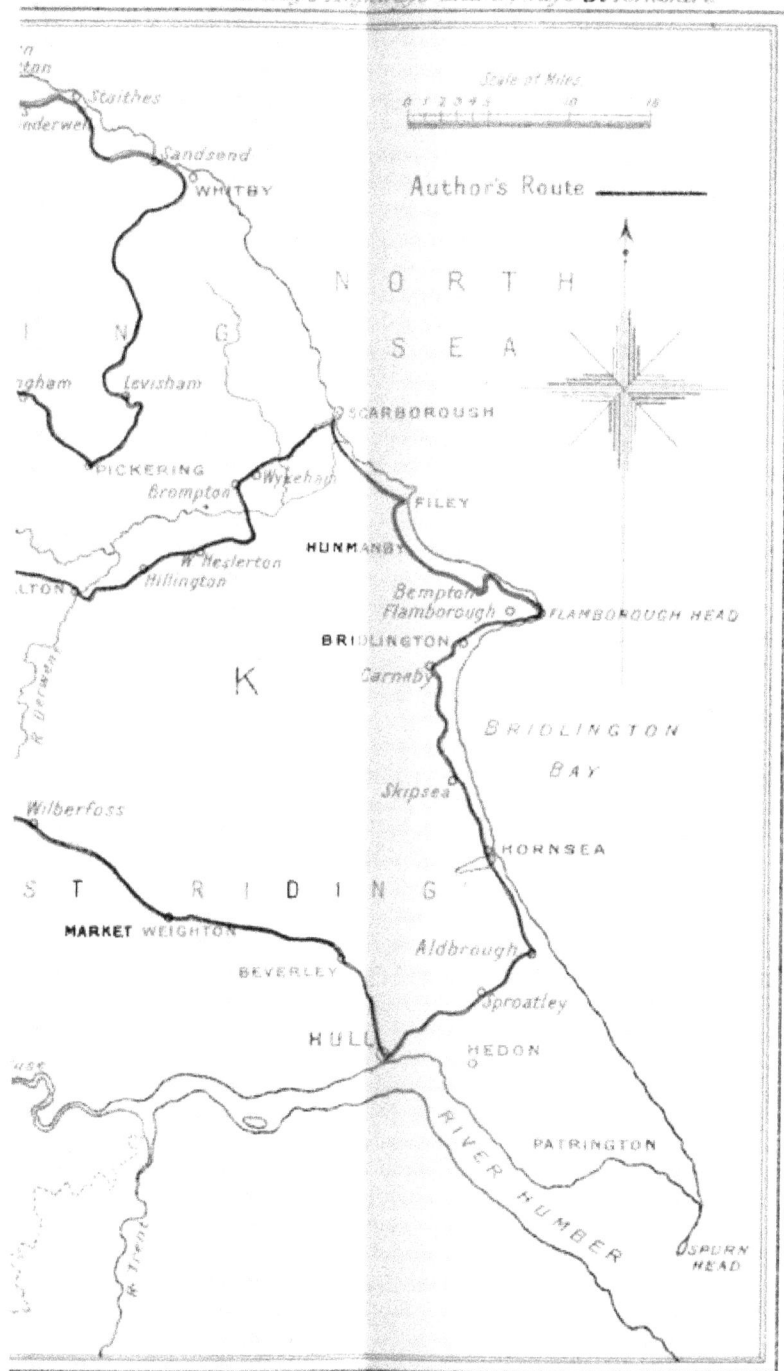

www.ingramcontent.com/pod-product-compliance
Lightning Source LLC
Chambersburg PA
CBHW032310280326

41932CB00009B/769